FATHER HUNGER

Fathers, Daughters, and the Pursuit of Thinness

Second Edition

Margo Maine, Ph.D.

Preface by Craig Johnson, Ph.D.

gürze books

Father Hunger: Fathers, Daughters,
and the Pursuit of Thinness, Second Edition
©2004 by Margo Maine, Ph.D.

Gürze Books
An imprint of Turner Publishing Company
Nashville, TN
(615) 255-2665
www.turnerpublishing.com

Cover design by Abacus Graphics, Carlsbad, CA
Painting: *Le Gourmet*, Pablo Picasso; National Gallery of Art,
Washington, DC; Chester Dale Collection

Library of Congress
Cataloging-in-Publication Data
Maine, Margo.
Father hunger: fathers, daughters, and the pursuit of thinness/
Margo Maine; preface by Craig Johnson.-- Rev. ed.
    p. cm.
Includes bibliographical references and text.
ISBN 0-936077-49-2 (alk. paper)
1. Eating disorders in adolescence. 2. Teenage girls--Mental
health. 3. Fathers and daughters.
    I. Title
RJ506.E18M35 2004   2004016127
616.85′26′008352-dc22   CIP

NOTE
The author and publisher of this book intend for this publication to
provide accurate information. It is sold with the understanding that
it is meant to complement, not substitute for, professional medical
and/or psychological services.

2 4 6 8 0 9 7 5 3

Contents

Acknowledgments   vi

Preface by Craig Johnson, Ph.D.   vii

Introduction   xi

PART 1: The Origins of Father Hunger

1. Father Hunger and the Pursuit of Thinness   21

2. Getting to Know Your Global Girl   31

3. Ten Myths About Fathers, Daughters, and Food   55

4. Fathers As Second-Class Citizens   69

5. Shaky Foundations for Fatherhood   83

6. The Daughter's Dilemma   97

PART 2: The Experience of Father Hunger

7. Damage to a Daughter's Emotions and Identity   113

8. Sexuality, Body Image, and Food   133

9. The Family's Functional Dysfunction   145

10. The Legacy of Loyalty   161

PART 3: The Solutions to Father Hunger

11. How Men Can Overcome Father Hunger   179
12. How Mothers Can Help   213
13. How Daughters Can Cope with Father Hunger   237
14. Impasses in the Treatment of Eating Disorders   257
Epilogue: Why We All Must Prevent Father Hunger   281

Appendixes

Appendix A: Suggested Strategies for Educators   287
Appendix B: Suggested Strategies for Physicians   295
Appendix C: Books and Internet Resources   299
Notes   303
Index   313

Acknowledgments

I am one of the fortunate few who escaped the experience of father hunger. My dad was available, affirming, and affectionate. He invited me into his world, but shared equally in mine and in the family's life. My mother supported and encouraged his involvement. I thank them both and dedicate this book in memory of them.

I also thank my husband, George Coppolo, for his endless patience and understanding when this project took precedence over our lives. His constant support has been essential to my accomplishing this and so many other goals. I am blessed with wonderful family, friends, and colleagues, and thank them for their presence in my life.

The support provided by Marianna Nelson, Research Coordinator at Newington Children's Hospital, now known as Connecticut Children's Medical Center, was priceless as I was writing the original text. Her editing, word processing, and understanding of the concepts I hoped to communicate in *Father Hunger* were invaluable. Matt Sawyers, another gifted editor, writer, and trusted resource, assisted my work in this newly revised edition. I am grateful to both of them.

The opportunity to work with Gürze Books has also been a great gift. I deeply appreciate the conceptual contributions provided by Lindsey Hall and Leigh Cohn, and the editorial assistance provided by Diane Chalfant, MFT. I thank them for their commitment to educating the public about eating disorders and their persistence and encouragement as my raw notions about father hunger evolved into a meaningful theory.

Finally, I thank the young women and their families who have let me into their lives and taught me so much. I hope this book enhances your healing.

Preface

by Craig Johnson, Ph.D.

Most experts agree that eating disorders are caused by an interplay of biogenetic, psychological, and sociocultural factors. Psychologically oriented theorists have hypothesized that those most at risk for developing problems with food and body image have had disappointing or traumatic relationships with people close to them.

This emphasis on relationship disappointment is the focus of Dr. Margo Maine's work. Previous explorations of this issue have concentrated almost exclusively on difficulties in the mother-daughter relationship, making many mothers feel that they were solely responsible for their daughter's problems. Refreshingly, this author shifts the lens to the importance of the father's role in the emotional development of a daughter.

Dr. Maine coined the phrase "father hunger" to describe the natural longing of children for their fathers, which, when unfulfilled, can lead to a variety of problems. In this book she examines how multigenerational and sociocultural factors have resulted in fathers becoming not only physically but also emotionally disconnected from their families, and how this distance affects girls' development of sexuality, body image, self-esteem, and identity.

Throughout the book, Dr. Maine translates sophisticated and difficult psychological theories into language that is understandable to the lay reader. She avoids "father bashing" by offering evenhanded explanations of the differences between social expectations for men and those for women, and how these affect our psychological development. One of the most serious effects is that modern society's prescribed roles cause men to have difficulty with emotional expression and nurturing skills, while women become increasingly isolated in the duties and responsibilities of parenting and caretaking.

I believe the success of a book is often determined by its appearing at the right time with the right information. Unquestionably, the time is right for a book that focuses on the importance of fathers as primary caretakers and as one of the most important men in a woman's life, In truth, it is frightening that books with such a premise are only now appearing.

This book also presents the right information. Dr. Maine has done a masterful job of integrating sociocultural influences, developmental data, and systems theory into a comprehensive and readable explanation of the ways in which impaired father-daughter relationships can increase the likelihood of a young woman developing problems with food, weight, and body image.

She then offers specific recommendations for how to repair the father-daughter relationship. She speaks to fathers directly, conveying changes they need to make, and explains what mothers can do to improve family relationships and assist in a daughter's recovery. Dr. Maine offers solid advice that is both challenging and accessible to all family members.

I wrote the previous ideas in 1991 for the preface of the first edition of *Father Hunger*. At that time I emphasized that the field had neglected the important role fathers should play in their daughters' development and recovery. So, has anything changed in the last decade and a half? Yes.

Professional treatment programs and consumer organizations are leading the way. For example, my eating disorders program at Laureate Psychiatric Hospital has conducted a family week for the past seven years. During the first week of every month, family members are invited to come to the center for a combination of education and intensive family intervention. They can attend as many family weeks as they want, and a concerted effort has been made to engage fathers. Last year more fathers than mothers attended and reported a very high level of satisfaction with their involvement in their daughter's treatment. This is a treatment trend throughout the field. Another sign is that fathers whose children have experienced eating disorders now make up half of the nonclinical board members of the National Eating Disorders Association compared to only one member when the original edition of this book was released. In fact, the relatively new nonprofit association, Dads and Daughters has adopted many of Margo's ideas in its approach to preventing eating disorders and body image problems. Clearly we have made progress, and I am confident that this newly revised edition of *Father Hunger* will accelerate the change.

This edition introduces a new focus on the crushing pressures being placed on today's contemporary girls by the global economy and worldwide media to live up to a painfully unrealistic body image that emphasizes slenderness beyond reason. For many girls, this extreme emphasis on thinness or appearance mistakenly becomes their main purpose, overshadowing the sense of value and worth that is their birthright and that would otherwise be cemented into place through developing their skills and making a contribution to the world. In this sense, our global culture has become a dysfunctional one that damages both women and men. Only an enlightened perspective can empower girls and women to rise above the cultural pressures and claim their own individuality. Fathers need to be part of this enlightened perspective.

Dr. Maine's other revisions have improved and expanded the original message that daughters need their fathers, fathers need their daughters, and wives need a vital working partnership with their husbands to help raise healthy women.

Craig Johnson, Ph.D., is Director of the Eating Disorders Program at Laureate Psychiatric Clinic and Hospital in Tulsa, Oklahoma. He is author of *The Etiology and Treatment of Bulimia Nervosa, Psychodynamic Treatment of Anorexia Nervosa and Bulimia* and *The Anorexia Diaries*. He is one of the world's foremost authorities on eating disorders and has published more than 70 scientific articles on their causes and treatment.

Introduction

Nearly a decade and a half have passed since I initially wrote *Father Hunger*. Some things have changed; some have not. Back in those early days, when I mentioned what I did for a living, a frequent response was, "Oh, I knew someone with an eating disorder." Too often today they say, "Oh, I knew someone who died from that." Then, I had never attended a patient's funeral. Today, I have. Years ago, most of my patients were teenagers. Today my waiting room sometimes looks like a pediatrician's, filled with young faces of children who are already struggling with eating disorders and body image issues.

In those early days, women called to get help for their daughters. Today, adult women are struggling with the same issues themselves. Despite the wisdom that normally comes with life experience, they are risking their lives to achieve a certain look and to feel acceptable to a society that does not respect real women, especially as they age. And fathers used to pay little attention to their looks, while today many of them are dieting and exercising excessively, engaging in *Body Wars*[1] much like the women in their lives.

Today we know so much more about what causes eating disorders, including the fact that toxic cultural standards for beauty and thinness put women at risk to develop them. Yet the standards, if anything, are worse. "Beauty" has become thinner than ever.

I used to believe that changing individual relationships in affected families could solve the problem. Today, I am convinced that our efforts should focus on broad-based cultural transformation: families alone cannot protect their daughters from the devastating effects of a predominant culture that reduces a woman's value to her weight and appearance. With that in mind, in 2000 I wrote *Body Wars,* an activist's guide to changing our culture and making it a safer place for women's bodies.[1] We still have far to go.

In the simpler world of the '80s and '90s, girls needed the right dress, hair, and flowers for the prom. These days, preparation for a special event takes weeks, starting with tanning; waxing their eyebrows, bikini line, and legs; manicure and pedicure; coloring their hair; having their makeup done by an expert; maybe even having a cosmetic plastic surgery procedure. The dress and the date have become almost incidental. The body is the project, and the process is endless.

Children and teenagers used to have many adult figures who were actively involved in their lives. Today we let them raise themselves, rarely intruding into the adolescent culture that can be so unpredictable and cruel. Girls used to feel pressure from peers, parents, and other people in their immediate community—they knew the faces. Today they can neither identify nor escape the incessant impact of faceless, impersonal global forces and influences, constantly telling them they are not enough—not thin enough, not pretty enough, not smart enough, not enough of anything.

Society's efforts to close the gender gap between boys' and girls' access to educational opportunities has had an unintended effect: the gender differences in addictive behaviors and violence are being eliminated. Girls are now smoking, drinking, using drugs, committing crimes, and acting as violently as boys. No longer is it just isolated families that are stressed, sick, or dysfunctional. Today our entire culture is sick, serving as a constant source of pressure and confusion for young people.

While eating disorders used to scare parents, doctors, and teachers into taking them seriously, today they are accepted as normal. People even joke about them. Years ago, a serious eating disorder usually resulted in hospitalization. Today managed care and cost containment rule, denying many critically ill people the treatment they urgently need.

In the 1980s I thought the end was in sight and that we could prevent eating disorders. Today I see no light at the end of the tunnel—I just see more and more people suffering. No one seems immune. And funding for research, treatment, and the development of prevention programs is woefully inadequate.

Back then, father hunger was a new concept. Today it is accepted as part of the vernacular in the discussion of eating disorders, but still we do little to address it. So many girls are missing out on a relationship with their dads. And the dads miss out too.

When I began to treat young people with eating disorders in 1980, I felt challenged as well as baffled by the complex interactions among mind, body, soul, and culture. I knew I had much to learn to become an effective therapist for these individuals. Many of my mentors and colleagues warned me about limiting the scope of my practice so early in my career. They believed that eating disorders were a fad that would last only a few years. In contrast, I strongly sensed that we would be seeing more and more people with problems concerning food and body image because of our culture's unrealistic and negative dictates about beauty, perfection, dieting, and emotional expression. Unfortunately, I was right.

Conservative estimates indicate that between 0.5 and 3.7 percent of adolescent girls and young adult women meet the criteria for anorexia nervosa, and between 1.1 and 4.2 percent meet the criteria for bulimia nervosa.[2] As many as 8 percent of otherwise healthy and vibrant young women suffer from these deadly disorders, and countless others are dabbling in disordered eating, extreme dieting, excessive exercise, and other pathogenic forms of weight control. It isn't a fad.

My clinical work has introduced me to thousands of people whose lives and psyches have been disrupted by problems with food. These people come from different socioeconomic and cultural backgrounds and have widely diverse family histories. They range in age from children to grandparents, and the extent of their illness varies from mild to severe.

I have seen how girls commonly grow up hating their bodies and expressing this and other pain through their relationship to food. Undereating, yo-yo dieting, overeating, compulsive eating, weight preoccupation, exercise abuse, eating disorders such as anorexia nervosa and bulimia, and the health problems associated with malnutrition are frequent results, as are difficulties with intimacy, relationships, and self-esteem. We need to reverse these trends soon. Too many people are suffering, and too many people are dying.

Probably the most important lesson I have learned over these years is to listen to my patients, for they hold the solutions to their problems. By listening carefully, I learned that the development of and recovery from eating problems does not concern only women and mother-daughter relationships, as much of the literature indicates. Fathers play a crucial role. This insight has come from my patients, not from books or journal articles.

When I first became involved in this field, I spent endless hours reading the clinical literature and latest research, determined to do the best for my patients and their families. I felt I was learning a lot, until one day I had an experience so powerful that it completely reshaped my thinking as a therapist.

I was sitting with a 15-year-old patient in her hospital room. Barbara had just been admitted, and I was seeing her for the first time. She had been in outpatient treatment for anorexia for a year and had recently developed bulimic symptoms as well. She was a beautiful, shy, emaciated girl. I asked her a few questions, and she gradually began to talk about herself, her family, her feelings of hopelessness, and her parents' marriage.

When Barbara talked about how she felt toward her father, I suddenly understood that I was interpreting what she said in terms of the theories I had just read—theories all about mothers and their impact on daughters. I realized that I could help Barbara more if I stopped sifting what she said through a theoretical framework. This meant that I would have to stop thinking like all the theorists I had been reading and begin to develop confidence in my ability to help patients like Barbara and in their ability to help themselves. This powerful intuitive moment became a turning point in my career as a therapist.

Coincidentally, Barbara had been talking about her dad when this revelation came to me, but fathers were almost completely absent in theories about both the causes and the treatment of eating disorders. This imbalance bothered me because of the role my own father played in my life. My development as a professional who could help others was strongly tied to our very close relationship, through which I felt my father's influence, values, love, and respect for me. As Barbara spoke, vivid images of my own father swept into my mind.

I wondered what my life would have been like if I had had a different kind of father. It was hard to picture growing up without his support and interest, his constant validation of my self-worth, and his desire to spend time with me. I remembered all the letters he wrote to me during that homesick first semester of college. Other memories surfaced, and I immediately understood how divergent Barbara's experience and mine were, because we had such different dads.

Suddenly, I felt I was venturing into uncharted territory. My personal experience stood in sharp contrast to this young woman's. I had never felt deprived of my father's love, and therefore I didn't hunger for him the way she did for her father. Turning to the clinical literature didn't help. Barbara's description of her dad did not match the theories about fathers of eating disordered daughters. He was neither uninterested nor uncaring, as fathers had typically been depicted. Instead, he was very concerned about his family, though inept as a parent. Meeting him, I observed a man who would do anything to help his daughter recover; yet he had little awareness of what she needed from him. He only knew how to buy her things, hoping she would be happy again. He didn't know how to give of *himself* because he had never been shown how.

Luckily for Barbara, he was willing to learn. Through family therapy, he became more emotionally expressive and actively involved in Barbara's life. The changes he made helped her recover.

Years later, I still think about Barbara and that first hour of therapy when she described her hunger for an emotional connection with her dad. She thought that having a different body would please him, so she had dieted, lost weight, overexercised, and purged, masking her pain and emptiness.

Treating Barbara and many others with eating problems has made me acutely aware of how much girls need their dads to help them develop into positive, strong, assertive, self-confident young women who are able to negotiate healthy relationships. When dads are uninvolved, absent, or inconsistent, their daughters experience what Barbara was describing—a deep, unrelenting father hunger.

Over the years I have discovered that father hunger is not restricted to female adolescents, nor is its expression limited to eating disorders. Both boys and girls grow up with this yearning for dad, which we have only recently begun to explore. Because of the cultural roles we have ascribed to men and women, father hunger is a nearly universal experience in most contemporary societies, and is expressed in many self-destructive behaviors.

The time has come to focus on the positive and crucial role that fathers can play in their daughters' emerging identity and self-esteem. There is no substitute for a father's love. Similarly, there may be nothing worse than being deprived of or feeling uncertain about it.

In this revised and updated edition of *Father Hunger,* I have added a chapter called "Getting to Know Your Global Girl," which describes the life of the average young woman today. The pressures on our "global girls" are enormous and universal, and many girls don't have the personal resources to escape them. Viewing an eating disorder in this context should help readers, especially fathers, understand the overwhelming intensity of the contemporary adolescent female experience. Girls often feel that their lives are spiraling out of control. Focusing on the body gives them a way to restore some sense of order. "Getting to Know Your Global Girl" is full of distressing facts. Get ready to be worked up as you read it.

The next section of this book examines the origins of father hunger. It demonstrates how our culture has influenced family functioning by perpetuating myths that attribute minimal importance to the father's role in the family, particularly in raising daughters. This section also clarifies the dilemmas young women face as they struggle to meet uncertain and conflicting expectations, subsequent to the rapid changes in sex roles during the latter half of the 20th century.

The third section describes how father hunger can become so devastating that young women wage war with their bodies to cope with their inner emptiness. It further illustrates how a limited paternal presence creates a loss for the whole family. Case presentations and vignettes are presented to portray how father hunger really feels.

The final section proposes ways in which we can change our culture's myths and role expectations so that men and women share power and responsibility more equitably and thus work together more effectively in both the family and the world. Separate chapters address fathers, mothers, and daughters. A new chapter discusses impasses that commonly arise in treatment focusing on family dynamics and healing the father-daughter relationship.

The Epilogue briefly explores what we can all do to create a more positive role for fathers and prevent the eating problems and body image dissatisfaction that plague so many young people. The appendixes include specific suggestions and resources for educators, physicians, and others who influence the lives of young people and their families.

I have tried to stimulate readers to think about their relationship with their father. You may uncover some old scars or open wounds in the process. Pay attention to these: they are opportunities for healing. When you finish reading this book, I hope you can find ways to create better relationships between men and women and between fathers and families. Imagine children feeling loved and secure in their relationship with their dad. Imagine men feeling comfortable and free to express emotions, nurture children, need others, and spend more time and energy with their families. Imagine fathers being more than family providers and protectors. Imagine men and women sharing power and responsibility both at home and at work. Imagine an end to father hunger—and to eating disorders.

PART 1

The Origins
of Father Hunger

CHAPTER 1

Father Hunger and
the Pursuit of Thinness

All children long for a close, loving relationship with their fathers. They are born with an innate drive to connect with them. Children literally yearn for this connection. And fathers have the capacity to respond. Kyle Pruett, a pediatrician who has researched this relationship for decades, writes: "Children and fathers hunger for each other early, often, and for a very long time."[1] When this normal craving is satisfied, children are likely to grow up feeling confident, secure, strong, and "good enough."

Often, however, this yearning is not acknowledged and the need for a bond with the father grows, causing self-doubt, pain, anxiety, and depression. *Father hunger* is a deep, persistent desire for emotional connection with the father that is experienced by all children. We will use the term to refer to the unfulfilled longing for father, which for girls and women often translates into conflicts about food and weight.

Like physical hunger, unsatisfied emotional hunger does not disappear; instead, it grows and grows. Adults who have not found a way to relate to their fathers or resolve their feelings of loss may continue to suffer this hunger indefinitely. They bring their longing to new relationships when they become spouses and parents. In this way, father hunger is passed down through generations. Although it is rarely identified, discussed, or confronted, it becomes a shared experience that we have come to accept as a normal aspect of our culture.

Thus, our society is organized around assumptions and practices that allow most children to grow up not really knowing their fathers—and often not even acknowledging the deep feelings of deprivation and loss that result. We have adapted to our father hunger despite the suffering it causes, especially to daughters. The accepted social roles for men and women—the family structure itself—have evolved to support this condition rather than challenge it. Cultural values and myths have limited men's roles, dictating that mothers are important but fathers are expendable.

Ultimately, this misguided system creates a debilitating loss that permeates families and affects all their members. Children must be satisfied with a minimal relationship with their fathers; mothers have to do most of the day-to-day parenting; and men feel inept and incapable in their roles at home—despite increasing expectations that they will be involved and present in their families.

From early in their development, males are forced to be separate, isolated, and unemotional. They are encouraged to *achieve* but not to *feel*. Consequently, when they become parents, fathering requires more intimacy than they have learned to handle. With their own emotional needs unmet and their emotional vocabulary undeveloped, they are ill prepared to meet the emotional needs of their children. Thus, each generation enters adulthood hungry for a connection with father but lacking awareness of these dysfunctional patterns and the skills needed to break them.

Father hunger is a special problem for daughters because they are taught from infancy to put relationships first. Since they value close connections, they find their father's distance very unsettling. They crave contact with their dads but are confused by this desire and feel guilty for wanting more than a father who seems spent or uninterested can give. Today more and more girls cope with this conflict by dieting and obsessing about their weight, in a misguided attempt to win their father's approval by conforming to cultural standards.

This book explores the ways in which father hunger affects both adult men and their daughters and promotes society's obsessions with food, weight, and body image. In the world of girls, father hunger too often leads to "If only I were skinny" reasoning and the rejection of critical physical and psychological needs. Recognition of these concepts will allow us to construct new ways for men and women to work together to decrease the prevalence of father hunger and give our girls the parenting and support they need to survive in this girl-toxic culture.

The "If Only" Trap

Girls may adopt the "If only I were skinny" approach to escape pain and reduce all their negative emotions into simply "feeling fat." Paradoxically, the problems therapists encounter in eating-disordered patients, chronic dieters, compulsive eaters, compulsive exercisers, and weight-preoccupied women do not really have to do with weight and food. Those are merely symptoms. The underlying issues are always rooted in deep pain and confusion, as the individual reaches for self-esteem and identity while dealing with depression, anxiety, fear, trauma, and disappointment.

For many, fathers figure prominently as a source of discomfort and longing. Patients describe how they've always wanted to please their fathers, how they never felt they "measured up," how they used their bodies to gain affection or approval, or how they now eat too much or too little to deal with their sadness. These women have found a seemingly simple solution to the pain of disconnection from their fathers. "If only I were skinny" and "If only I could stop eating" are their desperate refrains.

Modern culture promotes "If only I were skinny" solutions to many other problems as well. The media bombards us with messages equating thin, perfect bodies with wealth, success, status, and happiness. Such an environment suggests that a "perfect" body is the answer to any and all interpersonal problems and negative emotions. Elaborate, seductive, shared fantasies are displayed everywhere—on billboards, on the radio and TV, in magazines, movies, books, and advertising. Their constant presence perpetuates the "if only" trap and distorts our thinking and expectations.

"If only" reasoning is a common way we express our desires. We want simple explanations. Assigning cause and effect in difficult situations helps us make sense of life and put order into an often confusing existence. It gives us a feeling of control by suggesting that if we do a certain thing, we can change other things. A young woman thinks: "If I lose weight, Daddy will respect me and be proud of me." Manipulating her eating and body size is seen as a socially acceptable cure for her father hunger.

"If only" reasoning makes particular sense to children. In fact, until they reach a stage of cognitive development called *formal operations*, children naturally think in concrete terms and use reasoning patterns based on linear thinking such as "A causes B" and "if only" relationships. Only with maturation are children able to conceptualize problems in a more complex manner and begin to draw upon abstract concepts.

People with food issues may be very intelligent, but their reasoning remains stuck in the concrete "if only" approach when it comes to thinking through solutions to their sadness or low self-esteem. They are unable to recognize cultural contributions to their feelings about their bodies or to their family's patterns of interaction. Since "if only" reasoning represents a return to the simplicity of childhood, it may be seductive and comfortable—but it can be dangerous as well.

The focus on food, weight, or body shape inherent in the "If only I were skinny" approach to life helps us avoid dealing with reality. It simplifies, distorts, and hides the underlying problems. By masking the real issues, this approach actually prolongs the pain and sadness of disconnected relationships, especially with the father. It keeps both father and daughter from facing their feelings and confronting problems in the family's functioning and structure.

Parents or loved ones relating to someone with an eating disorder come up with their own set of "if only" statements, such as, "If only she would eat . . . " or "If only she could like herself . . . ." They too must shift away from "A causes B" reasoning. Whether you are a person with a preoccupation about food or a loved one trying to help, every time you find yourself saying "if only," stop and remember that this road leads only to a futile pattern of simplifying and avoiding underlying issues.

Relationships and Eating Problems: Systems Theory

We now can see why the simplistic A causes B, "if only" reasoning does not work. To understand eating problems and father hunger, a more inclusive and comprehensive perspective is necessary. Systems theory is one that can explain human behavior much more effectively. Simply stated, it suggests that "The whole is greater than the sum of its parts," largely because of interactions among those parts.

When this theory is applied to families, it becomes apparent that father not only affects daughter, but everyone influences everyone else, and all are in turn influenced by systems outside the immediate family nucleus. These other systems include the myths and patterns established and carried over from earlier generations, the social environment and the demands it places on individuals, and the cultural roles assigned to family members and to each sex.

In applying systems theory to father hunger, we see that we can no longer simply blame fathers for their absence and inability to support their daughters. Instead, we must consider how our culture has evolved to limit this important link between men and women of different generations. The answers are not linear (how dad affects his daughter); they are systemic (how all members of the family and external influences interact).

Family systems theorists[2,3,4,5] best explain how all these factors intersect to result in differing family patterns and problems. They describe the family as a cybernetic, dynamic system with all parts affecting each other through interactions, interconnections, and feedback. The components include the individual's physical, biochemical, and psychological functioning; vulnerabilities from early development and psychological experience; family functioning and organization; multigenerational family patterns; developmental stresses on the individuals; and pressures from outside the family.

In an interactive system, no one part has unilateral control over another. Mara Selvini Palazzoli, a family therapist from Italy, points out that whenever one family member appears to cause another's behavior, the interaction can only be understood by taking a closer look at the cumulative effect of past patterns within the whole family. Families develop "fixed behavioral responses" that may make one person look like the villain or the cause of all their problems when, in fact, everyone in the system contributes to the pattern—no one person creates it.

For example, regarding the father's minimal role in the family, Palazzoli says, "The so-called ineffective father is a product of cooperation among all members of the system and not an intrapsychic fact."[6] Women who suffer from eating disorders indicate this in their own words when they describe how multigenerational family patterns and cultural trends have prescribed certain roles for their parents. In these family systems, the father was scripted to be peripheral and authoritative because the culture, family structure, and role assignment supported that role. Their fathers did not simply choose to be uninvolved.

While traditions, myths, beliefs, and customary behaviors and roles from the past may be accepted without question by a family, they may not fit the current generation and may cause stress and pain. Body image dissatisfaction, problems with food, and eating disorders are potential responses to these cultural and familial conflicts for girls. Applying systems theory to your life may help you escape the "if only" trap and understand how to address father hunger more effectively.

Fathers: A Potential Antidote to the "If Only I Were Skinny" Fantasy

Culture contributes to eating problems and body dissatisfaction in many complicated ways. Historically, women have been socialized to focus on their appearance and to alter themselves to be pleasing to other people. Today, reflecting the impact of globalization, cultures place a high value on appearance and equate thinness with femininity and beauty. Furthermore, technology offers females many ways to attain the "perfect" body. Most experts in the field of eating disorders view these cultural and technological pressures as major reasons why so many young women are adopting severe diets and developing anorexia nervosa, bulimia, and other eating and body image conflicts.

Fathers can moderate the impact of these social dictates. For example, if a father agrees with our culture's shared misconception that all his daughter's problems would be solved if she had a perfect body, he may be contributing to the development of an eating disorder. In fact, girls whose fathers value weight control and appearance are much more likely to be dissatisfied with their bodies, to self-induce vomiting, and to engage in other unhealthy weight loss techniques.[7]

On the other hand, a father can give his daughter messages about beauty, self-worth, and body image that counteract these strong cultural influences. His words can be very powerful and reassuring antidotes for girls who are trying to balance the cultural pressure to be thin and sexy. As the age of onset for disordered eating and negative body image gets lower and lower, even very young girls come to believe that "If only I were thin, people would like me more; Mommy and Daddy would be proud of me." If fathers are not providing direct signs of acceptance and validation, the language of fat can easily take hold while daughters struggle to gain Dad's approval or attention.

Our society forces children to grow up quickly, treating little girls as sex objects almost as soon as they are out of diapers. Abercrombie and Fitch developed a strong marketing campaign for their thong underwear for 10-year-old girls, laced with highly suggestive language such as *eye candy* and *wink, wink*. Advertisements frequently show female children who are made to look grown up, and more and more products originally intended for adults are now aimed at children. For example, make-up is now marketed by cosmetics companies to 9- and 10-year-old girls because they have money to spend. The implication is that little girls need to make themselves more appealing, prettier, or sexier.

Many little girls respond to these messages by becoming preoccupied with their appearance or by dressing in a provocative or adult style. Fathers often feel overwhelmed by this premature sexuality and may attempt to distance themselves from their daughters rather than finding ways to remain close to them as they experiment with these behaviors. Girls may then conclude that their fathers simply do not care or do not accept them. Their sadness can lead to desperate attempts to please Dad or other men through their body and appearance.

For girls of all ages, being thin has become the answer to a myriad of uncertainties about their lives and identities. In the past 50 years, women's roles in our culture have expanded dramatically. Women are pursuing professions, interests, and lifestyles that previously were the exclusive domain of men. Many adult women live far different lives from those they expected, based on their observations of their mothers' lives. In *The Hungry Self: Women, Eating, and Identity*, Kim Chernin[8] was one of the first to explore this concept in great detail, particularly noting the difficulties young women experience when they surpass their mothers. These revolutionary changes have contributed to much inner turmoil and self-doubt, which in turn are conveyed to today's little girls and adolescents.

Obsession with physical appearance and weight have become a primary means of dealing with this anxiety: "If only I were thin, then I'd be sure of myself," or "If only I were thin, other people would see me as a success." And today, the means available to change a woman's body are endless. Diet pills, diuretics, laxatives, special diets, liquid meals, make-up, fitness programs, spas, and plastic surgery all promise an answer to the uncertainties women are experiencing. Unfortunately, these artificial solutions to a lack of identity and feelings of confusion and low self-esteem are often more available than are nurturing relationships.

Positive messages from a father can help a daughter face doubts about what being a woman means today. He can help her discern her life's direction, values, and identity. If he is supporting his wife emotionally and validating her work both at home and in the world, his wife will be more positively involved with the family, and the children will see men and women working together effectively.

When Dad's role is a constructive one, the daughter will be less likely to rely on "If only I had a perfect body" fantasies in order to feel competent and successful as a woman and comfortable with her femininity. The more a daughter's father hunger has been satisfied, the less she will resort to dangerous "if onlys" that lead to body image and eating conflicts as she attempts to forge her personal identity.

Recovery: The End to "If Only" Reasoning

An essential step in recovering from an eating or body image issue is understanding how multidetermined these problems are and how unconsciously and systematically we are influenced by our culture. Although the simplicity of the "if only" reasoning is seductive, it cannot change anything. It points fingers and it blames, but because it does not appreciate and resolve the larger and deeper issues, healing cannot occur. One woman who recovered from a severe eating disorder stated it this way:

> I used to love grade-school math. You can think things through and figure them out exactly. It works! I loved working at things like that. Recovery is kind of the opposite. It's like the end of all those easy math problems—you see things really aren't so simple.

I agree with her. Recovery is the end of the easy math problems. It is the beginning of figuring out how to change your responses to situations that are beyond your control. The problems of the families in this book are too complex to attribute to "if only" causes or solutions.

Eating problems are not simply signs of individual dysfunction. Although the individual with a preoccupation about food and body size must address these issues, our family structures and cultural expectations also need to change. With a heightened sensitivity to ways in which our systems promote father hunger, we may be able to transform our society to one that will foster more satisfying relationships between fathers and daughters and prevent the pain caused by eating and body image conflicts.

CHAPTER 2

Getting to Know Your Global Girl

Life is qualitatively different for girls growing up today. Their world and its influences on them have expanded exponentially. No longer are they shaped and formed only by their families and the neighborhoods in which they grow up. Today's young people are bombarded from every direction with demands that they look and act in narrowly prescribed ways and strive for impossible ideals.

Thanks to unprecedented advances in technology, globalization increasingly allows diverse cultures to interact and converge. Commerce, immigration, and shared resources, information, and ideas are bringing us closer together. With our world becoming more interdependent economically and telecommunications linking people instantly, personal and local influences such as the family, religion, and the community have gradually weakened. Our known universe has expanded, but our personal resources have shrunk. Social pressure and experts are more abundant than ever, advising girls covertly or overtly about how to act and what to be. But few of these faceless messengers are people who actually know them, let alone care about them. Global communications and global markets have made girls and young women global targets. We will use a new term to describe this recent social phenomenon: *global girls*.

Global girls' lives have become less intimate but more intricate. The increased mobility of modern life means more external opportunities, while less emphasis is placed on developing an internal sense of one's true self. This complicates the task of forging a personal identity at a time when moral authority, traditions, and core values are increasingly viewed as yesterday's news.

The younger the person, the greater the impact of globalization on her life. Developmentally, teens are the most vulnerable, readily pursuing and accepting influences from outside the family. But they haven't developed an internal set of values or strong sense of self by which to evaluate these messages and influences. Studies of gender inform us that the female psyche and socialization process make women very sensitive to external messages. As the number, force, and content of these messages intensify, girls' lives, already full of challenge and complexity, become ever more daunting.

Most adults, especially fathers, are largely unaware of the complex demands being made on their daughters. At the same time, society expects fathers to take charge, be the experts, and know everything. Admitting ignorance is a tough task for many men. It is far more comfortable to be the expert, the all-knowing one, than to be baffled by what you are hearing and try to figure out how best to help. But the only way to help anyone is to listen hard and long, while staying grounded in yourself. Attentive listening and caring can make a critical difference in your daughter's life. In fact, it could *save* her life.

The bottom line is: Your daughter needs you now more than ever. You have a chance to accept this challenge as a way to learn something that few others make the effort to discover. You have a precious opportunity to become a wise and reliable resource to the global girl you know and love.

The New, Improved Global Peer Pressure

One of the most troubling by-products of globalization is the ability to promote universal peer pressure. Market researchers focus on global teens, hoping to capitalize on the shared desires and insecurities of adolescents from different places and cultures.[1] Corporations develop global brands, from soft drinks to clothing, snack foods, beauty aids, and blue jeans.

Their strategy is working. Global girls have bought in. But they have bought far too much. They have fallen not just for the material goods, but also for the vacuity at the core of mindless consumerism, which can lead to problems like eating disorders.

The predisposition toward consumerism starts early. Global girls are taught to purchase before they are taught to read. Think about the not-so-subtle messages conveyed by Barbie dolls. Barbie lures millions of girls each year into the lifelong role of consumers. If you ask a little girl what she likes about Barbie, the answer is uniformly "her clothes" or "her stuff." Barbie is all about how you look, what you wear, and what you have—all image, no substance. Most American girls own Barbie by the age of 3 and have a collection of eight or nine by the time they are finished playing with them.[2]

Each new Barbie is more desirable than the last, and Mattel has commercialized its little supermodel to unprecedented extremes. Calvin Klein Barbie came with CK logos, and Shopper Barbie had her own charge card. Talking Barbie raised an uproar of protest when she came out with declarations such as "Math class is tough." And Slumber Party Barbie came with a scale permanently set at 110 and a booklet titled "How to Lose Weight," which offered the helpful instruction, "Don't eat." Barbie inspires global girls of completely different cultures, ethnicities, and body types to aspire to her unreal image. And they do.

Market Research, Corporate Greed, and Global Girls

A success story like Barbie's doesn't just happen: it is the result of a well-crafted, systematic, and painstaking attack on the minds of potential young consumers. Barbie's creator, Mattel, is a striking example of corporate America and its value system.

Recent market research found that Barbie's appeal had narrowed, with global girls over age 7 losing interest. Eager to recapture the "tween" market, Mattel developed a new set of dolls for 7–12-year-olds. The new line, called "The Scene," was updated and urban, focusing on fashion, music, and dating. The new Barbie sported pouty lips, a bigger head, a more hip attitude, and today's essential accessories—a PDA and cell phone. Capitalizing on the importance of female friendship, Mattel launched promotions of Barbie and her very modern friends to girls as young as seven, placing ads on *MTV, Teen Nick, WB,* and *Teen People.* Sales of "The Scene" quickly skyrocketed, justifying the $65 million per year spent on advertising Barbie, who brings $1.6 billion into Mattel's coffers each year.[3]

Some firms specialize in "psychocultural research," employing anthropologists and psychologists to analyze how young children react to images, how they use the Internet, and what appeals to them. Nintendo alone interviews 1,500 kids each week.[4] The goal of these marketers is to "*own* fun," "*own* kids," and sell "share of mind" to companies keen on hooking young consumers.

Much of this research is conducted on-line, in chat rooms, where innocent but computer-literate children spend much unsupervised time. Their spontaneous and direct responses are a virtual gold mine for market researchers. Parents sometimes unknowingly expose their children to these opportunists when they sign them up for what appear to be on-line educational activities.

No wonder we find that toddlers recognize corporate logos and that by kindergarten, girls are already worried about fashion, appearance, and body image. Using Disney characters and other beloved childhood images to promote cosmetics, fragrances, nail polish, and other adult products, advertisers urge girls to become someone else through their purchases. Sadly, advertising executives know more about children, what they want, and what motivates them, than many parents do.

Activists in the Stop Commercial Exploitation of Children movement draw a parallel between ways in which children are manipulated today to boost corporate earnings and how they were used in factories prior to child labor laws a century ago. Back then, manufacturers needed kids' bodies. Now they capture their minds, values, hopes, and dreams, selling them unnecessary things, tying their self-worth to purchasing power, and creating rampant materialism and inner emptiness.[5]

The children's marketing industry is a runaway train. Largely unregulated and growing rapidly, advertisers allocate more than $15 billion each year for marketing to children in the United States alone.[6] The average American child sees more than 40,000 television commercials annually.[7] Consumer culture consistently instructs global girls to "Be all that you can buy."

Apparently, all this money is well invested; children now influence the spending of more than $600 billion, including $28 billion of their own money.[8] Teenage girls spend more than $9 billion per year on makeup alone.[9]

The constant exposure to external messages that promise everything—from beauty to popularity, peace of mind, self-confidence, and great relationships—turns children, especially girls, into insatiable consumers. The quick fix of their next purchase robs them of self-determination, self-awareness, and self-esteem. Encouraged to look outside themselves for comfort, values, and direction, global girls fall easy prey to the addictive behaviors and unrealistic images that these ads promote. In fact, the diet, tobacco, and alcohol industries target women of all ages, but especially girls and teens, capitalizing on the body image, weight preoccupation, and beauty ideals that make them most vulnerable.[10]

The Global Image

Looking back at past ideals of beauty can help to put things in perspective. Marilyn Monroe, the dream girl of the 1950s and early '60s, would now likely be considered a plus-size figure. The first runway models all weighed 155 pounds or more, and in 1922, the first Miss America weighed 140 pounds at 5'7". By a half-century later, "beauty" had become 50 pounds leaner, with Twiggy weighing in at 91 pounds and 5'6".[11] Suddenly, it was necessary to meet the criteria for anorexia nervosa, the deadly eating disorder, in order to be considered model material.

Weighing less than 85 percent of the expected body weight for one's height and age is one of the criteria now used to diagnose anorexia. Twiggy's weight was approximately 70 percent of the norm—which, according to standard medical practice today, would suggest the need for tube-feeding.

Despite the fact that the average American woman today is 5'4" tall and weighs 140 pounds, the average fashion model is 5'11" and weighs 117 pounds—a shocking 75 percent of the normal body weight for that height.[12] Although girls are surrounded by average women's bodies in their families, schools, and communities, advertisers idealize only very thin and very "beautiful" Caucasian women. Despite the diversity of skin color seen in our global village, light skin and a very western look is the hottest global image around. Women of color who are pictured in fashion layouts or appear on prime-time TV tend to be whitewashed, further diminishing ethnic and racial pride among global girls.

Malevolent Media and Global Girls

By imposing impossible standards to keep women of all ages unsure, uneasy, and "in their place," the mass media relentlessly pressure global girls to be someone other than who they naturally are. By default, they develop a false self, constantly focusing on the outside, expressing their femininity through their appearance rather than their actions, accomplishments, feelings, and relationships.

Teenage girls are especially vulnerable to the media for several reasons. Adolescence is always a critical time in identity formation. Absorbing as much information as possible, teenagers' mission is to figure out who and what they want to become. Cognitively, they are keenly aware of cultural standards and ideals. Simultaneously, they are at a point of peak exposure to the media and its messages in all forms, while they are spending less and less time with their families, which are often viewed as categorically uncool. Taken together, the impact of these influences is multiplied exponentially.

Television accounts for a large part of the problem: TV rarely depicts women as powerful or prestigious, and it almost always portrays them as physically beautiful and extremely thin, fostering an image of perfection that few in the real world can live up to. Fifteen-year-old girls watch 20–25 hours of television each week during the school year. Watching soap operas, movies, music videos, and programs loaded with stereotypical roles for women has been associated with greater body dissatisfaction and a desire for thinness. Some of the "reality" shows actually follow women through cosmetic surgery as they craft a new image and compete in "beauty" pageants instead of dealing with more serious concerns. Among the most popular television shows, these set an even more distorted image for global girls.

Advertising also plays a major role. Female icons often look like boys with breasts and washboard stomachs. As a result, a recent survey of 2,600 teen girls[13] reported the following:

- 68 percent want to flatten their stomachs.
- 74 percent work out 2–3 times a week.
- 38 percent constantly think about their weight.
- 84 percent envy other girls' bodies.

Of course, the media's treatment of women did not evolve overnight. As far back as the 1970s, media critics pointed out the subliminal but systematic subservience of female images in print ads.[14] For example, female figures are generally pictured as smaller, shown in passive positions, and often placed literally below men. This discriminatory pattern continues despite the efforts of the women's movement and our increased awareness of gender and power issues.

A systematic review of magazine articles shows an inordinate emphasis on women's bodies as compared to men's; the not very subtle message being that, for men, many things may be important, while for women, only the body counts. Girls are constantly portrayed in silly and subservient positions, sometimes off-balance, often passively observing others, while boys are active, powerful, and in control.

In fact, women are actually more sexualized and objectified in magazine ads now than they were a decade ago. Female body exposure has increased, with almost 62 percent of white women and 53 percent of black women scantily clad, while only 25 percent of men were shown without dignified clothing. More than 17 percent of ads show women in lower status positions, such as on their knees or on the floor. Black women particularly were posed in sexualized, predatory positions, often wearing animal prints.[15]

Girls who compare themselves to media images of beauty are the most likely to develop eating disorders. Female undergrads report more stress, depression, guilt, shame, insecurity, and body dissatisfaction after exposure to ultrathin models,[16] and 70 percent of college women reported feeling worse about themselves after reading magazines.[17] The bad news is that global girls of all ages are constantly exposed to these images and messages. They rarely hear that they (or someone who looks like them) are beautiful just as they are. And, no surprise, men also see the average woman as less attractive following exposure to popular magazines.

Rites of Passage for Global Girls: Is Anyone Watching?

As media content related to women becomes increasingly sexualized, puberty now arrives sooner and hits harder than ever before. In the early 19th century, the average age of menarche was 15 or 16. Today most girls begin menstruating at age 12, and many have already had intercourse by their mid-teens. This contrasts sharply with teens in the 1890s, most of whom were virgins when they married in their early 20s.

Facing puberty earlier in life presents its own new set of difficulties. Global girls are forced to cope with tremendous changes in their bodies, the challenges of monthly menses, and the sense that they are supposed to be sexual, long before they are emotionally mature. They look and dress like grown-ups. Even if they should want to resist societal pressures and delay prematurely assuming the role of adults, rarely can they find clothes that allow them to look like the children they truly are. And sadly, fewer caring and understanding people are available to assist them through this critical passage. Girls find themselves less protected and less nurtured than ever before.

And so menarche pushes global girls into a "consumer culture that seduces them into thinking that their body and sexual expression are their most important projects."[18] The pubescent body has to be managed rather than experienced, and there's a product for everything, from high tech pads and tampons to medicines and special products to wash or spray away any natural scent or trace of the changing body.

Support through this rite of passage is sought from all kinds of money-making moguls, including drug companies, "feminine hygiene products," magazines, glossy educational materials, and videos, instead of the mothers, grandmothers, aunts, cousins, and older friends who were once so available during this critical psychosexual transition. Information about birth control and sexually transmitted diseases is readily available, but a heart-to-heart talk about what it means to be a woman is a rare occurrence for global girls.

The medical system also lets down global girls. Despite how open we believe we are about sex and other sensitive topics, 35 percent of girls report that they are too embarrassed to discuss with their doctors issues including sexuality, menstruation, cramps, physical changes, abuse, birth control, and pregnancy.[19] Bombarded with information and stimulation, there seems to be no one to talk to at this critical point in development. The mass media have taken over parenting, and they make very impersonal and manipulative mothers and fathers.

On the other hand, thanks to magazines and the Internet, global girls do have access to information. Seventy percent of girls aged 10–14 who read magazines like *Teen*, *Sassy*, or *Seventeen* say that these are important sources of information for them on all kinds of issues, including beauty, fitness, and health.[20] Unfortunately, with the absence of real people to talk to about these and other confusing issues, many see the fashion models in the magazines as the ideals to emulate.

Living in the cyber age, global girls have cyber relationships and give credence to cyber information, without truly knowing the source. The Internet provides intimacy as well as education about the most critical issues in life. Global girls surf the Net and discover the latest diet products to send for—no parent or doctor needed. Easily they come upon the pro-Ana or pro-Mia websites, short for pro-anorexia or pro-bulimia, where severe eating disorders are promoted as a lifestyle choice and not an illness. Girls who are already dabbling in disordered eating find a script for self-destruction here. The Web, then, is a tangled mixture of good and bad information, equally readily available 24 hours a day, 7 days a week.

The Language of Global Girls

The global village is a harsh environment for girls. Generally taught not to express negative feelings or strong opinions, they are left with few ways to deal with difficult emotions or experiences. Lacking other resources, they too often translate any and all emotional conflicts and concerns into the language of fat.[21]

Convinced that fat is bad, global girls begin to convert feeling bad or unsure of themselves into feeling fat. They struggle to succeed in a girl-destroying culture[22] full of mixed messages and paradoxes. They are expected to achieve, but not to achieve too much. Be true to themselves, but be polite and submissive to others. Be aware of the culture, but never mention its inherent sexism. Be feminine and adult, but sexy and coy, whatever that means. They are trained to sacrifice their true selves and become less, rather than more, individualistic.

In the midst of these competing demands and double binds, the more complex issues of identity, relationships, anxiety, and insecurity can all be avoided when "fat" is the only acknowledged feeling. In our global village, the language of fat is fast becoming universal parlance.

The Changing Face of Eating Disorders

Globalization allows western culture to export many products and ideas. Unfortunately, for global girls, part of this legacy promotes a relationship to food and to the body that takes away more than it gives and puts their lives at risk.

For many years, eating disorders were found almost exclusively in highly industrialized western nations like the United States, Canada, and some western European countries. Other cultures seemed immune to them. As globalization proceeds, however, this pattern has changed dramatically. Now the list of nearly 40 countries reporting eating disorders includes places as unexpected as Nigeria, India, China, South Korea, South Africa, the former Soviet Union, and Mexico.[23] Yet there is a common factor among these seemingly disparate countries: each, in its own way, has begun to idealize thinness in women. In contrast, eating disorders simply do not appear in cultures that reflect more reasonable body-image norms.

Many dynamics drive the spread of eating disorders. Cultural risk factors include sophisticated and fast-growing economies and rapid technology and market changes that affect women's status. With greater access to education, new positions in the workplace, and the accompanying gender equity issues, women's lives are in an unsettling process of transformation. Factor in changes in the modern diet, now filled with prepared foods that are high in calories and fat, and a more sedentary lifestyle, which have both led to an increase in obesity. The body reality conflicts radically with the body ideal, bringing up a myriad of issues for global girls.

This conflict and its many cultural risk factors make what has happened in countries like Japan sadly predictable. Having rapidly assimilated western technological and social influences after World War II, Japan quickly developed a significant rate of eating disorders: 5.5 percent of Japanese women currently meet the criteria for anorexia nervosa alone.[24]

An even more dramatic example of the impact of globalization occurred in Fiji. This was a culture where large female bodies were valued for their strength and contribution to family and community life, and where food was celebrated and enjoyed with rich traditions and meanings. Eating disorders were virtually nonexistent.

Then in 1995, limited exposure to western network television was introduced. Within three years, eating disorders had run rampant. From little concern with dieting or weight in 1995, by 1998 11 percent of the population had begun to practice self-induced vomiting, 29 percent were at risk for clinical eating disorders, 69 percent had dieted to lose weight, and 74 percent felt "too fat." Watching popular female images on TV created a desire for the kind of life these stars seemed to have, and these new "global girls" committed to changing their body to get it.[25] Evidently, powerful global influences can overturn strong local cultural traditions and values almost overnight.

Sexual Violence: Whose Body Is It?

Situations that earlier generations faced in college—drugs, drinking, smoking, sex, to name a few—today confront many girls by middle school and sometimes even earlier. One young woman innocently explained that she had been a "late bloomer," not sexually active till she was in college. She spoke apologetically, embarrassed and ashamed to reveal how "old" she was at her first sexual experience. Her next statement was also a sad commentary on the sexual revolution: "I'm the only one of all my friends who didn't lose her virginity in a date rape."

In a very real sense, global girls do not own their own bodies, which are constantly violated by a culture that objectifies, degrades, and attacks them. As a result, many global girls expect forced sex to be part of the female experience. An on-line poll of teen girls indicated that 28 percent of them had been pressured to engage in intercourse or another sexual act against their will. The majority, 54 percent, blamed themselves, and another 10 percent were unsure if it was their fault or not. Twenty-one percent of the girls surveyed said that they didn't know how to refuse.[26]

Another study found that 21 percent of high school girls had been abused, physically (17 percent), sexually (12 percent), or both.[27] Teens are twice as likely to be victims of violent crime than the general population and are quite likely to be victimized repeatedly. Of women who were sexually assaulted in college, 38 percent had already been victimized prior to entering college. African-American girls aged 12–15 face the highest risk, but no girl is safe.[28]

These statistics make a simple point: the more objectified young women are, the more their self-esteem is diminished and the less able they are to assert their own will over their lives. Such abuse dramatically increases the risk for both substance abuse and eating disorders, since both serve to "self-medicate" or numb a person from pain and anguish.

In fact, eating disorders serve a variety of psychological functions for someone dealing with trauma. Starving, bingeing, purging, and other self-punitive behaviors may be an expression of hatred for the body that experienced abuse, a means of expressing anger or rage without lashing out at anyone else, an attempt to impose control over what enters or stays in the body, or a desire to fade away into oblivion or to be repugnant and unattractive.

Global girls grow up in a culture that is both overtly and covertly abusive. Film, television, magazines, and the Internet all make violence against women seem the norm. Men are indoctrinated into this attitude from boyhood on. Video games are notorious for this, but most parents don't have a clue about what their young children are seeing and absorbing. *Grand Theft Auto 3*, the most popular video game sold in 2002, is full of violence toward both sexes. It rewards players for having sex with a prostitute and then killing her. *Vice City*, produced by the same company, Rockstar Games, features abusive pimps and powerless prostitutes, and glorifies brutal murders of women.[29] If we accept this as normal childhood play, our society is doomed to misogyny and violence against women. We can't change girls' experiences without changing boys'.

Is Any Body (Anybody) Real?

A supermodel once claimed that the only way she can recognize herself in ads is by a distinctive mole.[30] The airbrushing and computer-enhanced effects are so extensive, she cannot even identify her own body.

Many photography services for school yearbooks offer extensive retouching: glasses, braces, and blemishes can be removed; hair can be added, removed, shortened, or lengthened; clothes and colors can be changed. When a global girl sees this offer, it may be hard to refuse— she can look like someone she isn't and be remembered that way for years to come.

Everywhere we look, it is becoming more and more difficult to find authentic women who are unafraid of being who they are. One magazine cover featuring a woman's face was actually made up of five different images all blended together. Julia Roberts was not considered thin enough for the sex scenes in *Pretty Woman,* so a body double was used.

And even ordinary people now have plastic surgery to cater to the demand for bodily "perfection."

Some stars are defying these expectations. At the age of 43, critically acclaimed movie star Jamie Lee Curtis decided to come out of the closet as a woman with a real woman's body—a gutsy act for any Hollywood actress. Having written a series of children's books emphasizing the importance of "just being you," she decided to take part in a photo shoot without any makeup, jewelry, or professional assistance, under bright and unforgiving studio lights, in nothing more than a sports bra and spandex briefs. The image appeared in a major women's magazine. But on the next page, the other Jamie Lee Curtis appeared, made up, dressed up, and fully airbrushed. That image took three hours and a staff of 13 professionals to create.[31]

Even when female stars want to model a more realistic shape or body type, they may not succeed. Kate Winslett, known for many leading roles, especially coupled with Leo DiCaprio in *Titanic*, has spoken out against dieting and the waiflike images promoted in today's films. She admitted that she likes herself better when she weighs more. Despite this, the British *GQ* airbrushed and retouched her to slim her down for their cover. She fought back in the press, saying, "I do not look like that. And, more important, I don't desire to look like that."[32]

These are two examples of brave women who defied society's expectations. While their courage may have placed their careers at some risk, both have already achieved fame and wealth and could more easily afford to take this stand. The average global girl knows that being real has a price. And she may not be able or willing to afford it.

The Plastic Self

Cosmetic plastic surgery is hot. It's the fastest growing medical specialty in the global village. It is one way to emulate Barbie, the ultimate plastic icon. Technological culture constantly, but subliminally, suggests that global girls accept nothing as is. Everything needs to be changed, improved, transformed for the better. It is a culture of conformity rather than of acceptance, encouraging global girls to pursue solutions as radical as surgery to feel more attractive and accepted.

Not too long ago, anyone who opted for surgery without an extreme disfigurement was seen as insecure, unstable, or neurotic. Next, plastic surgery was reserved for older, wealthy, vain women clinging to the illusion of youth. But now, plastic surgery is seen as an affordable investment for normal people of all ages who just want to "improve" their appearance.

Marketing self-actualization and self-esteem through medicine has worked. In fact, plastic surgery for teens increased by nearly 50 percent in just two years during the late 1990s.[33] A poll found that 25 percent of the readers of *Seventeen* magazine had already considered cosmetic plastic surgery.[34] Before their bodies are even mature, teens are opting at record rates for nose jobs, body sculpting, liposuction, and breast reduction or augmentation. Many of their favorite stars and role models have led the way. No longer seen as unusual or a luxury, surgery is now an everyday necessity in the minds of many global girls.

No matter what a girl's culture or ethnicity, the standard for global girls is Caucasian. When it comes to female beauty in the global village, the value of seeing diversity or multiculturalism as "beautiful" is outdated. The most frequent plastic surgery in eastern countries is a technique called "upper lid westernization," in which the natural Asian eye is reshaped to appear Caucasian.[35] Although globalization could have brought an appreciation of many different types of beauty, we instead see global girls of all ages pursuing only one ideal and paying any price for it.

Global Girls and Dangerous Diets

A study of more than 80,000 9th and 12th graders in the United States found that among 9th graders, 56 percent of females and 28 percent of males were engaged in unsafe dieting practices. Among 12th graders, 57 percent of females and 31 percent of males were involved in dangerous diet modification, including skipping meals, ingesting diet pills or laxatives, inducing vomiting, smoking cigarettes, and binge eating. These rates were highest among Hispanic and Native American students.

The good news from this study is that positive self-esteem, emotional well-being, school achievement, and family connectedness serve to protect kids from dangerous diet practices.[36] However, girls who perceive their families as troubled or feel the home is a negative environment are more likely to develop body image concerns and disordered eating practices.[37]

The Centers for Disease Control and Prevention[38] also reports epidemic rates of weight loss attempts among high school students. For example, the CDC's extensive study of teenage diet-related behaviors exhibited in the previous month found that:

1. 46% were trying to lose weight.

2. 44% were actively dieting.

3. 60% were exercising to lose or avoid gaining weight.

A breakdown by gender showed that, while both sexes are troubled by weight concerns, girls are engaging in dangerous dieting much more often than boys are.

In the global village, dieting has become the acceptable standard of behavior. In 2004, *Amazon.com* listed nearly 90,000 titles under the category of "Diet." Popular magazines are full of weight loss plans and diet products. The health food store, the supermarket, and the drugstore all sell various diet pills and metabolism boosters, some of which have no active ingredients while others contain potentially dangerous substances such as amphetamines and ephedrine. Many global girls believe herbs are safe, but ephedra and other "natural products" can be powerful stimulants, and when misused can cause cardiac irregularities, high blood pressure, tremors, anxiety, headaches, heart attacks, strokes, and even death.

The tragedy is that dieting in these global times can be dangerous and even deadly. Global girls who develop clinical eating disorders are 12 times more likely than their peers to die from a medical problem and 75 times more likely to commit suicide.[39] These are problems that no culture should import.

Equal Opportunity Obsessions

Teenage dieting is an equal opportunity activity, although many still believe that disordered eating and eating disorders are primarily found in upper middle class Caucasian girls. With the impact of the media and the stress of rapid social change, these problems are now taking hold of most cultures, ethnic groups, and classes throughout the United States. The Centers for Disease Control and Prevention[40] surveyed teenage girls about their dieting in the past month and found these results:

	White	Black	Hispanic
Exercising to lose weight	72.5%	53.4%	66.2%
Dieting	63.1%	40.2%	56.5%
Fasting	19.7%	15.2%	23.1%
Using diet pills	13.6%	7.5%	13.5%
Purging	8.2%	4.2%	10.8%

Contrary to public opinion, global girls of any color or class are at risk, but biased beliefs about who suffers from these problems may prevent many from getting help.

In fact, assimilating into American culture significantly increases the likelihood that non-Caucasian individuals and those from non-mainstream cultures will begin to demonstrate body image and food concerns, although the behaviors may emerge differently. For example, women from a lower socioeconomic status may develop binge-eating disorder rather than anorexia or bulimia.[41] Furthermore, a study of African American girls found significant fears regarding maturity and a strong drive for perfection, characteristics that are commonly seen in girls who later develop eating disorders.[42]

Many global girls cannot resist the impulse to diet. As the media bombards them with ads, programs, and infomercials filled with images of unattainable bodies, they also learn that 65 percent of adults in America are overweight, with as many as 25 percent meeting the criteria for obesity. Even more disturbing, the obesity rate in children has doubled in the past 40 years.[43] The reality is that dieting has actually made us fatter, but that may be difficult for global girls to comprehend in light of the weight loss propaganda and commercial campaigns that assail them from every angle.

Learning Their ABCs

Despite the attention paid in recent years to gender equity in schools, global girls still encounter major obstacles that affect their learning. They are treated differently based on gender, and they experience sexual harassment earlier and more repeatedly than boys do.[44]

The "fairer sex" is still encouraged to be quiet, restrained, and unobtrusive in the classroom. One study found that preschool teachers tell girls three times more frequently than boys to speak more softly and use a "nicer voice."[45] Girls suffer as a result, being less able to speak or advocate for themselves both inside and outside school.

As they pass from grade to grade, girls often grow less and less self-confident. Approaching puberty, they change from being self-assured, capable, clear-thinking individuals to uncertain, insecure, anxious self-doubters. Having been encouraged for so many years to be quiet and passive, global girls confronting the hostile hallways of middle school and high school are poorly equipped for self-defense. According to the American Association of University Women, 81 percent of 8th –11th graders experience sexual harassment, with 27 percent reporting that this occurs often. Some face it as early as 3rd grade. Many will avoid school or cut classes, others will be less able to pay attention and learn, and as many as 24 percent will speak out less in class as a result.[46]

This continues in college. One study found that 35 percent of female college students reported sexual harassment on campus, including behaviors such as punching, cornering, verbal abuse, or assault. However, fewer than 20 percent of these filed any complaint. Another study reported that 40 percent of undergraduate and graduate women were harassed during their first year on campus, with more than 10 percent saying they had been sexually assaulted. Many coeds also experience computer-based harassment, being stalked on the Internet, threatened, and sent gruesome images.[47] Having never developed ways to respond and fight back, the shame they feel about these experiences leads to depression, self-injury, and even eating disorders.

Other Issues for Global Schoolgirls

Title IX of the Educational Amendments of 1972 provided a great impetus for increasing the opportunities available to global girls. It mandates gender equity in high school and junior high school athletics by prohibiting sexual discrimination in educational institutions that receive federal funds. Since its enactment, girls' sports have flourished. In 1972 only 2 percent of girls participated in organized athletics.

Now, more than 40 percent do. Sports create opportunities for leadership, teamwork, achievement, and competition, providing an arena where positive adult role models are generally present. Girls who participate in sports are less likely to use drugs or become pregnant and are more likely to graduate from high school. An impressive 80 percent of the women in upper-level positions of Fortune 500 companies played sports in school.[48] Unfortunately, Title IX is under siege as critics assert that money is being taken from boys' sports to fund girls' sports.

Despite all the benefits of sports for global girls, some risks are also present. Many girls do find that athletics build a stronger sense of pride and confidence in their bodies, which is not contingent on their appearance. On the other hand, some girls become less satisfied with their bodies and more keen on weight loss. The risks for this outcome are generally higher in sports that emphasize a trim, lean body (such as rowing and track) or are judged (such as gymnastics and diving). Individual personality traits, such as perfectionism, and pressure from parents or coaches make some girls more likely to develop body image problems and eating disorders.[49]

Today, many global girls feel they must play sports to be "good enough" and socially accepted in the very competitive teen world. Families who think that athletic prowess will increase their daughter's chances for college scholarships may exert undue pressure on her to excel. Other girls conclude that sports are the only way to please their father and assure his continuing involvement in their lives. Despite the potential benefits, organized athletics are not for everyone. Even so, many global girls feel tremendous pressure to compete.

Another positive trend has also emerged for global schoolgirls: their opportunities in math and science have increased. Yet because of gender-biased career preparation programs, girls still lag behind in technology skills. By 2010, 65 percent of workplace jobs will require computer skills, but few girls are encouraged to take computer programming rather than data entry classes. As a result, they find themselves being prepared for passive rather than active roles in industry. Although girls take Advanced Placement courses as frequently as boys, only 17 percent take AP computer science.[50]

Critics say that gender equity attempts have gone too far, but in fact, both boys *and* girls have serious gender-related gaps in their academic preparation. Just as girls take less science and math coursework, boys take less language, psychology, sociology, and fine arts. So girls are handicapped in their computer skills, while boys are handicapped in their communication skills.

Another gender equity issue is the disparity between grades and standardized tests. While girls get better overall grades in high school, boys outscore them on standardized tests, including the SAT, ACT, and AP exams. This has major implications for college acceptance and similar opportunities.[51]

All of these areas require attention if we are to level the playing field for global girls. Until we do, global girls will focus on image, weight, and appearance as their primary keys to success.

What Dads Can Do to Help Their Global Girls

Daughters need their dads now more than ever. Fathers can make a huge difference in their daughters' lives just by showing up, standing by, and listening. Here are some more suggestions.

Know what you don't know. Learn about your daughter's life. Don't believe that your experience and hers are similar; in fact, you are years and cultures apart. Respect the differences.

Consider the many impacts globalization will have on her life. Think about the variety of skills and coping mechanisms she will need to succeed in her world. Do whatever you can to help her develop these.

Show interest in her activities. Don't just expect her to tag along with you or to like the things you like. Enter her world by sharing her music, going places that she wants to visit, and doing things she enjoys.

Take the quiz, "How Well Am I Doing as My Daughter's Father?" (included at the end of this chapter). It will help you assess the gaps in your knowledge about your daughter's life. Commit to improving your score and take it again in 2 months.

Encourage her to identify and discuss her emotions and opinions. Let her disagree with you without withdrawing your affection. Show respect for differences between the two of you.

Teach her to say no and set limits. This will prepare her for situations that might compromise or even endanger her.

Help your daughter develop values other than consumerism. Share some of your values and create opportunities to enjoy nature, reading, the arts, sports, music, cultivation of friendships, volunteerism, or other interests and activities.

Show respect for real women of substance. Be aware of your attitudes toward women, their appearance, and their achievements. Point out the important contributions women make in your community and family.

Watch what you say about women's bodies. Criticizing and focusing on women's weight and appearance has become a cultural norm, so commonly accepted that men may not realize the power of what they say in the presence of their daughters.

Be Your Brother's Keeper. Challenge your male friends and associates when they show disrespect for women, objectify women, or make sexist remarks. A little bit of courage can go a long way toward helping to create a better world for your daughter.

Promote respect for all shapes and sizes. Weightism is rampant today. Take stock of your attitudes toward fat people. Become aware of your prejudices and work to overcome them.

Examine your own weight, eating, and body image issues. Men are not immune to these concerns, as today they are experiencing more and more pressure about their appearance. Make peace with your own body and treat it well.

Maintain a diet-free home. Encourage enjoyment of food, moderate exercise, and a healthy, balanced lifestyle. Rules about food only backfire and contribute to eating and weight problems.

Emphasize inner beauty. Talk about what you value in people and especially in her. Help her to see that she is more than an image to you.

Become more media-literate and help her to do so too. Discuss unrealistic images when you see them on billboards, on TV, or at the movies. Help her to identify and think critically about the distorted images presented in visual media.

Rid your home and work environment of anything that objectifies or degrades women. Magazines like the *Sports Illustrated*

Swimsuit Issue and *Playboy*, and items such as pin-up calendars, breed body dissatisfaction and self-degradation. Many standard men's magazines are full of demeaning images of women. Look around carefully and clean up your space.

Monitor what she is exposed to on TV and the Internet. Set rules about both. Endless solitary hours with either are likely to be unhealthy. Locate the computer and TV where they can be casually overseen.

Let her find and follow her passions. Encourage her interest in academics, sports, the arts, and other activities, whether they are traditionally feminine or masculine.

Find out if her school has gender equity and sexual harassment policies. If it doesn't, set up a task force. This will make her world safer.

Don't let adolescence scare you away. When she starts to develop sexually, stay close and involved while respecting her maturing need for more control and boundaries.

Encourage positive female role models. Be sure she has caring women in her life who can help her learn about her body and sexuality as she moves through puberty, especially if her mother is not part of her life.

Raise better boys. Spend time with sons and boys, sharing your values and helping them to become sensitive to women, instead of leaving them to a misogynistic culture.

Let her get to know you. Share your life and interests with her. Be real and honest, and get out of the role of Superman. Talk about your feelings. This will help her negotiate other relationships with male authority figures.

How Well Am I Doing As My Daughter's Father?

Here is a short Dads and Daughters self-assessment quiz. It will give you a quick way to understand how well you're doing as your daughter's father. Answer honestly and add up your score before peeking at the scoring key. If your daughter isn't school-aged, skip the school-related items and subtract 15 points from your score. (Reproduced with permission from J. Kelly, *Dads and Daughters: How to Inspire, Understand, and Support Your Daughter When She's Growing Up So Fast.* New York: Broadway Books, 2002.)

	Often	Some-times	Hardly Ever
1. I can name my daughter's three best friends.	1	2	3
2. I know my daughter's goals.	1	2	3
3. I comment on my wife/partner's weight.	3	2	1
4. I'm physically active with my daughter (shoot hoops, jog, etc.)	1	2	3
5. I make dinner for my family.	1	2	3
6. I talk to my daughter about managing money.	1	2	3
7. I spend 1/2 hour, one-on-one with her, doing something we both enjoy.	1	2	3
8. I talk to other fathers about raising kids.	1	2	3
9. I talk to other fathers about raising daughters.	1	2	3
10. I restrict her activities more than I do/would do for a son.	3	2	1
11. I talk to my daughter about advertising.	1	2	3
12. I tell my daughter what her strengths are.	1	2	3
13. I comment on my daughter's weight.	3	2	1
14. I know what school projects she's working on.	1	2	3
15. I protest negative media portrayals of girls.	1	2	3

16. I view pornographic material.	3	2	1
17. I participate in parenting organizations.	1	2	3
18. I yell at my daughter's mother.	3	2	1
19. I suggest that my daughter go on a diet.	3	2	1
20. I object when others suggest that she go on a diet.	1	2	3
21. I converse with my daughter, and she does most of the talking.	1	2	3
22. I know what my daughter is concerned about today.	1	2	3
23. I know how many student government officers at her school are girls.	1	2	3
24. I have read her school's sexual harassment policy.	1	2	3
25. I help boys learn to respect girls.	1	2	3
26. I tell my daughter stories about my own youth.	1	2	3
(27-30 - For dads who live AWAY from their daughters)			
27. I initiate contact with her at least 5 times a week.	1	2	3
28. I ask how she feels transitioning to and from my home.	1	2	3
29. I demonstrate respect for her mother and stepparent.	1	2	3
30. I fulfill my visitation and support commitments.	1	2	3
(31-34 - For dads who live WITH their daughters)			
31. I volunteer to help with her extracurricular activities.	1	2	3
32. I take my daughter to school.	1	2	3
33. I visit my daughter's school during the school day.	1	2	3
34. I take my daughter to work with me.	1	2	3

Scoring:

If your daughter isn't school-aged and you skipped the school-related items, subtract 15 points from your total score.

If you scored:

30–35: Your relationship with your daughter looks like it's on very solid ground.

36–45: You appear to have a good foundation, but there are areas to improve.

46–60: You probably need to take active steps to reexamine your attitudes and learn ways to build deeper respect for each other.

61–90: It's time to consider serious change. Your actions and attitudes may be undermining your daughter.

Your exact score is not as important as noticing how you answered the questions. Take some time to review your responses and identify some of the areas in which you can make improvements.

and beliefs about femininity. Today, because women's roles have changed tremendously and are still in flux, girls need as much direction and guidance as they can get from both the significant women and the significant men in their lives.

Myth #10: Girls need their mothers, not their fathers, during adolescence.

Again, girls require both their mother and their father; it's not an either/or option. Especially when parents are separated or divorced, girls need contact with both parents and should not have to choose one over the other. A mother must accept her daughter's interest in her father and her husband's interest in his daughters. Young boys who lose contact with their father show the impact of this loss early in life. In girls, the effect is generally not apparent until adolescence or adulthood, when they become aware of their own sexuality and move into an expanded arena of personal and social relationships with men.

Fathers play a particularly special role in their daughter's passage from childhood to adolescence. Girls need to have their rites of passage honored by their fathers. They want to feel attractive, womanly, and acceptable to the most important man in their lives—their father. Their father's approval and encouragement helps them accept their changing bodies and gives them confidence with boys. In the absence of this acceptance, girls often experience self-doubt, self-deprecation, and depression. They may act out their distress in many ways—by withdrawing from social contact, by being promiscuous, or by the self-loathing and rejection of self that is expressed through an eating disorder.

Adolescent girls may experience the loss of their father's attention for many reasons. Because fathers believe they are unimportant to their children, particularly to their daughters, they may not devote the energy necessary to work at the changing relationship that naturally occurs when girls leave childhood and enter adolescence. Fathers frequently do not enjoy their daughters' new interests and the attention they pay to their appearance and to the intricate details of their relationships. Their daughters no longer seek them out for childhood games and bedtime stories, so fathers may not know how to reach out and interact with them in new ways that are more appropriate to an older child. Girls may make a painful association between developing a more sexual body and becoming a young woman and losing their father. When growing up means losing significant relationships, the maturation process is neither attractive nor promising.

On the positive side, numerous studies have shown that women who report having had a close and caring relationship with their father during childhood developed a strong sense of personal identity and positive self-esteem, as well as enjoying greater confidence in their adult relationships with men.[13] A supportive father-daughter relationship significantly influences women over a long period of time, improving their likelihood for positive self-esteem, body image, moral strength, and intellectual and social competence. Girls who witness parents who are compatible and respectful of each other identify positively with both and develop a comfortable sense of gender identity.[14]

How lucky girls are to have dads who are involved and caring. In fact, they are twice as likely to go to college or find a stable job after high school, 75 percent less likely to give birth as a teenager, 80 percent less likely to ever be in jail, and half as likely to experience significant depression.[15] To further illustrate this point, when fathers support their daughters' physical and athletic development during adolescence, girls display less sex-role rigidity, more social independence, and more success both in school and in their later work lives.[16]

In contrast, girls who grow up without a close relationship to dad are likely to have difficulties with men in general, being unable to assert themselves, speak directly, and negotiate issues. Forced to develop indirect ways to communicate, they may act coy, seductive, or manipulative to get their needs met.[17] In general, successful women are more likely than their peers to report having experienced strong paternal support and involvement and the perception that father believed in their competence.

Fathers need to be available to their daughters to make their development a positive process, to guide them into adulthood, and to help them separate from mother while retaining their sense of female identity. Young women integrate their own sexual maturity through their relationship with their father. A secure bond with him makes the new experiences, challenges, and responsibilities of adolescence and adulthood feel safer. Most important, it assures them that their dads still love them. Daughters need this reassurance no matter how old they are.

New Myths for a New Day

Historically, our old myths have served a functional purpose, prescribing stable family roles for each new generation. Even today, some families adhering to cultural traditions appear to function well on a superficial level. But times have changed, and these limiting roles and rules have become obsolete. Continuing to adhere to them is like refusing to abandon a sinking ship. It contributes to great personal dissatisfaction and family dysfunction. To fully address the issues and consequences of father hunger, changes and healing must occur not only at the level of the individual and family, but also in the larger culture as a whole.

To challenge the myths and notions that accept these imbalanced roles and promote father hunger in each succeeding generation will require creative changes in the life scripts of both men and women. In the home as well as the work environment, power and responsibility must be redistributed more evenly.

To begin this process in your own life, take some time to think about new myths that could promote a deeper, closer relationship between children and their fathers and that would gradually decrease the epidemic and long-term consequences of father hunger.

Questions and New Connections

- How many of the 10 myths did you agree with before you read this chapter?
- How many do you agree with now?
- How have these myths affected your life and your own relationship with your father and or daughter?
- How would our lives change if fathers were more available and involved in the family?
- Conceptualize ten myths that would promote a positive father-daughter relationship, and write them down. What would your life be like if these myths had guided your relationship with your father? If you are a father, how will your new myths influence your relationship with your daughter?
- What can you do to put your new myths into practice in your family?

CHAPTER 4

Fathers As Second-Class Citizens

The traditions and myths of many societies have long treated men as second-class citizens or shadows in families, perpetuating generation after generation of paternal deprivation. Yet fathers are seen by one expert in child development as: "the single greatest untapped resource in the lives of American children."[1] If we are serious about meeting the needs of children and families, we must find ways to connect fathers to their families and especially to their global girls.

While we still focus far more research on mothers alone, we have learned a fair amount about fathers in the past 25 years. Now we know that when fathers are absent, it is not simply a sex role that is missing; fathers have a much greater impact than that alone. We have learned that fathers and mothers influence children in similar ways: parental warmth, nurturance, and closeness lead to positive outcomes whether the parent is male or female. Individual characteristics of a father (such as masculinity or intellect) and the amount of time spent with his child are less important than the kind of relationship he develops with his child. Furthermore, individual relationships between parents and children are actually less important than the overall family con- text: a well-functioning, warm, nonhostile environment is associated with positive child adjustment, while marital conflict often leads to child maladjustment. To be a success as fathers, men need to respond to the needs of their individual families; there is no one-size-fits-all script.

By denying men their rightful role as involved parents, we cheat children, for "once a baby is weaned, there is absolutely nothing that ... can't be done just as well by a man as by a woman."[2] We must stop cheating children and fathers of the joys of a close relationship. We desperately need dads.

This chapter examines how the paternal role has evolved historically, so we can understand how to maximize it today and satisfy the father hunger that global girls experience.

Father's Role in the Family: A Historical Perspective

One of the earliest social structures that has been extensively studied is the prehistoric hunting and gathering society. We might think that fathers in such early societies were less available than fathers in today's families because of their long absences in search of food. However, a closer look will show that this conclusion is not supported. In these early communities, fathers could be completely absent for extended periods of time. But as soon as the hunt was over, they returned home. Men left only to obtain their families' basic essentials. The length of time they were away depended on the season, the weather, their success in the hunt, and various other factors.

Actually, the hunting and gathering family was not deprived of contact with paternal figures. They experienced few family problems when father was absent because of the ongoing structure and support given to both parental roles. When father was present, he was available and involved, instructing his sons to hunt and conveying the society's customs to his children. Older men who were no longer strong enough to hunt stayed behind, teaching survival skills as they helped to raise the children. Essentially, men were visible and active in the family.

Despite their distinct division of labor, the two sexes shared power. For example, when men were away, women assumed undisputed authority, and their role as gatherers and preparers of food was acknowledged as essential to survival. When the men returned, they were welcomed back to camp and were appreciated for their contributions. Present or absent, their position of importance was unquestioned. In these ways, division of labor actually crystallized and supported each sex's role. Men and women enjoyed a fairly egalitarian existence, being equally involved with the family and equally important contributors as parents. Because the subsistence societies were relatively classless, issues of power and control between the sexes were not as divisive as they would become later.

Family structure and sex roles changed significantly with the transition from subsistence-based hunting and gathering to more agrarian societies. Since agricultural work requires great physical strength, men became more active farmers while women cared for the children and developed the home environment. Permanent houses and villages replaced the nomadic living of hunters and gatherers. Youngsters interacted minimally with their fathers until they were strong enough to work in the fields.

The advent of the agrarian era, with its consequent impact on parental roles, may mark the origin of the father hunger of modern society. The transition to an agricultural base brought with it the potential for surplus supplies, which resulted in the ability to accrue wealth and gain power. Farmers could accumulate supplies; and wealth, status, and class were based more on men's work than on the joint effort of men and women working together. The family structure became more patriarchal, with men less immediately involved in family life but more dominant as decision makers. One historian who has chronicled the evolution of the father's role believes that as men made the transition from being hunters to becoming farmers, they developed a strong need to assume authority in the family. He concludes: "The hunter dominates his prey, whereas the farmer governs his family."[3]

During this agrarian period, newly married couples usually moved onto the property of the husband's family. This move by the wife to her husband's family symbolized the man's authority. Fathers became increasingly inaccessible to children, assuming the role of remote patriarchs as they established power bases outside the family.

Impact of the Industrial Revolution

The Industrial Revolution, which began in the late 18th century, was probably the most significant factor in the evolution and decline of the father's role in families. Until this time, the father's work had centered around the home. Children saw their fathers and other men during the day and understood the nature of their work. With industrialization, however, men began working long hours away from home.

They became nearly invisible to their children, and mothers assumed almost all responsibility for child rearing.

The traditional father's role had stressed teaching moral and religious values as well as survival skills such as hunting or farming. His new role now became more specialized and limited in scope, primarily providing economically for the family, being the breadwinner, "bringing home the bacon." The transition from nonindustrial to industrial society thus moved father out of the home and changed the family environment dramatically.

Innovations in fashion and physical adornment reflected this transformation of men's and women's roles. Prior to industrialization, men and women equally pursued beauty, physical adornment, and fashion. (Paintings from the Renaissance portray this. Men were extremely fashion-conscious at that time. They wore wigs and makeup, and pampered themselves as much as women did.) Once men began to work in factories, they started to dress more plainly. To demonstrate the fruits of their labor—their money, power, and status—men took new interest in adorning their wives. Historically, women had always altered their appearance to please others, but with the Industrial Revolution, the wife's appearance and adherence to fashion became an expression of her husband's status. The increased emphasis on female beauty is one of the negative outcomes of the shift in sex roles that accompanied industrialization. It contributed largely to today's obsession with body image.

As the Industrial Revolution proceeded, the fields of education, child development, and psychology emerged. They emphasized the importance of motherhood and all but ignored fatherhood, while emerging lifestyles lent increasing support to the growing myth that children need their mothers exclusively and that fathers are extraneous. Still nominally responsible for moral education and for the unpleasant task of disciplining, the father's role was limited to that of judge, policeman, and breadwinner, effectively undermining their positive relationships with their children. Moving the father out of the family and leaving intact only his role as economic provider and disciplinarian placed him in an untenable position.

We are still experiencing the aftershocks of industrialization. Before examining more recent trends, let's summarize the important effects of these economic and social changes. The Industrial Revolution removed the father from a visible role in the family and began the movement toward raising fatherless children. Success outside of the home became the primary goal for men. Women assumed sole responsibility for child rearing, and enhancing their beauty and appearance became a means to signify their husband's success. Highly differentiated scripts for men and women limited families' intimacy, trust, and expression of emotions. These cultural patterns laid the groundwork for the eating and body image problems that plague so many women today.

Contemporary Trends

Trends in the 20th century evolved to place today's father in the proverbial double bind. The more he works away from his family, the better he fulfills his role as provider, and the better father he is seen to be—even if his kids hardly know him! Since children need concrete and physical evidence of affection and caring, however, they feel ignored and insecure when dad doesn't spend time with them. This is the dilemma in which the modern father finds himself.

Until the late 1920s and early 1930s, the father's role as breadwinner and disciplinarian continued unchallenged. The Great Depression, however, dealt a significant blow to the self-esteem and identity of American men. In a failing economy, despite all their hard work and the money they had acquired, they could no longer provide economically for their families. Being the breadwinner had been the core of their identity because they had little, if any, other function in the family. When so many men either lost their jobs or worked far fewer hours, they became quite depressed. Some committed suicide, while others numbed their despair with alcohol. Although fathers might spend more time at home, they no longer held a position of prominence and were probably not emotionally present for their struggling families.

Since then, we have seen more and more fathers disenfranchised and unhappy, weary of the obligation to support the family financially without the rewards of close interaction in the family's emotional life. Some speculate that the pressures placed on fathers to achieve in their roles, together with the lack of emotional support, have contributed to the type A personality and the prevalence of stress-related illnesses that we see so frequently in men. Finally, some men have begun to question the wisdom of defining themselves and their lives almost exclusively through their work.

World War II was the next major influence on the American family. By the late 1930s the American economic scene had begun to improve, with factories operating at full force on defense contracts and fathers once again able to provide for their families. When the United States went to war, women assumed the industrial jobs and men left to fight overseas. The new climate was one of wide support for the war and acknowledgment of men's crucial responsibility to protect their families and defend the world against the destructive forces of Nazism and Imperialism. The father's importance outside the home was once again supported and endorsed. During this period, the roles of both sexes stabilized. The war strengthened women's positions, as they now had to maintain both the family and the country's economy. An aura of mutual respect and support developed.

After the war, however, many women experienced a loss of status when they were again relegated to the role of homemaker. Men resumed their places in the workforce, taking advantage of postwar economic opportunities and becoming ever more distant from the family. During this time of consolidation, the family was highly valued, sex roles were rigidly defined, and father's task was to succeed at work, while mother's was to take care of the home and family. Father remained the disciplinarian, moral teacher, and provider, but a new trend emerged: he was now expected to be a strong role model for his sons, setting a standard of economic and vocational success, personal strength, self-control, and reserved, unemotional logic. Daughters were encouraged to model their mother's behavior, which emphasized homemaking skills and family harmony. In this way, the prescribed roles for men and women were widely divergent.

Despite these significant changes, life for families after World War II was fairly placid. This was certainly the calm before the storm. By the late 1960s, the conflicts brewing beneath the surface of this tranquil period would challenge all the traditional family values and roles. Two key events that contributed to this unrest were the Vietnam War and the women's movement.

American involvement in Vietnam stimulated extreme intergenerational conflict, divisiveness, and persistent doubts about the wisdom of male authority figures. The antiwar movement, largely composed of college students, challenged the establishment's position more loudly and forcefully than any other group had ever challenged a war. The younger generation rejected the decisions and power of their fathers and openly questioned the morality and values of both parents. The rift that developed between the generations led to a widespread rejection of traditional beliefs and customs.

It was not an easy time for parents who had worked hard to provide their children with material wealth and security. The older generation, which had grown up accepting war as a fact of life and believing in the importance of the United States as a safeguard of democracy in the free world, could not understand youth's incessant questioning and disputes over the morality and purpose of America's role in Southeast Asia. Many people still have unhealed wounds from such intergenerational conflicts brought on by the war in Vietnam.

While the Vietnam War stimulated a compelling need to examine our values as a society, the women's movement, rekindled in the late 1960s, further prompted us to look at sex roles in a different light. The effect of this movement has been a gradual reorganization of society to allow women more room to function outside the family and men more room to function within it. Many young men who rejected the war and were disgusted by their fathers' values began to view traditional masculinity as invalid and misguided. They were attracted to the women's movement because it questioned the culturally accepted male roles. However, without alternative role models or blueprints for effective fathering, the status quo persisted.

The Times May Be Changing

Other contemporary factors are contributing to the possibility for change in fathers' roles within the modern family. Although pressure is still placed on fathers to work hard and provide well, men generally work fewer hours today than they did 100 years ago. Actually, men are being forced to assume more active roles in the family, because women are now working full-time and are much more involved outside the family. When women participated as active soldiers in the recent wars in the Persian Gulf and Iraq, fathers were left at home to take care of the children. As women progress into the more traditionally male arenas, men have more opportunities to experience their nurturing female side. Society needs to support both sexes through these changes.

This transformation is not easy. Most men still see work as the key to their identity, and they feel torn between the competing demands of their jobs and their families. Employers expect men to travel and to sacrifice personal time to advance or just to maintain their positions. Men will often accept overwhelming demands at work because supporting the family financially remains crucial to male self-concept and self-esteem, and to being a "good enough" father. Furthermore, many jobs today require advanced technical skills, are personally isolating, and require aggressive behaviors that are incompatible with family life. The competitive win-lose mentality and quick, logical decisiveness that bring success in the office can be disastrous at home.

The increased number of women in the workforce can also cause uneasiness. Men who find themselves competing with women may feel intimidated or angry. Although most grew up in families in which husbands were encouraged to be workaholics and wives were supposed to stand behind them no matter what, they can no longer expect this. Instead, they may find women competing with them at work and demanding more of them at home. As a result, they feel confused, unsuccessful, threatened, and unsupported in both environments.

Despite this, most men want their role in the family to encompass more than just providing for its material needs. In fact, when asked about tensions between work and family, many men say that they want more time with their families. Their responses tend to be age-specific. While 79 percent of men aged 40–49 feel that a challenging job with career advancement is more important than family time, 82 percent of men aged 20–39 put family ahead of work, and 71 percent of younger men would even give up some income for this.[4]

Thus we can see that new trends are emerging. Younger couples, in contrast to their parents, expect to coparent their children.[5] This significant shift in a single generation is indicative of our great potential for change. Since 1995 alone, acceptance of paternity has increased threefold. In fact, more than 90 percent of teen fathers now say they want to be involved in their children's lives. The benefit is mutual: those who are involved are more likely to finish school, maintain a job, and stay out of trouble.[6]

What Is Fathering?

Unfortunately, the methods and hypotheses used in traditional psychological research have largely supported the notion of the father as a second-class citizen and have reinforced the cycle of father hunger. We know little about fathering because, until very recently, social science has completely ignored this important area of human behavior.

Setting the tone for how psychology and psychiatry came to view fathers, Sigmund Freud showed a nearly exclusive interest in the mother-child relationship. Although he acknowledged that the father's protection of his children is the "central childhood imperative"[7] and that the most significant event in a man's life is the death of his father, Freud never addressed the nurturing, or generative, aspects of fathering.

Later in the 20th century John Bowlby, who wrote seminal works on the attachment and bonding of young children, also concentrated on the mother-child relationship, relegating the father's function to "economic and emotional support of the mother."[8]

As the fields of psychology and child development flourished in the mid-20th century, prevailing research consistently emphasized mother-infant relationships. Studying dyadic (one-to-one) relationships is much easier than studying the interactions of a whole family system. Also, since research is generally done during the day when fathers are at work, mothers were often the only parent available. So, consciously or unconsciously, mental health theories served to maintain the myth that fathers are unimportant. The result is that historically, little effort has been devoted to examining the impact of fathers' presence on the family, and even less attention has been paid to how we can help fathers to become more involved, other than to get them to pay child support more readily.

Only in the past 30 years have researchers become interested in the father and his role in child development. Several factors stimulated this closer look. First, the prevailing sociocultural conditions served as important catalysts. By the 1970s, the traditional family structure began to change dramatically. The divorce rate increased, and many homes had no father physically present. Consequently, the impact of paternal absence became a primary research interest. Reflecting the myths about father-child relationships, however, most studies examined the impact of the father's absence on boys but ignored its effect on girls.

Another trend also accelerated our interest in the father's role in the family. Collectively, we began to realize that children can develop strong relationships with caregivers other than their mothers. Infant research indicated that babies were more than passive recipients of interactions and hypothesized that we had underestimated their ability to develop relationships. Subsequent studies have shown that infants form attachments to both parents around the same time in their first year of life.[9] In recent years, many divorced fathers have made tremendous efforts to be actively involved in their children's lives despite their absence from the home. Fourteen percent of fathers win physical custody of their children today.[10]

Waking up to the fact that a child's development is influenced by multiple complex factors, the mental health field began to appreciate the contributions of the larger family environment. Simple concepts such as the mother-child relationship no longer sufficed to explain a child's behavior. Therapists recognized that the parents' relationship with each other had important effects on their children. New work in adult development found that the experience of parenting affects both men and women.

All these factors converged to pave the way toward a new appreciation of the father's significance in the family. Once our vision broadened, we even recognized the child's impact on the father, a phenomenon called "engrossment." Researchers have called the dawn of this realization "the click" or the "aha," noting the sense of accomplishment and enhanced self-image that it brings.[11] According to their observations, within the first few days of the infant's life, both mother and father develop a bond of affection for the child. The fathers they studied also reported feeling a definite sense of accomplishment and an enhanced self-image with the birth of their children. They observed, however, that few social supports are available to help a father maintain this connection and feel comfortable around the baby.

Being a parent awakens many strong and startling emotions for men. One father described his feelings as "fireballs of love [that] swoop through me all the time," so that he feels "like the Fourth of July is happening inside me."[12] When men allow themselves to experience the richness and variety of their feelings, fathering can help them discover wonderful parts of themselves they would not otherwise know.

Even before a baby's birth, a father can become very involved in the psychological preparation for parenting. Expectant fathers often worry a great deal and experience anxiety and mood changes. In a study of normal pregnancies, one-fourth of the expectant fathers sought medical help for gastrointestinal symptoms they had never before experienced. In some tribal societies, the phenomenon of *couvade* (in which the father simulates labor and delivery) is common. The husband's parallel physical participation is believed to ease his wife's pain and protect her and the baby during the birth process.[13]

Recent research shows that in both complicated and uncomplicated pregnancies, both parents become emotionally attached to the fetus and are likely to experience prenatal and postnatal depression and anxiety.[14] Fathers appear very invested despite how disenfranchised they have been from the responsibility of parenting. The potential of this bond is remarkable.

Research in anthropology and other fields may shed light on how to help men be active fathers, for history has found fathering to be a plastic or moldable behavior, very much affected by the social environment. Fathering has been unexpectedly observed even in animal species in which the males are characteristically independent and aggressive. This suggests that fathering must be an innate capacity, largely dependent on external opportunities and encouragement.[15]

Anthropologists point out that no single natural or correct way of fathering exists, and that a culture's expression of fathering will be either enhanced or denied by the roles it prescribes for men and women. The greatest degree of paternal involvement can usually be found in cultures in which local warfare is absent, spousal relationships are monogamous, the division of labor allows fathers access to children, and women's work, other than child care, is considered important.[16] Could there be a simple lesson here? Fathering is most effective when men and women work together as partners. It sounds easy, doesn't it?

Not only is fathering an innate male potential, but research also informs us that both sexes have equal capacity to nurture. In both animal and human studies, no documented gender-based differences in competent parenting have been found. Any differences are culturally constructed rather than biologically based.[17] While the sexes may differ slightly in how they play with young children, with fathers encouraging more gender-stereotyped play, these trends fade as the children grow. Mothers and fathers who are closely involved with their children will resemble each other more and more as the children grow older.[18]

It is time to put to rest the myth that the instinct to parent is stronger in women, or is the exclusive prerogative of women. In fact, parenting skills develop "on the job." Mothers become experts by practicing. Likewise, fathers do not, unless they practice. Surely they can develop the reciprocal attachment we associate with good mothering, if cultural expectations don't interfere and push them into the background.

Children with involved fathers have been found to have higher cognitive and developmental functioning, greater empathy, a stronger internal locus of control, and less rigid sex stereotypes,[19] as well as being more successful academically, athletically, and socially.[20] When fathers have to, choose to, or are encouraged to parent effectively, they can do it. While they may express their parenting differently, both sexes have the capacity to nurture and care for children. Fathers can be first-class parents instead of second-class citizens.

Parenting in the Global Village

The day is gone when either parent can feel secure and supported in his or her role. Both mothers and fathers are bombarded with advice from the media and pop psychology, incessantly promoting the latest trends and best techniques and equipment for the task of child rearing. With extended family support less available because of the mobility of our society, most parents have nowhere else to turn. Living in the age of "experts," they come to doubt their own instincts. Becoming the perfect parent is the dream of so many, and there is always a prescription available for this: it just may not fit the needs of the individuals involved.

The global girl's family is constantly changing. In the United States, half of first marriages end in divorce, and many more couples separate temporarily or permanently. While 66 percent of women and 76.5 percent of men will remarry, the divorce rate for second marriages is 10 percent.[21] More than half of all U.S. children will spend at least part of their lives in single-parent families, and a similar trend is evolving in other industrialized nations.[22] Projections are that only 34 percent of children born in the U.S. in the year 2000 will be living with both their parents at the age of 18.[23] Economics and social policies may play a part: only 33 percent of poor children live with both parents, while 70 percent of more affluent children live in intact families.[24]

While in some circumstances, fathers actually become closer to their children after divorce, this is still the exception. Most surveys find that divorce severely disrupts the father-child relationship, with one-third of divorced fathers maintaining no further contact with their children.[25] Only 25 percent of the children of divorce see their fathers weekly or more often. Contact decreases as parental conflict increases, and when fathers relocate, lured by global opportunities, they leave their global girls (and boys) behind in the dust.[26]

Despite the tremendous desire for coparenting discussed earlier, this seems difficult to achieve. The global village is tough on marriages and families. While we have seen significant changes in some men's fathering behavior, this "has occurred against a background of dramatic increases in the number of children who barely know or have almost no contact with their fathers."[27] Now, more than ever, there are haves and have-nots: Far too many children and fathers are missing out on something really special. Despite what we know about the benefits to both of a close relationship, the global village, with the pressures it places on both generations, is a breeding ground for father hunger.

The ancient Chinese symbol for *crisis* is made up of two parts. The top is the symbol for "danger." The bottom is the symbol for "opportunity." In crisis we find both danger and opportunity. Our global society has reached such a crisis, a time when encroaching disaster can provide the impetus for change. More and more global girls have serious eating disorders that could cost them their health or their life. More and more families are torn apart by the pressures of living in an era of consumerism, competition, and constant change. More and more fathers want to be there for their children but either do not know how or cannot manage active parenting along with the other relentless demands being made on them.

While many mothers do work to support their families, men still earn more. In fact, on average, women must work for 16 months to earn what men earn in 12.[28] Consequently, many fathers feel they must maintain a high profile in the increasingly competitive work environment, chained to their laptop, cell phone, and beeper even outside the office, in order to assure that they can meet their families' economic needs.

Coparenting would be easier if the workplace rewarded men and women equally. Until it does, men are going to be less likely to feel they can set limits at their jobs and put the family first. Thus, major changes must occur in our culture and economic system to make dads a more important part of their families' lives and make father hunger a thing of the past.

Questions and New Connections

- Think about what children raised in this global era need from their fathers. Are their needs today different from the needs of children in previous eras? Are children less or more likely to get their most important needs met?

- Imagine what your relationship with your father would be like if you lived in a different historical period. What cultural supports were available to fathers of that time?

- What can employers do to support men in being more available to their families? What effects would paternity leave and flexible working hours have on children and families?

- How should custody and visitation plans be designed to allow greater access to fathers?

CHAPTER 5

Shaky Foundations for Fatherhood

Fathers and their adolescent daughters each have worries, dreams, insecurities, needs, drives, and desires that may have been dormant, more manageable, or less important during the girl's earlier years. When she becomes a teenager, however, the differences and conflicts between them are accentuated. Adolescence challenges the equilibrium between the sexes as well as between the generations. This is the time when many fathers and daughters experience a complete breakdown in their relationship, leading young women to long for paternal affection and approval—to hunger for daddy.

Fathering an adolescent daughter can be challenging. Father and daughter may be equally bothered by unfinished business from their childhood and by the changes brewing as they enter a new life stage. For both young and old, developmental transitions are disruptive. When we leave one life stage to enter another, social roles and expectations evolve, requiring adaptive changes in our behavior. We also transform internally: we see ourselves differently and may be unsure who we are becoming.

For men, aging brings up many issues. Some react by becoming more preoccupied with themselves or their work. Many, still feeling the old, familiar pressure to be the breadwinner, push themselves to make more money and cannot rest until they have climbed to the top rung of the ladder. Other men may decide to focus on their own needs and spend more time on hobbies or sports, devoting less energy and time to parenting. Still others may reevaluate their role in the family and adjust their priorities to become more involved with their children.

Some fathers find their children more interesting as they mature. Many others become rigid and rejecting as they confront the challenging needs of teenagers. Whatever change a father makes may be confusing to his daughter as she traverses the rocky road of adolescence. The struggle to form an individual identity and become an independent young woman raises tremendous uncertainty. She needs support, security, and acceptance—especially from the most important man in her life. Unfortunately, fathers are often ill-prepared to provide what global girls need most.

The differences between the male and female psyche, which contribute to father hunger and which are so evident in families with eating problems, begin at birth and become firmly rooted by early childhood. In fact, these differences may even precede birth, because they are derived in part from the collective consciousness that has unfolded throughout human history and includes:

- Past and present attitudes, expectations, and personal experiences of parents, extended family, and other key caregivers

- Complex genetic contributions to development and behavior

- Physiological variations in development and functioning

Regardless of when the differences begin or why they occur, socialization and cultural experience exert powerful and divergent influences on both men and women. For at least the past two decades, feminist psychologists have delineated how modern culture can disable and destroy the potential of girls and young women.[1] But these influences are also disabling to young men, who too often grow up devoid of deep connections and particularly deprived of meaningful relationships with father figures. In our current manner of raising children, then, neither sex appears to be getting a healthy or easy start in life. Each feels disenfranchised, incomplete, and unsupported by the other.

This chapter will explore the influences of culture on the psychological development of males in modern society and how our expectations of fathers perpetuate the cycle of father hunger wherein men who have been deprived of satisfying contact with their fathers find themselves unprepared to nurture the next generation effectively. Parenting global girls is particularly challenging for men because of the differences between their skills and their daughters' needs.

Society's Message to Men:
Separate, Separate, Separate!

Differentiation of the self and creation of an individual identity is a complex lifelong process, which provides the basis of personality formation. It involves the primary caretaker to a great extent. In most cultures, this is usually the mother, and so the progression unfolds differently in boys than in girls and will have divergent and long-lasting consequences later in life, affecting personal adjustment, the marital relationship, and parenting.

For boys, developing an identity and differentiating oneself means separating from the warmth and cuddling of mom and connecting to dad, who is often a more remote, less demonstrative, and more demanding parent. Separation is difficult because of the special relationship between mothers and male children. Studies have shown that mothers frequently allow sons more opportunity to play with their food and to develop their own feeding schedule, while they expect their daughters to adjust more to external demands, such as being neat and eating on schedule. Boys are weaned and toilet-trained later than girls, as well. Thus, the mother-son relationship is often very special and loving, and can tend to become overly indulgent.

Indulgence experienced by males during infancy can cause difficulties in the later phases of development that require separation. In contrast to the earlier cuddling, mothers begin pushing their sons out of the nest. Sons instinctively understand the need to be separate and independent. Still, the loss of mom can be very traumatic. During this phase a father's absence, disinterest, harsh criticism, unrealistic expectations, or outright rejection will intensify the boy's distress. On the other hand, a strong connection with dad can help boys cope with their changing relationship with mom.

When men are unavailable to children, boys are denied the encouragement, affection, and support they long for from their dads. Having lost the warm relationship with mother and being unable to find intimacy with men, many boys today grow up never having experienced real intimacy in relationships with any adult males. They carry a heavy burden of unmet emotional needs.

Research informs us how emotionally neglected and physically abandoned by their fathers some males feel, and literature affirms and echoes this theme. The yearning of an abandoned son for his absent father is a common, nearly universal theme in religion and literature. This archetype is frequently found in classics such as Shakespeare's *Hamlet*, Homer's *Odyssey*, and the biblical story of Joseph.[2] Boys ill equipped by their family-of-origin experience may not know how to seek support or even how to have close friendships with their same-sex peers.

Much of the emotional atmosphere outside the family environment is also one of disconnection and harshness for many boys. Contemporary mental health experts have called the boy's masculine environment a "culture of cruelty," in which boys are immersed in unspoken pacts of dominance, fear, and betrayal. Instead of learning to trust and develop empathy, boys in such a culture learn to be guarded and defensive. Their emotional growth is stunted, and they become emotionally illiterate. Many will live their whole lives impaired and blunted as a result.[3]

The culture of cruelty teaches boys and men to hide any feelings of inadequacy and guard their emotional distance, so no one sees their human vulnerability. At their core lies a deep longing for their father's love and approval, and the toll it takes can be truly devastating. Unable to identify or discuss feelings and problems, men are 4-5 times more likely than women to commit suicide and are more likely to be killed accidentally or to engage in self-destructive behaviors. Raised to deny feelings and take action instead, far too many men act out their pain through hypermasculine, nonemotional, and sometimes deadly means.[4]

A young man's unmet emotional needs are generally tabled until he establishes a meaningful relationship with a woman. Then, sex becomes an acceptable way of expressing and seeking affection. Being held and loved may help him reconnect with earlier points in his development when he felt cared for and loved by his mother.

However, the unfinished business and disappointment in the male's relationship with his parents profoundly affect his adult behavior as a father. For example, if a man has only felt close to women through sexual relationships, he may not know how to remain close to his daughter as she matures sexually. Many fathers choose to distance themselves from their daughters to avoid this uneasiness. Unfortunately, this occurs just when their daughters most need support, validation, and input from them as they wrestle with moving away from their moms and becoming adult women.

Some men, longing for the female nurturance they have missed since early childhood, may become overly dependent on their daughters. Girls who have been constantly encouraged to attend to others' feelings and needs may easily tune in to their father's emptiness and try to please him or make him happy. Such relationships can range from "codependent" to seductive, if the father inadvertently makes his daughter into a second mother or wife, or even steps over the line to pursue a sexual relationship with her.

The Cost of Separation

A closer look at the psychological and social pressures experienced by males as they grow up will help us understand their lifelong struggle to find satisfaction in themselves and in their relationships. Think for a minute about the messages we give to little boys as we push them to separate and develop. From infancy on, we tell them: "Be a big boy," "Stand on your own two feet," "Be tough," "Don't cry," "It doesn't hurt," among many other invalidating messages. We teach little boys not to be aware of their emotions, or at least not to express them, and we tell them not to need anything from anyone.

These constant directives leave them feeling empty, alone, scared, and vulnerable, but they aren't supposed to experience such sentiments, so they pretend nothing is wrong. Little boys pick up early that emotions are "feminine"—only for "sissies." Since they are learning to be "masculine," they begin to devalue feelings and disown their needs. In this way, we actually encourage boys to separate not only from both their parents, but also from their own inner emotional lives.

Surrounded by messages that belittle male emotional expressions, boys are unable to let others know how sad and alone they feel as they separate from mom and try to identify with and model dad. They recognize their father's strength and power in the world but also perceive that he is a man who functions minimally in the family and who is often emotionally and socially inadequate. Since fathers can't admit to such "weaknesses," sons deny their perceptions and cover up their own weak or needy feelings as they attempt in indirect ways to win attention and approval from their fathers.

The costs boys pay for complying with these messages to separate, be tough, achieve, and *do* rather than *feel* are very high. Performance-oriented behaviors begin quite early as a logical attempt to obtain contact and feedback from fathers, to lessen the pain of separation. We see tough little boys playing on midget football teams, getting teeth knocked out, and ruining their knees. They push themselves to excel, imitating their father's behavior and hoping for their attention and a deeper connection.

While many boys try to achieve, and in some cases, to live out their father's fantasies, others will reject these values. Instead they will rebel, perhaps have trouble in school, or even engage in criminal activities. These boys develop a hard shell to cover up loneliness and rejection. Still, the underlying drive is the same: they crave a close connection that feels good. They are, however, unlikely to find satisfaction, love, and a close connection to themselves and others by any of these misguided means, because they have learned so well to ignore and avoid their emotions.

When boys leave childhood and enter adolescence without making satisfying attachments, they arrive wounded. They have learned to keep their feelings inside and try to get their needs met in indirect ways. They have also accepted that men belong on the periphery of the family and are valued for their accomplishments rather than their presence. Although they may have felt let down by their fathers, they also believe they should not need them. Many have heard how their fathers have sacrificed for them, so they may not feel entitled to make further demands for closeness.

A son's guilt about his needs may soon be transformed into a subtle form of loyalty. This is evident in young men who attempt to resolve feelings of loss, anger, and guilt by adopting a lifestyle and values similar to their father's. Those who went through a period of rebellion may feel especially remorseful, and may cope by becoming excessively loyal.

Under these circumstances, the development of family loyalty can be an unconscious, insidious, and powerful motivator with the unrecognized goal of finding some connection. For example, young men whose fathers were absent because of career demands often become workaholics to create a bond with their fathers. Their father hunger is converted into accomplishments at work. Much like their dads, they play a minimal role in their children's lives and put most of their energy into achieving out in the world. On the other hand, men who do not succeed at work may become depressed and even abandon their families because of their inability to live up to the allegiance they feel they owe their fathers and to follow the life script that has been written for them.

Men who succeed in surpassing their fathers economically sometimes discover that, instead of finding the connection they sought, they have abandoned the family's value system and are facing an unfamiliar high-pressure lifestyle. As these men confront adult experiences for which their fathers did not prepare them, they feel especially let down and neglected. Workaholics with no energy left for personal relationships, they lack a connection with both their fathers and their families, with both the past and the present.

Most men in today's society, despite the variant paths their significant relationships may take, had absent, uninvolved fathers. They enter adulthood, marriage, and parenthood with serious wounds caused by a socialization process that has alienated them from their feelings. They are left with a deep despair and yearning for connection with their dads. Having paid dearly for separation, they experience little satisfaction in relationships with themselves and with others, and are poorly equipped to parent their children, particularly their adolescent daughters.

The pressures on men to separate so completely result in a value system, world view, and repertoire of sex-specific behaviors that handicap fathers in their role in the family. The beat goes on: men who were raised fatherless end up raising their children the same way. Father hunger, perpetuated as loyalty to the old myths and traditions, remains unchallenged.

Value Systems Clash

The emphasis on separation affords men much power in the world. Self-control, independence, autonomy, and individuality emerge from it. Males are further encouraged by a socialization process that teaches boys to need no one, to be in charge of themselves, and not to let others boss them around. They learn to assert themselves, protect their turf or reputation, and fight for their rights. The use of physical aggression or violence, when necessary, is acceptable. If a boy lacks the brawn or inclination to fight, he is considered inadequate, a "sissy," and will probably be socially ostracized. He is expected to exude self-direction and power over himself and others at any cost.

Taught to ignore the opinions of others, boys are pressured to focus on independence, skills, competence, and achievement. They are typically less concerned about feelings—their own and others'—and they take more frequent risks as a result. Even if they are afraid to attempt something, males feel a push to "just do it" and not worry so much about interpersonal consequences.

The decision-making process is thus very different for the two sexes. Men feel pressed to make quicker, more purely rational choices, while women constantly consider the implications for their relationships. So while "the moral imperative ... with women is an injunction to care,"[5] for men it is to respect individual rights and independence.

These opposing values cause boys and girls to react differently to many social experiences. Watching children on a playground will tell the story. In general, boys' play is more physically active, as they have been encouraged to take risks with little concern for how they look or the possible consequences of their behavior. Compared to girls, they are less aware of others' watching and judging them. Boys' play lasts longer than girls' and is apt to continue even when there are misunderstandings. They tolerate disputes (maybe even enjoy them) and settle them so the game can continue. If a controversy erupts when girls play, however, they are more likely to end the game or change the rules rather than risk causing animosity. In fact, fearing disagreements, girls will gravitate toward playing less competitive games. So, during play, boys are learning how to organize people and negotiate problems, while girls learn that it is more important to show caring for others and to avoid competition.

With such divergent backgrounds, a father and his daughter will bring very different skills and attitudes to their interactions with each other. Fathers will tend to enjoy doing and accomplishing things, while daughters may just want to talk and share emotions. While men may emphasize a product, principle, or achievement, girls may value the process more. Fathers may stress and reward competition, but daughters may hesitate to compete and achieve, not wanting to hurt anyone. Finally, while men value independence, their daughters may appear dependent because they crave connections.

This discrepancy between masculine and feminine values and perspectives causes much misunderstanding between men and women and certainly influences how a father and his adolescent daughter negotiate their relationship. Men become fathers prepared to be separate, independent, and unemotional; while their daughters need to be connected, interdependent, and expressive. What fertile ground for father hunger.

Body Image, Sexuality, Food, and Nurturance

The male socialization process also determines how men feel about their bodies, sexuality, food, and nurturance. Their distinctively male perspective severely limits their understanding of their global girls' experience in these areas.

From early on, boys and girls receive opposite messages about physical pleasure. Parents make unconscious decisions on issues as simple as clothing, which may have a lasting impact on the bodily experience. They clothe male babies and toddlers in comfortable garments designed for activity and exploration. Boys are thus encouraged to have fun and not to be constrained by their clothing. They see their bodies as tools for pleasure and enjoyment—their own property, not mom's.

As they grow, boys often consider a bigger body an advantage because it brings opportunities to pursue sports or other activities that require size and strength and allows them to "perform." In fact, boys in preadolescence and adolescence often want to gain weight to be like many of their sports figure heroes with large physiques.

In the past few years, however, more and more men are experiencing discomfort with their bodies. Increasing numbers of men today engage in self-destructive activities such as steroid abuse, dietary changes, and excessive exercise to attain a bigger, more muscular body. New terms such as *muscle dysmorphia* and *reverse anorexia* have been coined to describe their eating disorders, reflecting society's emphasis on strength and power and the changing ideals for men's bodies. Just as the Barbie doll has influenced the female body image, male action toys may be affecting boys. Originally, these figures had basically normal, although very muscular, proportions. But now they are totally unrealistic and unattainable, with proportions (such as biceps of 32 inches) that far exceed the physiques of even the largest body builders. [6]

However, for most men their body image accounts for only a small part of their overall self-image. In contrast, the global girl who is dissatisfied with her body is also dissatisfied with herself. In the female frame of reference, body and self are one.

The experience of emerging sexuality also varies greatly between males and females. Many boys expect their bodies to give them pleasure and power, so they welcome getting bigger and stronger during puberty. While performance anxiety may be troublesome, males are less conflicted about sexual activity because they are more accepting of their physical shape, size, and impulses.

Sex may be a release for men, but women tend to worry about it. They criticize their bodies, believe that men will never really like them, and worry about society's moral expectations of them and the very real possibility of pregnancy. Overall, whereas boys associate puberty, maturation, and sexuality with enhanced status and prowess, these changes raise conflicts and increased self-doubt for women.

The experience of aging is also very different for men and women. While according to prevailing cultural values men are seen as more attractive and powerful as they grow older, women's beauty and influence decline. A birthday card expresses this contrast aptly. On the cover is a cartoon showing a woman looking somewhat sad and a man smiling. The text reads: "Women get old. Men get distinguished. Women get wrinkled. Men get rugged. Women get senile. Men get charming." Inside is the message, "I was going to wish you a happy birthday, but I'm not sure if I like you anymore."[7]

Just as men typically experience their bodies as bringing them freedom, they have historically viewed aging as ensuring control and power. In contrast, many women experience both their bodies and the aging process as prisons. While men feel empowered as they grow older, women feel equally disempowered.

Aging, however, is not completely free of conflict for men. Many experience mid-life crisis and anxiety when their physical and sexual prowess begins to decline. Age discrimination in the workplace and unemployment among older workers have become major problems. Just as for daughters, a man's body may become his receptacle for anxiety over such issues. In response, some men may exercise excessively to stay fit or become involved with younger women to prove their virility.

When a man is experiencing such conflicts, which often arise just as his daughter is going through puberty, the relationship between father and daughter may suffer. His discomfort with himself and insecurity

or impulsivity regarding sexuality may frighten her. If he seems preoccupied by sex or becomes more overt in his own sexual behaviors, she
becomes confused, not knowing how to react because her needs for
parental support and stability during her adolescence are so strong. In
addition, a father's tendency toward separation and denial may make
him oblivious to his daughter's needs and reactions. The widening
chasm in their relationship results in the daughter's deepening sense
of father hunger.

Men and women may also differ in the ways they relate to food.
Men are usually more accepting of themselves physically and may feel
freer to enjoy eating because they worry less about their weight. They
receive fewer messages from advertisers in the diet and fashion industries, pressing them to change their bodies. In contrast, women often
see food as an enemy, something they must conquer. Also, since men
often have other areas in which they feel in charge and derive a measure of self-worth, they don't need to control what they eat for this
purpose. Moreover, men usually do not feel compelled to cook, since
this duty generally falls on women. Again, their relationship to food,
be it cooking or eating, can be one of pleasure.

Similarly, nurturing others, through food and other caretaking
behaviors, is optional rather than required for many men. On the other
hand, men may avoid opportunities to cook and do other domestic
tasks because they are afraid to fail or because they are guarding a rigid
idea of "masculinity." The strong achievement orientation they have
learned since childhood raises many obstacles to engaging in the
parental behaviors that children find reassuring. Men miss valuable
opportunities to nurture when they view the kitchen as off-limits. And
the constant messages to achieve and to be autonomous can overpower
their natural desire to connect with others.

Even men who sincerely want to be nurturing fathers may lack
role models or guides to show them successful parenting techniques.
Like their counterparts who are trying to surpass their fathers materi-
ally, they may also feel fatherless, abandoned, and ill-prepared. The
path of least resistance, the traditional masculine role of leaving
parenting up to mothers, is attractive and seductive when there is so
little support for more active fathering.

All these societal pressures and expectations result in chronic
intimacy problems for both sexes. Men feel disconnected from the father who was never there for them, and consequently they are unable

to be there for their daughters. Since the daughter's relationship with her father is the prototype for her relationships with other men, her father hunger will color the rest of her life. Both daughters and dads seek, but do not find, connection.

Let's summarize the factors that may lead men to experience difficulties in close relationships such as parenting. Because of the way boys are raised and the denial they are taught, they become cut off from their feelings and mechanical in their actions. They are not born this way, but are pressed into this mold by cultural expectations. As little boys move away from their mothers, they have no one to move toward. Their fathers are frequently unavailable, so the pressure to separate from mom leaves little boys feeling alone and isolated. As they mature, they have difficulty getting close to other people, because past example has taught them that closeness eventually leads to abandonment. Boys who have few opportunities to seek nurturance from men do not see male relationships as being helpful or comforting. In the rare instances when closeness for men is endorsed, such as a mentor or sports coach for a young man, the relationship is typically time-limited.

In short, men are taught that to develop, they must separate from the important people in their lives. We constantly endorse this separateness and isolation. Consequently, when men become husbands and fathers, building close relationships is not easy for them. Their life script tells them to work and support other people financially, but not to express emotions or expect much from others emotionally. This developmental process produces adult men and fathers who are wounded, fearful of close relationships, and inexperienced at feeling and expressing emotions. They are ill prepared to meet the needs of their global girls. Consequently, father hunger persists.

Contemporary society needs a whole new model of masculinity. Some pioneers are venturing into new territory by becoming more emotionally involved with their families and assuming more equal roles in the home. We see more men taking their children to school, playing with them on playgrounds, and participating in their lives. This is a promising trend. Helping men overcome the problem of father hunger is the subject of Chapter 11 of this book.

Questions and New Connections

- How has the pressure on men to be separate and independent affected the men in your life? How has it affected your relationships with them?

- Do you agree that most men grow up wanting more from their fathers? How has this been evident in your life? How has this affected your relationships as a child or parent?

- Do you believe that your father was satisfied in his role as a parent? Did he feel connected to you?

- What do you know about your father's experiences as a son and what his relationship with *his* father was like?

- If you are a daughter: What experiences would satisfy your father hunger?

- If you are a father: How has your relationship with your dad affected your parenting? What have you been trying to do differently from your dad? How are you similar? Was your dad a different father to his sons than to his daughters? Are you?

CHAPTER 6

The Daughter's Dilemma

This chapter shifts our attention from how male psychological development perpetuates father hunger to how female psychological development reflects it and, in turn, also perpetuates it. Traditionally, much research in the field of psychology has been based on a male model of development. Since the women's movement, however, feminists have challenged and gradually influenced this disparity. Psychologists now realize that male-oriented theories stressing independence, separateness, autonomy, and individual rights do not apply to women's modes of thinking and functioning. Men and women need to understand these differences in order to establish positive, mutually fulfilling relationships.

A new appreciation of the differences between men and women can help us understand the origins of father hunger. In short, males are pressed into separation and isolation, which results in pervasive problems with intimacy. Thus, they may not know how to father. Females are pressured to put others first and form close relationships; thus, they need to feel connected and may not be satisfied by a peripheral father.

The yearning to be close to dad and be part of his world leads many women to develop severe problems with food and their body image. Denied permission to express their true feelings, global girls displace their focus onto eating and weight, areas over which they feel they have control.

Because girls have learned to express themselves in such indirect ways, fathers rarely understand the agony of their father hunger. Neither father nor daughter is likely to find satisfaction in their relationship until they come to understand the uniqueness of the male and female experiences. Articulating these differences will help each find common ground so that father hunger can be satisfied.

Society's Message to Women: Connect, Connect, Connect!

While separation is the unrelenting theme as males develop, connections and relationships are equivalent mandates for women. Pleasing people supersedes satisfying oneself, because it promises the deeply desired bonds with others. Paradoxically, caring for others forms the center of the self for females. Men are encouraged to be independent and to focus on themselves, while females receive subtle and not so subtle messages that they should ignore their own needs and devote themselves to gratifying others.

Jean Baker Miller was one of the first authors to write extensively on the psychology of women. She recognized that "Women's sense of self becomes very much organized around being able to make and then maintain affiliation and relationships."[1] This tradition continues because, as little girls watch their mothers and identify with them, they learn not only that relationships and connections are very important to women, but also that taking care of others is central to their lives. Mothers make special efforts to teach little girls to take care of younger children and male family members, but rarely do they encourage their sons to act this way. Beginning very early in the socialization process, these other-directed behaviors become the female's way of ensuring the all-important attachments and connections.

Women easily adopt a pattern called *otheration*,[2] which is defined by overreacting to external demands and underreacting to internal cues. This starts early. While mothers more frequently allow boys to set their own schedule, play with their food, and experience mealtime in a manner that suits their own impulses, they discourage their daughters' active play and experimentation with food. This conveys the expectation that little girls should control their appetites and look neat, clean, and tidy, thereby helping to make their environment look attractive. Such subliminal pressures on little girls support the principle that cooperation and attention to the desires of others must be put above satisfying their own natural curiosity and meeting their own needs.

Fulfillment for males may mean pleasing the self and being

autonomous, but for females it usually denotes satisfying everyone else. In fact, when girls as young as seven are asked to describe themselves, they give examples of how others have depicted them. In marked contrast, boys report their own self-perceptions.[3]

Otheration leads to many problems, particularly a lack of self-assertion in relationships and deficits in self-awareness. Extreme expressions of this common pattern include eating problems and denial of the body's physical and nutritional needs, which endanger many women today.

Since we emphasize relationships for girls, we also allow girls much greater closeness with mother than we allow boys. In adolescence, however, when girls are expected to become more separate from the family, many find it difficult to do this without losing their most intimate attachment, to their mother. Today, global girls experience additional pressure because cultural changes in women's roles require that they achieve outside of traditional female realms. As their life experience diverges from their mother's, they may fear surpassing her and losing her approval by being more successful in school achievement or work accomplishments.

For global girls, adolescence represents a culmination of the conflicts between traditional caretaking values of femininity and the achievement and performance expectations of the masculine world. Facing these tensions and feeling insecure with peers, girls may begin to associate the adolescent period with a loss of important relationships. This feeling is especially intense for girls whose fathers are not available to them at a time when they are feeling the pressure to be more separate from mom. A connection with father could assure them that future relationships have the potential for intimacy and caring, and that they will find a comfortable balance between dependence and independence, and between femininity and masculinity.

Costs of Connections: Self-Denial, Confusion, Guilt, Codependence

Just as the costs of separating are high for men, so the costs of making connections an exclusive priority are high for women. Self-denial easily leads to identity confusion, guilt, and codependency, providing fertile ground for eating and body image problems.

Generally, these consequences do not surface until adolescence. Preadolescent girls more characteristically assert strong opinions and appear confident and self-assured. Carol Gilligan described this healthy resistance simply: "Eleven-year-olds are not for sale."[4] Prior to adolescence, girls appear capable of balancing the needs of self and others fairly effectively.

Something changes, however, when girls move into adolescence. During this time, most girls switch from confidence to confusion and from self-assertion to self-denial. Though they may *appear* cool and competent, they rarely feel that way. Instead, they are unsure and often ashamed of their thoughts, desires, and feelings.

This transformation reflects some of the dilemmas we have regarding sex roles and values. Specifically, Gilligan attributes it to the feelings aroused in girls as they become more aware of the culture and social structure around them. They see women as having little power and being told to keep quiet, look good, and say nothing of importance. Girls who had been strong, opinionated, confident preadolescents suddenly seem uncertain of themselves. When asked a question, they are likely to answer, "I don't know."

Adolescent girls have not been well prepared to face the new demands of a modern world that appears to value separation and autonomy. They have learned to suppress their needs, take care of others, and avoid initiating activities—especially ones that involve taking risks or asserting oneself. Thus, teenaged girls doubt themselves. They may perceive that traditional women's strengths—their attentive and caring attitude and their emphasis on building relationships—are required but not rewarded in our masculine culture. They find it difficult to articulate their confused feelings and assert themselves. The more uninvolved the father, the more gut-wrenching this developmental passage will be as they try to find a place in the male-oriented systems outside the family.

Many global girls sidestep their confusion by obsessing about food and appearance. For example, as they pursue sports, math, science, and other traditionally male areas, they may begin to wonder if they are losing some of their femininity and becoming too masculine. Some react by becoming overly attentive to other people, by dieting to attain the perfect body, and by being meticulous about their appearance to assure that their femininity will not be lost. In their desperation to conform, they risk their health and become alienated from their natural hunger. On the other hand, if they resist the mandate to please everyone else, these young women are filled with guilt and become increasingly confused about the priority of their own feelings and needs in the overall scheme of things.

Regardless of their own desires, most girls believe they should at least try to fulfill the world's expectations. Thus, the pattern of otheration that began in early childhood continues, but it runs at cross-purposes to the global society's newer emphasis on the woman's individual development. The conflict results in chronic self-blame and remorse.

Guilt pervades the female psyche the way isolation haunts the male psyche. Men learn to ignore feelings, and women obsess about how they caused the underlying problem. Globalization's advances in mass communication have only intensified this self-reproach and denial. Global girls are bombarded with advice on how to raise children, please a man, keep the family healthy with good cooking, pursue a successful career, and earn lots of money—and do all these things effortlessly while maintaining a perfect figure and a trendy appearance! Judging themselves by such impossible standards, these aspiring "superwomen" conclude, "I'm just not good enough, and perhaps I never will be."

This provides fertile ground for female guilt to grow. Founded on a deep father hunger and their frustrating inability to be good enough to win their dad's love and attention, girls worry that, whatever path they choose, they will never be able to please men. Girls are more confused about this dilemma today because they have more options than ever before. They can pursue higher education, athletics, business, and other areas previously seen as masculine. Even though they may follow these interests primarily to satisfy their father hunger, they often fail in that regard, still finding the longed-for connection with dad to be tentative or inadequate. They blame themselves for this disconnection, believing that they alone are responsible for it. Their guilt is compounded.

Young women bring their self-blame and their longing for paternal approval to their marriages and other interactions with men. As adults, they try harder than ever to take care of their husbands and families and to be sure that their own activities or interests do not detract from the family. They constantly juggle roles and duties, hoping to satisfy others first, but usually experiencing the unpleasant effects of chronic guilt despite their extreme efforts. Years of sacrifice and denying their own interests and identity to please others eventually results in resentment for the unfulfilling nature of the relationships that have developed.

Similarly, women who choose a single or lesbian lifestyle may feel inadequate as well. In a male-dominated culture, a woman without a man receives many negative messages. Thus, it may be very difficult to feel good about the path she has taken.

Guilt can also overshadow women's self-esteem and mental health when they work outside the home. Consequently, they will continue to place their husband's and family's needs first, further ignoring their own. This result of years of otheration helps to explain why so many family relationships deteriorate into codependence. Codependency becomes a defense that helps one avoid facing problems directly in order to preserve stability and maintain the status quo.

Consider the example of a wife who, feeling guilty for taking time away from the family to pursue her own career, overlooks or excuses her husband's alcoholism. This woman may fear that her work distresses her husband and may conclude that she should not complain about his drinking. If only she took better care of him, he wouldn't need to drink, or so she thinks. In this way, codependency becomes a means of both managing guilt and maintaining connections.

Unfortunately, guilt about desires for personal growth, subordination of feelings, and excessive caregiving continues to be transmitted from mothers to daughters today. Global girls learn this legacy early. Their chronic attempts to feel connected by satisfying others, coupled with an exaggerated sense of responsibility, place them at great risk for problems with food, self-image, and relationships.

Appearance and Identity: A Special Correlation for Women

Physical appearance has a unique meaning for many women, reflecting their connections with themselves and with others. Most women are accustomed to pleasing others through their bodies. As a result of their increasing hunger for approval from men and the demanding social norms for female "beauty," many women begin waging war with their bodies at extremely young ages.

Earlier, we discussed the powerful force of "otheration," a tendency to overvalue the opinions or needs of others and undervalue one's own feelings. We also explained why women feel it is important to make and maintain relationships. Looking pretty or sexy is a way to do this, and we begin instilling this idea in global girls as early as infancy. For example, parents dress their female infants in pretty ruffled, lacy, matching outfits, which are often impractical and uncomfortable. Boys' clothes seem to say "Go ahead, have fun, move around!" Girls' clothes seem to say, "Be careful, stay clean, restrain your activities, and guard your appearance so everyone will admire how pretty you look."

When girls are only infants, we teach them tidy eating and gentle play to keep them pretty and clean; when they start school, we encourage neat drawings and written work. We emphasize attention to detail and appearance over fun and learning. Furthermore, we begin the strange phenomenon of the beauty contest when they are as young as three or four. As in the adult version of these events, these miniature women must smile prettily, act coy, and be dressed in feminine, frilly outfits—complete with makeup and sophisticated coiffure—to win adult praise and rewards.

Even before adolescence, a girl's perception of her weight affects her self-esteem. By 4th grade, girls strongly believe that being thin will bring popularity and social success. One writer describes women's self-scrutiny as a "devastatingly fierce visual acuity" that "operates almost as a third eye."[5]

Global girls learn these lessons well; for the rest of their lives most will spend countless hours and dollars in an insatiable pursuit of fashion and beauty. Ironically, though, they fight a losing battle, because although some cultures have recognized the grace and charm in maturity, the global economy does not. As women age, they face the harsh reality that natural maturation changes their appearance in ways that run counter to society's prevailing standards of beauty. Consequently, mothers who feel that their own looks are declining may place special emphasis on their daughters' physical presentation.

Some girls do choose to abstain from today's relentless beauty and appearance rituals. They may come from a family or cultural group that has different values and rejects these norms for femininity. Or they may believe they will never measure up, so they decide not to try. In either case, unless they have a strong social support network giving them unconditional positive regard, they are apt to feel alienated and alone, like social outcasts.

The attention to female appearance is not new. It has been present throughout human history, but today the pressure is more pervasive and universally endorsed. What's more, girls' other-orientation makes them easy targets for the advertisers of any fashion item or beauty product that promises acceptance or approval. Global girls are barraged by magazines and other media that present only "perfect," "beautiful," thin female bodies and promote all kinds of unhealthy products promising to miraculously deliver such unrealistic results. Pick up any women's magazine (including those for preteens) or tune in to any television program (even those for preschoolers). You will see pretty, thin, outwardly successful and happy females advertising cosmetics, laxatives, diuretics, diet pills, liquid diets, exercise equipment, and even cosmetic surgery. All promise the "perfect" body that will please others and show how much the female consumer cares about her appearance. Even when the beauty and fashion industries are marketing "the natural look," they manage to convince people that men will be attracted only to thin women who are preoccupied above all with their appearance.

The models we see in these ads have become increasingly thin over the past 30 years, establishing a standard of beauty that few can, or should, attain. But women will try hard to attain that look because of their oversensitivity to what they perceive as the wishes of others. So, not only do advertisers use women's bodies to market consumer goods, but women themselves obligingly offer their bodies as commodities to obtain power or acceptance in the depersonalized world. Being thin and attractive seems to be a necessity for many global girls who are unsure of themselves, and our consumer culture works hard to instill self-doubt and uncertainty.

We can appreciate how easy it is for external factors to take hold when we realize how natural it is for a woman to scrutinize her body. Girls experience dramatic changes as they mature physically. In boys, the onset of puberty brings a growth of body and facial hair, a deeper voice, and a rush of hormones. But in girls it produces marked changes in their entire physical self. The flat breasts, undefined waist, and straight hips of childhood are replaced with very noticeable curves and contours.

Menstrual periods may cause cramping and discomfort, as well as uneasiness and self-consciousness about the possibility of spotting through one's clothes. Every month, hormonal fluctuations cause ups and downs in mood, as well as changes such as bloating, pimples, and an increased desire for food—all of which focus a woman's attention on her body.

A woman's awareness and natural examination of the physical changes associated with menses, pregnancy, postpartum reaction, and menopause make her an easy mark for the fashion and beauty industries throughout her life span. Because advertisers have found so many ways to capitalize on women's self-scrutiny and self-criticism, physical processes that are in fact natural have come to assume unnatural proportions.

When we consider the effects of normal body scrutiny combined with the pressures exerted on women by the beauty and fashion industries and the uncertainty today's women feel about their female identity, it is easy to understand why many women are overly concerned about their appearance. Compared to men, women tend to be more discriminating, more exacting, and more critical of their bodies. When a woman describes her shape, she is likely to be less accepting of its natural contours, as well as her weight and her overall image; often she will overestimate her size. A woman can be her own worst enemy when she engages in excessive ruminations about what will satisfy men. If only men and women would talk more together in true heart-to-heart conversations about body image and appearance concerns, women might be kinder to themselves!

Men often have difficulty understanding why women expend so much energy and suffer so many inconveniences just to be fashionable. This brings us back to the differences in our socialization of males and females. Boys are encouraged to be independent and to take risks; girls are encouraged to be nurturing and to seek approval. By adolescence, females have been steeped in ways of relating that rely on other-directed behaviors. Their self-knowledge is minimal, while their desire to satisfy the world is maximal. Thus, global girls tend to look at themselves through the eyes of others. Their self-image is dependent on what they believe people think of them as they constantly contrast the pretty and thin fashion images portrayed in the media with the reflection they see in the mirror.

One recovered anorexic wrote:

> *When a man looks in the mirror, he can tell himself, "You may be an ugly old devil, but you're brilliant, successful, virile." When a woman looks in the mirror she sees the totality of her being.*

Because of the social brainwashing to which she has been subjected, the mirror seems to tell her more than it can tell a man.[6]

Men often enjoy their bodies and see them as the means for experiencing pleasure, but women wage war with their bodies, believing that they will finally receive the approval they need from their fathers or other men only if they force themselves to have the perfect body.

The Feminine Catch-22: Cooking and Dieting

Another look back at human history can help us understand the differences between the attitudes of men and women toward food. Anthropological studies show that in almost every era and culture, women have borne the important responsibility of feeding others,[7] just as they have had a near monopoly on child care.

In many families today, men are cooking and helping in the kitchen, but their role is more often that of assistant, not the person in charge. Primary responsibility for any task brings a deeper investment in the outcome of the activity, and along with it, a sense of burden. So men and women approach cooking with different purposes and emotions.

Little girls raised in traditional families learn that food and meal preparation will become their responsibility when they grow up. Watching their mothers, aunts, and grandmothers manage the daily kitchen chores, they may observe that women often don't enjoy this activity. This lack of pleasure may serve as a forewarning of the central but sometimes negative role food will play in their lives. Today, even though many mothers work outside the home, they still hold the primary responsibility for meals. Food preparation and eating together as a family may have become less important and less time-consuming because of the changes in our lifestyle and the availability of convenience foods. But, as we shall see, they still cause conflict. Food is one more area of life that is experienced quite differently by the two sexes.

Cooking causes more conflicts for women today than ever before. One reason is that food and its preparation have become more visible to us. New studies about nutrition contradict old ones and confuse people about which foods are the right ones to give our families. Furthermore, new technology has enabled the manufacture of many sophisticated devices for food preparation, and advertising incessantly announces their availability to us. Thus, meal preparation has become the newest field in which women must seek to be fashionably up-to-date.

Like the fashion world, the food industry constantly urges us to change our ways and try something different, new, and better. Women are particularly receptive to these messages because they believe that they are responsible for taking care of others and assuring the good health of their families. The media promote this conviction by promising women that the right foods and their correct preparation will assure a family's well-being. Every week, television shows, commercials, newspapers, and magazines deluge us with claims about some new food that is declared to be an anticancer, antiaging, or anticholesterol agent. Even when the underlying research is faulty, the news makes a good story or promotion. These reports can be perplexing to all of us.

Women's changing roles in society further complicate how they interpret these messages about food and cooking. As more and more women work outside the home, they feel increasingly guilty about not being full-time homemakers. Taking care of their family's health and looking after their nutritional needs is one way of compensating for this guilt. Despite role changes and new responsibilities, many women continue to hold on to the role of cook, probably as a way to assure continuity with the past and to retain a connection with traditional female behavior. Just as men often use sports or other physical activities to prove their masculinity and to gain approval, women may express their femininity and their desire for relationships through cooking.

The dilemmas women experience regarding food are intensified by the ubiquitous pressure to be thin. Although the way to a man's heart may be through his stomach, as tradition dictates, the way to attract male attention is to be thin. To satisfy the need for connection with men, women have to feed them, but restrict their own intake.

Enter the diet industry, which, like the food and fashion industries, aims its advertising and recruitment at women for whom dieting has become a normal activity. In fact, at any given moment, 43 million women are dieting to lose weight and another 26 million are dieting just to maintain their current weight.[8] It's no wonder that little girls believe that dieting is an essential part of being female—one could say that it has become a rite of passage. So we find that younger and younger children are expressing significant weight concerns; in fact, 80 percent of 4th grade girls have already dieted, and the number one wish of girls aged 11–17 is to lose weight.[9]

Dieting is now so well accepted, and even expected, that the amount of money spent on it nearly doubled between 1990 and 2000. In 1990 alone, Americans spent over $33 billion on weight loss classes and products.[10] By the late 1990s, annual income from the diet industry in the United States had exceeded $50 billion:[11] $5–10 billion more than the annual projections for the entire federal budget for education, training, employment, and social services together.[12]

Of course, most of this money is being spent by women. Their dilemma is a difficult one: how can I feed my family well but suppress my own appetite so I can be thin? Some women try to solve this conflict by preparing full dinners for their family while they heat frozen meals of less than 300 calories for themselves. Watching this, their daughters get a preview of the struggles with food that they seem doomed to inherit.

In today's global culture, food problems have no age limit. Older women worry about their weight and appearance almost as much as younger women. They relate being thin to the all-important value of looking youthful and attractive. Women who struggle with their eating are engrossed in a search for meaning, identity, and a place in the world. Searching for themselves, without an internal structure strong enough to resist conflicting messages, they translate the unrelenting pressure into a conflict with their feminine body over issues of food.

To summarize the main points discussed in this chapter, global girls bring a very different psychological history and sense of self to their relationship with their fathers. A father who is raised with a mandate to be separate, strong, and independent may not understand his daughter's need for close, intimate, emotionally self-disclosing interactions and her equally strong drive to please others. Nor do many fathers comprehend the conflicts women experience surrounding their bodies and weight, their appearance, and food. Men find power and satisfaction through larger, stronger, active bodies, but their daughters seek approval and status from diminished size and through cosmetic enhancements.

Fathers rarely understand the impact on their daughters of the media and its images of thin women, because they were raised not to be influenced by outside sources; they have constantly been encouraged to be independent and make their own decisions. These differences, and the estrangement they engender, exacerbate father hunger.

One of the dilemmas daughters face is how to balance the pressure to achieve and be autonomous in a masculine world with their feminine need to nurture and please others. Many women are experts at caring for others, but they have not yet mastered the means of caring for their own needs without being plagued by guilt.

Global girls need help and guidance from both parents to know how to surmount these problems and forge a personal identity. As the role of women has changed in modern society, fathers have become much more important to their global girls, and father hunger carries greater risks. Girls need their fathers to help them understand masculinity and femininity, so they can negotiate a balance between the needs of others and their own needs. However, most continue to experience father deprivation rather than reassuring father contact.

Girls starved by father hunger may choose physical hunger by dieting or abusing their bodies, desperately hoping for a dad's attention and fleeing from the pain of his neglect. Perpetuating the pattern, they will bring their father hunger to all their other relationships in the continuing quest for approval, acceptance, and love.

Questions and New Connections

- How has the pressure to connect affected you and other women in your life? If you are a female, is it difficult for you to focus on your own needs? How does otheration play out in your life? If you are a male, is it difficult for you to be receptive to others' needs?

- Do you agree that most girls want a closer, more supportive relationship with their fathers? Have you wanted more of a relationship with your father? How has this been evident in your life?

- What are the most difficult issues females face as they grow up? How can their fathers help them with these?

- How do men and women differ in their relationship to food and their bodies? How do these differences affect their relationships with themselves and each other?

PART 2

The Experience of
Father Hunger

CHAPTER 7

Damage to a Daughter's Emotions and Identity

The central problem in the father-daughter relationship is the discrepancy between what daughters need and what fathers are equipped to provide. Daughters, with their deep desire for connections and intimacy, hunger for dads who can provide closeness. But fathers, valuing separateness and independence, remain distant. This dichotomy leads to conflicting definitions of personal power, identity, self-direction, pleasure, self-esteem, affective expression, communication, goals, and values. As a result, fathers and daughters rarely understand each other.

The next chapters move from the theoretical and historical basis of father hunger to the feelings that result. The emotional consequences of father hunger become apparent as daughters approach adolescence and their need for contact and love from their fathers intensifies. Left unsatisfied, father hunger may be converted into problems with food, body image, self-esteem, and relationships. In this chapter we will look at issues central to women's emotional development, as illustrated by the words and life stories of some who have suffered from eating disorders and from the damaging long-term effects of not getting enough attention from dad.

Emotional Connectedness

A woman needs to feel connected to others. Beginning very early in her development and usually continuing throughout her life, her sense of self and personal identity are derived from relationships. In fact, emotional connectedness is usually her strongest drive, so taking care of others can easily become more important than taking care of herself.

Adolescence is a time when a girl's identity is forming and consolidating. Relationships are particularly critical at this time, and a young woman's interests may naturally turn toward men. A father whose own upbringing has diminished the importance of interpersonal connections and whose sense of self emanates from separateness may not recognize his daughter's need for intimate relationships. The daughter begins to feel ashamed of her desire for contact with dad, assuming that something is wrong with her for wanting more from him.

She may begin to doubt the validity of her appetites, be they for relationships, food, or sex. Surrounded by a culture built on myths that girls need only mothers and that fathers are a luxury, an adolescent female will do her best to deny her need for dad. Furthermore, convinced that she is unworthy of his affection, she may punish herself by not eating, overeating, purging, or overexercising. Thus, instead of acknowledging the desire for a connection to dad and either correcting the problem or mourning her loss, she silently blames herself for her father hunger.

Even though I had a close relationship with my dad, I still was strongly influenced by cultural norms to underestimate the importance of this emotional connection. It took me a long time to realize how essential my dad was to my development and how significant the fathers of my patients are to them. Once I learned how to listen, I discovered that most adolescent and adult women suffer from their father's emotional distance and lack of involvement in the family's life. In their words, dad was "self-absorbed," "unavailable," "tied up in his own ego," and "incapable of dealing with feelings."

A father's inability to connect with his daughter causes her to feel rejected, abandoned, anxious, fearful, sad, and insecure. The father's disengaged emotional style undermines young women in many ways, the most important of which is that their daughters never feel loved. Many women in recovery see this relationship as one of the most significant contributions to their eating problems. When Liz (whose story you will read later) described what led to her anorexia, she said quite simply, "All I wanted was my father's love." What she craved and needed was an emotional connection to her father.

Unrequited Love

Women who struggle with eating and body image problems often talk of unrequited love when they speak of their fathers. "I never felt good enough for him" is a common refrain. Many report having felt their father's disappointment with them throughout their lives: as a person, they never quite measured up to his expectations. The chronic perception of unrequited love can be especially damaging to girls, since as a rule they attach earlier and more intensely than do boys.

In most families with eating disorders, the fathers are good providers. In fact, many take their traditional role as the economic head of the household so seriously that they have few emotional reserves left for their family. In the few cases I have known where the fathers were not described as good providers, more often than not these men had illnesses or suffered from depression. Unable to fulfill their traditional role, these fathers' self-esteem suffered, and this interfered with their ability to give their daughters love and affection.

Some women who develop eating disorders believe that their fathers' disappointment began at birth when they were born female instead of male. One woman recounted:

> My parents had always wanted a boy. I was their last try. My father would tell me how disappointed he was. I felt close to him when I was little, but it was very traumatic for me when I realized there was no relationship there. It crushed me. I realized I would never meet his expectations.

Sensing a father's preference for sons and discomfort with daughters, many young women act out their father hunger by pursuing sports, academic achievement, or other interests of their fathers. Some begin by exercising excessively, with their dads or independently, pushing their bodies to the point of exhaustion. They strive for a hard, lean body, believing that their dads will accept them if they achieve this. Often they pursue sports hoping to please their father rather than to fulfill any personal desires of their own. Like little boys, they convince themselves that if their performance is good enough, they will win dad's love, conditional though it may be. Today's global girls have more and more opportunities to pursue sports, and many feel tremendous pressure to participate, whether they enjoy them or not.

While some daughters pursue more masculine activities and may be labeled tomboys, others exaggerate their femininity in response to their unrequited love. Through dieting, exercising, using laxatives, or taking diuretics or appetite suppressants, they attempt to sculpt their bodies. Some even have plastic surgery; still others undereat to punish themselves or eat uncontrollably to stuff down the painful realization of unrequited love. All are endangering their health—even risking their lives—for love.

Running on Empty

Both fathers and daughters in traditional families feel this unrequited love. Fathers, brought up to believe that economic support of the family is their most important duty, bear many burdens for which they feel unappreciated. They come home at the end of the day, worried about work and money, with little energy left for the family. They "gave at the office" and are emotionally spent. Rather than being accosted with still more demands, when they walk in the door they want some peaceful time to relax. They hope the family will appreciate how hard they have worked for them and will provide a welcoming haven.

Conflicting expectations may fill the air with negativity and resentment, further validating the daughter's feeling that she is unloved. According to one woman's description: "My father was always involved in his business, and he was never affectionate. When he was there, he was just negative and critical."

An atmosphere of stress, fatigue, unhappiness, and disapproval cannot create the secure home life that young people need. Adolescence brings with it tremendous insecurity. Its passengers need to feel comforted, accepted, and loved at home to survive these turbulent tides. Teenaged daughters need to be emotionally supported and refueled by their fathers, since men's opinions are so central to them. Accepting the many changes associated with adolescence, particularly sexuality, is not just an internal process. Global girls rely on others, especially their fathers, to help them integrate sexual maturity into their personal identities and lifestyles. When fathers are depleted, they have little to give their daughters. Both are running on empty.

Constricted Communication

Communication problems and deficits in self-assertion reflect basic differences between what each sex has learned to value. For example, females want to know what others think and feel. They bring this intense need to their fathers during adolescence as they try to understand and negotiate their position with the opposite sex. Males, however, have been socialized not to show or verbalize their feelings, and so denial and control are the skills a father brings to the relationship with his daughter.

Usually, fathers who have most completely internalized the economic-provider role are the least proficient at personal communication. One consequence of keeping a lid on their feelings, however, may be outbursts of anger that are very frightening to a daughter who is eager to please her father. As one woman described: "I was afraid of Dad. He never talked much, but he got angry easily. I guess he shut off all his feelings because of his temper."

The myth that men do not feel has devastating effects on young people who are learning how to communicate. Perceiving that emotions are off-limits, they will discuss the bare essentials but ignore deeper issues. This communication pattern expresses only external, not internal, reality. It is like window-shopping, rather than going inside the store to touch and feel and try on the garments. It can be confusing and limiting to children.

And constricted communication is a communicable disease—it spreads easily. So although a father may have a severe case, everyone else in the family also suffers. For example, one young woman whose father was unable to talk about feelings finally expressed her pain through her extreme weight loss.

> My father had arthritis. I knew he was miserable, but he would never talk about it. I felt so guilty whenever I complained, because he never did. I think I'm a lot like my dad—I have a hard time talking about how I feel. Maybe that's why I had anorexia.

Many global girls grow up not knowing much about how their fathers feel about anything. Without receiving the feedback needed to validate their attempts to reach out and assert themselves, they begin to doubt the validity of their own impulses and needs. "If Dad doesn't have any feelings, should I?" becomes an underlying question, and they may adopt the same denial system their dads have modeled so well. Lacking the avenues for direct communication with her father, a global girl may then use her body to say indirectly what she feels.

Pleasing Others

One of the damaging effects of constricted communication between fathers and daughters is the absence of even the most basic messages of acceptance. The result is that daughters grow up wondering how their dads feel about them, but having no way of knowing since they never receive any feedback. They are quick to conclude that they have not "measured up" in some basic ways. They are desperate to please but don't know how.

Some daughters cope with the need to please or satisfy their dads by trying to be like them. After all, imitation is the highest form of flattery! For example, one woman who recovered from anorexia described her father this way:

> Dad would never get into feelings with us. He did things for us but didn't talk. I used to fear him. He expected a lot from us and had a hot temper. He had no use for people who didn't carry their weight. So I was always on the go—go—go. I never wanted to be a slacker. I wanted to please him, but he never seemed to notice.

Trying to please her father, this woman rejected her body's needs and stopped eating so she would not be seen as a "slacker." She and many other women who develop eating problems describe childhoods in which they would do anything to satisfy their dads, whom they often saw as overburdened and unhappy. Here's an example of the results:

> When I was six years old, my father told me I was too old to play with dolls. I never did it again. I couldn't play. To gain acceptance from him, I had to act mature instead. I tried hard to win his approval. It may be why I became a lawyer. The only way to get his attention was to do something drastic. My weight loss was the only thing that ever worked in getting his concern. But then he was as angry as he was worried.

Such experiences lead women to expect nongratifying, critical, negative interactions with men. The die has been cast, and they may go through life attracted to men who are just like their fathers, hoping sooner or later to please either daddy or his substitute. In this way, father hunger assumes a powerful position in a young woman's life. For future relationships with men and with a masculine culture, it creates a blueprint based on the willingness to do anything to get male approval.

One woman described this as follows:

> *My father never talked to us much. I never knew how he was really feeling . . . I never got feedback about how I was. It would have helped if he had talked to me more. Recently I've been talking about him in therapy. I'm realizing that his ignoring me had an effect. I wanted his approval and probably have tried to get it from other men, not in a healthy way.*

Power

A healthy personal identity requires that we feel a sense of mastery and independence in the world. This, however, is a tricky process for women, since pleasing others is also necessary to their self-identity. Many women are at a loss for how to assume power in a culture that rewards masculine characteristics more than feminine ones, and where independence, autonomy, control, achievement, and economic productivity are valued more highly than nurturance and relationships. As young women today struggle to balance femininity and masculinity, they find it difficult to meet their own needs, to continue to please others, and also to assume a desired, possibly influential place in the world. They may also find that although self-assertion brings with it a sense of power and connection to those masculine values, it may jeopardize their relationships.

On the other hand, global girls who grow up feeling loved and respected by their fathers generate a sense of personal power, which enables them to make and stand by decisions that balance the needs of the self with the demands of others. Those who don't enjoy this kind of connection will not easily achieve this equilibrium. One young woman described the impact of her father's absence on her inability to assert herself in relationships:

I don't have any childhood memories of him. He's quiet. I don't remember him saying "I love you" until I was 17 . . . . If I had known him and if he had been an example for me, he could have taught me that all men are not lechers and bastards. I had many experiences with that kind of man. I felt powerless as a woman and didn't know how to gain control of my life. If my father had been there for me, he could have shown me that I'm not less than a man, that a woman can have her own ambitions, desires, needs, and can say what she needs.

A more open and accepting relationship with her father might have empowered this woman to make decisions, assert herself, and feel effective as a woman. Instead, she denied her femininity and withdrew from relationships. Not eating and losing weight became the one area in which she felt permission to exert her own personal power.

Control

Food and control go hand in hand. Giving or withholding basic sustenance is some families' easiest and most frequent method of behavior modification. Parents use food to reward, punish, or alter a child's behavior. So, quite naturally, children may engage in battles over food in order to gain some influence in their families.

People who develop significant eating problems come to see changing their nutritional intake as the only way they can exert autonomy. For example, one young woman whose parents had been very authoritative in all their interactions, including at mealtime, described how eating became her sole means of control.

I was fed up with everything, sick of having to answer to everyone and follow what they wanted. I had always pleased my parents by being a good eater . . . My mother liked to cook, and I always thought I was pleasing her when I ate . . . . And mealtimes were very important in my home. I started to feel that I had no power in the world––even eating was for others, not for me. I had to find something that was mine. I learned that I could control what I ate, how much––that's all I had, the only thing that was mine. So I used food to subvert my parents' control over me.

Although this young woman felt more pressure from her mother to conform to prescribed eating habits, she felt dominated and unappreciated by both parents. What an interesting and symbolic expression she used: *fed up*. She expressed a desire to gain more control of her life through food, because mealtime was her only access to her father. She wanted him to hear her. Not eating was a plea for father to respond to her as a person rather than just dictate to her.

Excessive constraint over eating, however, soon leads the person to being tyrannized in a new way: worries about food, calories, fat, exercise, and ways to avoid eating or to get thin come to dictate every waking moment and interaction. As the same woman said:

> The ironic thing is that I only wanted control, and for a while I guess I had it. But before long, my life was totally out of control. First I was anorexic, then bulimic. I had to be hospitalized three times. I was sick for about four years. If only I had known how to gain real control in my life. I was really asking for my father to help me with this.

For many women, denying their need for food is an effort to reject their femininity and curb their appetite for connections with others. By taming their hunger for food, they hope they will also tame their hunger for Daddy, for love, and for acceptance from men. Such constraint may be an attempt not only to conform to the male pattern of being less connected to food, but also to make their bodies more masculine. Eating problems thus can symbolize a different way of connecting with dad—through control.

Achievement

Global girls learn early that men value achievement, so they search for ways to succeed in order to get dad's approval. Today in many people's minds, the ultimate female accomplishment is a well-toned, slim, "perfect" body. The food, fashion, diet, and fitness industries constantly remind us that changing our food intake and our body shape will bring personal happiness and acceptance from others. As one woman said:

> I really wanted, needed, my dad to be proud of me. I wasn't sure how to get that—nothing I did seemed to work, but I knew he thought

*being thin was good, so I started to diet. It was the beginning of an
eating disorder—but all I wanted was to please my dad. This was
my only way to achieve. It showed self-control and all the things I
thought he valued. But in the process, I nearly ruined my body and
could have lost the basis of being a woman: being able to have kids.
I didn't realize all that back then. I only knew I needed a way to
achieve—I needed to be outstanding in order to feel OK, to get approval from my dad.*

Today we tend to define achievement in masculine terms. Objective measures, especially numbers—how much money a person makes, or how much a person weighs—determine an individual's worth to society. Competing and winning are considered accomplishments, while nurturing and caring are not. Consequently, to attain some sense of personal success, many young women will abuse their bodies in the attempt to win an unspoken, global beauty contest.

Attention

As you have read, girls who grow up without a positive connection to their fathers suffer tremendously from a father's lack of attention. They hunger for a basic essential: knowing that they are worthy of love, approval, and affection. Since they have been denied positive responses and approval from this most important man, they feel unworthy and undeserving. Stuck in this web of father hunger, some are unable to move forward in their lives. In their minds, developing an eating disorder may represent their only chance of connecting with their fathers and getting the attention that all children need in order to grow.

Looking back at their eating problems, many women have told me that meals were the only times they saw their dads on a regular basis, so this was the logical time to try to get attention. If dad notices, then the eating problem is successful. Therefore, changing these behaviors and recovering may be a frightening prospect: what if they lose what they have worked so hard to attain? As one woman said,

*Finally my father came into my life a bit when I started to lose
weight. That kept it going. I knew that I needed him and I had done*

a lot of other things, good and bad, to get [his attention], but this was the only thing that worked, and I was reluctant to stop.

Many men simply do not know how important they are to their daughters' self-esteem. The gap between the attention most fathers give and what their daughters need has tremendous implications. Global girls who hunger for their dads to notice them are bound to have a shaky sense of self as they enter adolescence and adulthood. If they do not feel acknowledged by dad, they will wonder how they can become part of the world he represents.

Identity

The whole notion of female identity—what it is to be a woman—is in flux today. Young women are expected and encouraged to do many things they could never consider doing 25 years ago. As a result, women of all ages are bewildered as they consider which roles they should assume, what they should be like, what interests to pursue, and how to balance what they know they must do (take care of others) with new expectations that they achieve and be independent. Finding one's personal identity, a sense of a unified self and social role, is a great challenge to young people growing up in this period of rapid change.

Our families shape our identities by both their actions and their attitudes. Parents today are struggling with old roles and definitions of masculinity and femininity that no longer fit and that confuse their daughters, who are trying to consolidate their sense of self and find a way to live in today's society. Jessica, who developed a serious eating disorder as a teenager, talked about the conflicting pressures she felt as she struggled with her female identity:

In the world I grew up in, women were second-class citizens. I was tuned in to that. I got angry with what my mother took. I think that's still lurking back there. I was getting double messages. I felt a need to achieve and I knew I was smart, but I had iron shackles on my feet at the same time. I was getting the masculine push to achieve and the feminine go-to-college-so-you-can-raise-better-children. That's still going on—the only time my father said he was proud of me was when I had my son. Anybody can have a kid!

Like many other young women today, Jessica was ambivalent and confused about growing up and preparing for the future: should she achieve, or should she just prepare to be a good wife? She knew she did not want a life of self-sacrifice like her mother's, spent "holding my dad on a pedestal." When she looked at her family and the surrounding culture, she did not anticipate finding a comfortable role as a woman.

Gradually, Jessica solved the dilemma about her feminine identity. Recognizing what she did *not* want was a big step for her, but that was followed by much turmoil. As an adult she finally did reach a compromise—she is now a wife and mother, works part-time, and feels quite fulfilled. Like many of her peers, she unfortunately battled her body and her appetites for food and relationships before she figured out how to *be* as a young woman.

For Jessica, an important part of finding her own path was understanding the impact of the culture on her perceptions and on her family's functioning. She concluded that culturally prescribed limitations on her father's role caused many of her problems. She now knows that her father's lack of involvement was not necessarily an active choice. Instead, it was prescribed by the social patterns at that time.

Jessica also determined that her childhood, adolescence, and identity formation might have been different if her father had been more involved with the family. If her parents had been able to work together more effectively, she might have grown up with clearer, more constructive views about being a woman. A father's attitude and behavior toward his wife has a significant impact on his daughter's emerging female identity. For example, when Jessica's father belittled her mother and did not support her importance in the family, Jessica responded to this perceived lack of respect by deciding to be different from her mother. She had no other model, however, so she became very confused about femininity and adulthood. Regrettably, like many other women, Jessica attempted to resolve the questions about who she was, where she was going, and what place to occupy in the world by changing her eating and her body. She thought that losing weight would win approval and power from a masculine culture.

An eating disorder can function as a developmental passage from childhood to adulthood, a way to forge a personal identity. By slowing down the process, it allows the person to avoid or delay facing the issues of adolescence and young adulthood. One young woman said she could not imagine how she would have become an adult woman without her eating disorder. In her words:

> *The anorexia is part of becoming who you are. It's like being in a cocoon, building a wall around you for a while. Finally I could understand why I did it and feel OK about that.*

For many young women suffering from father hunger, conflicts with their bodies and food become their protective cocoon. Just as a caterpillar breaks out of the cocoon to become a butterfly, those who manage to survive will be transformed by the experience. This metamorphosis often includes a heightened awareness of their father's influence in their lives. This is apparent in the examples that follow.

Liz: "All I wanted was my father's love."

Liz said plaintively, "All I wanted was my father's love." These words, quoted earlier in this chapter, were hers. Her story illustrates many of the themes we have discussed, especially the longing for dad's attention. It also challenges many of the myths discussed earlier. Liz's childhood memories speak to the importance of the father in the family, especially to his daughters.

Liz was the youngest of three girls. They all knew that their father had wanted sons. She "went all out to be the son," playing softball and soccer, "but it was never enough." Being the youngest in the family put her in a difficult position. Not only did Liz feel she was her father's last chance for a son, but also she was the only child still at home when her parents eventually divorced.

The family environment included many stressors that converged in an eating disorder for Liz. Her mother was weight-conscious; her father was achievement-oriented. He was a physician, devoted to his practice and profession, which did not leave much time for his wife or family. Liz noted that her mother expressed anger with her father by not cooking. They never even ate meals together! But, because her parents had lived like that for a long time before they began fighting, her mother's matter-of-fact announcement that they were getting divorced really surprised Liz. Then her home life began to change. Her sisters left for college and until the divorce was final, her parents still lived together but fought a lot.

Liz felt no one cared about her. Her sisters had left, her father was more preoccupied and distant than ever, and her mother was tense, angry, and began drinking. Her mother had never seemed happy as a homemaker and had not put much effort into providing meals or nurturing her daughters, but now she became even less involved. After her parents' divorce, Liz had less contact and time with her father, and her doubts about his love for her grew. She wanted desperately to please him, so she pursued academics and athletics. She tried to be more like a boy, but nothing worked; nothing evoked her father's affection and approval.

Liz's adolescence was miserable. From the age of 12, when her parents decided to divorce, she had problems in school. One year she nearly failed. Later she began smoking marijuana and drinking, leaving evidence of this in both her parents' homes. They never responded to these behaviors, so Liz assumed they didn't care. They didn't seem to realize that she felt isolated, sad, and lonely. At her request, she went away to boarding school. Both parents remarried, and her mom spent a great deal of time with her new husband. Her father remained overinvolved in his work.

Liz's eating problems began at age 20 while she was away at college. She had become engaged to a man who was much older than she. She later questioned whether he was a replacement for her father. Their engagement and wedding plans brought her closer to her parents, but Liz soon realized she did not feel ready for a long-term commitment and broke up with her fiancé. Sadly, she felt she had also lost the new relationship she was beginning to build with her parents. Because she had always tried to be "the best" and "the strongest," she could not let her guard down and tell her parents she needed their help.

Until this time, Liz had not dieted or been unhappy with her body, although her roommate and many of the young women on campus seemed to be. After the breakup with her boyfriend, however, she needed something to take his place, so she started to diet. Her father had always stressed the need to have a goal and a plan, and suddenly weight loss became her life's purpose. She said:

> I was so weak and vulnerable. I had no one. I had nothing else to do but to compete with my roommate in dieting and exercise. I was always striving to be perfect, to please my parents. When I realized that would never happen, I just stopped eating. I wanted just to slowly, passively waste away and not bother anyone.

Before she began dieting, Liz was 5'4" and weighed 120 pounds. Then she lost 35 pounds. Her father, though he was a physician, never mentioned her weight loss. Her mother never talked about it either, but did try to get her to eat. Liz did not find her mother's attempts helpful. Her stepmother appeared aware but didn't say anything until one day when she told Liz that her father was concerned and offered to go to therapy with her. Both her mother and stepmother tried to support her in their own ways, but Liz said, "I was looking for my dad. That's all I wanted. I wanted something from him."

Gradually, with her stepmother's help, Liz realized that her father's inability to show affection did not mean he didn't love her. Although she never took advantage of their offers to attend family therapy with her, their willingness to do so helped her, and she began to accept her father's love through her stepmother.

Liz had been seeing a therapist and she continued to do so, although her recovery process continued long after she had stopped regular sessions. As she spoke about the importance of her sessions and the therapist's gentle, accepting support of her, it became evident that a male therapist was especially appropriate for her.

Through the therapeutic relationship, Liz found that men can pay attention to feelings, can show caring and nurturance, can listen and be available, and can understand her complex problems. While her father's behavior had supported the myths about men being unable to care, feel, or understand, her therapist's contrasting behavior challenged them. Gradually she began to open up to men and to anticipate that they might understand. Although it was initially difficult, Liz found that developing a relationship of trust with a male therapist helped to restore her self-confidence and her ability to trust.

During her recovery, Liz felt she was becoming closer to her father, but she went through a long "anti-male phase" when she did not want to be alone with him. Gradually, though, she developed friendships with other men. She went on to finish college, then graduate school, and began a professional career. She is now married and has a family of her own.

Liz and many other women have repeated the belief that "If only Dad had been there, maybe all this would not have happened." They speak to the long-term and painful impact of father hunger.

Patricia: "I never felt that I was enough."

"I never felt that I was enough." This is how Patricia described her childhood. Now in her 40s with a rewarding marriage, career, and three children, Patricia developed anorexia when she was a teenager. She feels her eating disorder was directly related to her father, who was a diabetic and became severely depressed. An only child and a bright little girl who was very talented in music, Patricia felt great pressure to achieve and make up for her father's disappointments. "Because I did well, I think I created expectations in him that I would excel. My father felt he was a failure. I think he looked to me to fill some of his own hopes."

Patricia did everything she could to try to make her father happy. She began cooking for him as soon as she was old enough, even paying attention to his special dietary needs as a diabetic, but mealtimes were tense and unpleasant. Her parents argued when her father did not eat properly. Patricia had always been a picky eater herself, and having to think about her father's dietary problems might have contributed to her own preoccupation with food. As her father became more depressed and withdrawn, her mother grew increasingly angry. Patricia, who desperately wanted to please them both and take their minds off their problems, became an overachiever:

> By the age of 15, I was a workaholic. I used to stay up till 2:00 or 3:00 a.m. doing homework. I felt there was no room for failure. I had to make up for their disappointments. I had to make up for my dad's depression and feelings of failure, but there was no room for failure for me. I remember I failed a test in driver education. My father was so angry—he called his friends demanding another test, but I refused to take it. I could have really used help with failing. I couldn't fail. Anorexia was another achievement and, at the same time, it was a way of rebelling against my father's demands.

Patricia suffered from anorexia nervosa for seven years. She sees it as a response to her perceptions of what her family expected of her:

> There was a demand to be beyond my years, to make up for my dad's failures and their unhappiness. For me, I think I finally rejected that responsibility and refused to become independent. I think I was saying, "I'm not grown up enough to handle this."

Patricia was 5'5" and got down to 75 pounds. Despite her weight loss, her parents could not face up to her problems. Although her mother would try to get her to eat, she never talked about why she wasn't eating. Patricia knows her father was concerned and remembers seeing tears in his eyes, but he was discouraged and preoccupied with his own concerns. Her parents took her to their medical doctor, who encouraged her to gain weight, but nothing really changed until after she went to college.

If Patricia's high school teachers worried about her weight loss, they didn't mention it, and as Patricia continued to achieve in school, they most likely discounted their worries. When a young person seems so competent, so perfect, and so able to take care of others, adults may not recognize the emotional needs and deficits underlying this veneer. No one knew how much Patricia was suffering and how her father's illness, problems, and special needs were impacting her relationships, identity, and self-concept. She was sick, preoccupied, and isolated throughout high school, and her eating disorder worsened.

As a freshman in a prestigious women's college, Patricia continued eating very little and losing weight. Still, no one tried to find out why this was happening and no one referred her for therapy. This was more than 20 years ago. Hopefully, if her situation happened today, it would be handled differently. Now most colleges have counseling and health services that can help students identify their problems and work on recovery.

Late in her freshman year, the dean of the college took notice of Patricia's wasted body. He told her that if she continued to lose weight, they would hospitalize her. By this time Patricia had internalized her father's expectations, and the threat of not being able to continue her pattern of achievement was frightening. Paradoxically, the same fear of failure that had contributed to her eating disorder now helped her begin to gain control of her symptoms. She didn't want to disappoint her dad or anyone else. The dean's words shook her up, and she slowly began to give her body what it needed.

In addition to regaining weight and her health, Patricia worked very hard to correct the patterns in her relationships that had led her to focus on others rather than on herself. Gradually she learned how to develop relationships with men that were not based on self-sacrifice and otheration. As a result, she now has many satisfying connections, including a happy marriage. Although it took three years for Patricia to gain weight and begin menstruating again, she has recovered both physically and psychologically. However, she still wishes she could have experienced a better relationship with her now deceased father and mourns this loss and the loss of her adolescence.

Patricia now sees her eating disorder as causing her years of misery, self-doubt, isolation, and poor health. Although she has been able to overcome these problems, her father hunger had costly consequences and could have destroyed her. To heal, she had to admit the sadness she experienced in her relationship with her dad and acknowledge its effects on her life.

Questions and New Connections

- As a father, what can you do to overcome the separateness and give your daughter the connectedness and support she needs from you? How can you express your approval and love for her?

- As a daughter, what can you say to communicate more directly about what you need from your father?

- How can families refuel so they are no longer running on empty, and their emotional resources are renewed?

- As a father, what can you do to debunk the myths and show your daughter that men do feel and can be understanding? What can you do to be more available to her?

- What are some healthy ways for women to express their power and feel a sense of being in control in the world today?

- If you are a daughter, write three ways you can work on these normal human needs without resorting to food and eating: power, control, achievement, attention, a unique personal identity.

CHAPTER 8

Sexuality, Body Image, and Food

A father has a significant influence on his daughter's acceptance or rejection of sexuality and body image, and on her eating and health habits. Still, old myths that minimize the father's contributions continue to flourish. By default, more than by intention, the role fathers play in their daughters' critical passage through adolescence to sexual maturity is inadequate and disappointing, and fails to meet the needs of global girls.

Part of the problem is that the two sexes learn to experience life so differently. For example, because we teach men to fear, distrust, and deny feelings, we give them few opportunities to be emotionally open to others. Consequently, for many men, sex is the only time they feel permission to be close. So as the typical father watches his global girl mature and become increasingly sexual, he may be worried about boundaries and withdraw from her even more. Dad's anxiety compounds the daughter's own fear of her body's changes and becomes a powerful deterrent to a close, supportive relationship and to her sense of herself as a budding young woman. The result can be denial not only of her sexuality but of all her body's needs. This is apparent in anorexia, exercise abuse, bulimia, compulsive or binge eating, and body dissatisfaction.

Father Hunger and Sexuality

Father hunger becomes increasingly detrimental when girls enter puberty, because this is the developmental phase during which their curiosity about men and the male perspective, their interest in heterosexual relationships, and their own physical attractiveness emerge and intensify. When a father responds by withdrawing and being aloof, his daughter suffers from low self-esteem, and her confidence in her sexuality is undermined. She is denied valuable opportunities to gain experience and practical knowledge about how to act around men and how to talk to them.

For many, dieting is a response, an effort to please men, to be sexually attractive, or to get attention. For others, the same behavior may be an effort to deny their physical maturity. One woman who developed eating problems during adolescence said, "In the back of my mind I was trying to have a body that wouldn't attract men, and then I wouldn't have to worry." By reverting to a more juvenile body, she hoped to regress to her childhood, when relationships with her father and other men were unencumbered by sexuality.

Some women with eating problems describe having been close to their fathers during childhood, but feeling abandoned or rejected by them as they matured. The daughter then interprets dad's absence as a sign of her own failure, her fault. However, when fathers retreat or withdraw because of their own discomfort with their daughter's sexuality, the daughter is left with no explanation. She can only assume that the breakdown in her relationship with her dad has some unspeakable connection to her puberty. For girls, physical maturation is traumatic enough, but when they also perceive that it means they can no longer be close to their fathers, it becomes even less inviting. Those who unconsciously long for the happy years of being daddy's little girl may limit their eating to halt or reverse the growing up process.

Patricia had many fond memories of her dad from early in her life. When she was eight or nine years old, however, he became distant. She wonders if her dad was afraid of her approaching puberty. His lack of emotional support during her formative adolescent years contributed to discomfort with her self, her sexuality, and relationships to men:

> I remember playing with him when I was little. He was fun and really liked small children. But I don't remember his presence in my middle years at all. He became sick and very depressed, drinking and retreating into himself. I never felt I had a real conversation with him. As an adolescent, I knew nothing about relating to males, although I was interested. I guess his absence was a big factor. It wasn't until graduate school that I learned how to relate to men. I believe my anorexia has a lot to do with this fear of sex.

Women who develop eating and body image problems sometimes perceive that their parents, especially their fathers, are conflicted about sex or disapprove of it. These young women begin to feel that their bodies are disgusting and their impulses are immoral. They use self-destructive eating to achieve a less sexual body and diminish their guilt. One woman said:

> *I knew if I reached a certain weight, I wouldn't have to worry about doing wrong—no one would be attracted to me so I wouldn't have any guilt. It was a way to work around the guilt . . . . I knew my father's attitudes about sex. I felt I should be punished for being curious about sex and interested in guys, that I was bad—there was nothing good in me. Not eating was a way to take things out on myself.*

Many global girls today dread the physical changes of adolescence because they assume that physical maturity means they should suddenly be ready and willing to have intimate relationships. Since they have hoped so desperately to please their fathers, they cannot imagine being able to say no to men. Their solution is to abuse themselves through not eating, excess exercise, or other self-destructive behaviors so they will be unattractive and avoid temptation. They know no way to cope other than to reject their bodies, their sexuality, and their need for food.

For some, an eating disorder reflects both an interest in and an anxiety about sexuality, a conflict that arises from experiences in their families. These words describe the dilemma:

> *I was very fearful of sex. All of my parents' taboos and limits seemed to really cover their fears of my sexuality. I was afraid, but I wanted it. My anorexia was a way to delay having sex.*

One woman, whose problems with food began after her first sexual relationship, realized that her eating was a way of dealing with her guilt, discomfort, and inability to assert her needs:

> *Sex was real scary to me. My anorexia has more to do with that than with food. Once I was involved sexually, I thought I had to marry my boyfriend. But it wasn't a good relationship. It wasn't at all satisfying. I saw it as another performance. I really felt guilty*

and bad about the sex. That may have been why I stopped eating. I
had never really known my father, although he was there. Maybe if
I had felt close to him, my relationships with other men would have
been better.

These words reveal how father hunger, when it goes unsatisfied, impairs a daughter's feelings about sexuality and affects her relationships with other men. If this woman had had positive experiences relating to her father as a person, she might have been able to negotiate her first sexual encounter more successfully. Instead, she could not set limits and experienced tremendous guilt. She could, however, set limits on her eating, and this lessened the guilt. When she finally began to explore the disappointments she had felt with her father, she discovered the underlying reasons for her problems with sex and food.

Father Hunger and Early Maturation

Global girls who enter puberty early may be at special risk for developing eating problems and body dissatisfaction. Visibly standing out from their peers, they worry whether they will be able to maintain friendships or will be ostracized for their noticeably different bodies. These girls are often extremely self-conscious, fretting about how to cover up the signs of puberty—breasts and menstrual periods.

Early maturers are also the target of teasing by boys, and sometimes by adult men. This makes them feel more ashamed of their figures. Often, the end result is a generalized feeling of losing control of all aspects of their lives. Since their bodies are doing new and unpredictable things, they expect the same kind of uncertainty and powerlessness across the board. Neither a daughter nor her parents are ready for her to have a teenaged body when she is 9 or 10 years old. Fathers may be particularly uneasy and unsure when this happens. They may withdraw more dramatically and quickly when their little girl develops a woman's body as early as the 4th or 5th grade.

The eating and body image difficulties associated with early maturation are illustrated in the story of Nicole, who matured when she was just 10 and developed an eating disorder when she was 14. She recalls that puberty happened quickly: as if she "went to bed one night after playing with dolls and woke up the next morning with breasts." She had always been shy and reserved, and she felt even more uncomfortable about the male attention she began to attract when she developed physically. Her new breasts drew comments from the adult men in her life—her father, his friends, her uncles, and strangers as well. Suddenly, their expectations of her changed dramatically. She felt she was being forced to act like an adult woman, while she would have preferred to continue playing with dolls:

> I wasn't ready for my body. Nobody mentioned this as part of growing up, but once my body changed, everyone started responding to me differently, even adult men—friends of my father. I thought, this is the way it is. This is how life is going to be. Inside I hadn't changed—my body just looked different, and people were only responding to that. I didn't feel I had any control over it. I decided I should look a certain way—the way I thought they wanted—so I started to lose weight. I got even more attention then. Each time, I hadn't changed inside, but people were responding to me differently. It seemed that people cared only about my body, not about me.

Nicole felt she had little control over her destiny once she had developed a sexual body. In her first dating experience, the boy, who was a few years older than she, became physically violent and tried to rape her. This trauma marked the beginning of her eating problems. She believes that if she had experienced a more affirming relationship with her father, she might have felt a greater sense of control over her body and her life. Hungry for male approval, she was unable to refuse when this boy took advantage of her. She began to believe that becoming an adult woman "was not very enticing," and that it would bring her less, not more, control over her life. She turned to anorexia as a way of gaining control over her life, only to find that the anorexia soon took control over her!

By the time Nicole was a college student, she had made much progress in overcoming her eating disorder. However, she recognized that she still had some difficulty handling relationships. She was afraid of getting close to men, so she dated only casually, not seriously. For many years, she remained hypercritical of her body and afraid of sexual intimacy, always expecting disapproval and rejection.

After Nicole started therapy and began to acknowledge her feelings about her dad, she made much progress in many areas, including her relationship with him. The positive changes she experienced with her father through working on this relationship gave her confidence that other interactions with men could also improve.

Nicole's story is representative of the serious consequences father hunger can have on a daughter's adolescent development. As Nicole described her father, he did not seem to be a man who deliberately rejected his daughter or who had negative attitudes toward all women and their bodies. He sounded like a normal man who had little idea what his daughter needed from him.

Once again, we can see the damage done by our discrepancies between male and female experiences and values. If only Nicole's father's upbringing had not been so traditionally masculine, he might have understood how important he was to her, and she might have avoided the anguish of her eating disorder. Instead, anorexia seemed to be the only way she could cope with her disappointment with her body and with men.

Father Hunger and Sexual Trauma

As we have seen, eating and body image problems are often the result of unhealthy attitudes and feelings about sexuality conveyed by the family or culture. In many cases, inappropriate sexual experiences lead to disordered eating and body dissatisfaction.

Exact data about the incidence of sexual trauma affecting women with food and body image problems are impossible to attain because such violence is generally underreported. Many victims are afraid of repercussions. Others are ashamed and feel guilty of having provoked or caused the abuse. People who have been abused often try to make sense of it by convincing themselves that they deserved or provoked it—instead of realizing that no one, under any circumstances, deserves to be abused; and no one, for any reason, has a right to abuse someone else. (If you or someone you know is in an abusive relationship, please urge them to seek professional help for this dangerous dynamic that can escalate uncontrollably toward a life-threatening crisis.)

Still others cope with sexual trauma by denying the event. Often, people who have been victimized defend themselves against the pain so completely that they remember it only after months or years of therapy. Nevertheless, the powerful and confusing feelings evoked by sexual trauma certainly contribute to eating and body image conflicts. Starving or bingeing and purging may be efforts to:

- Establish personal boundaries
- Punish oneself
- Express anger
- Control one's life

A man who violates the socially accepted physical boundaries with his daughter causes severe anguish. A child's lifetime ability to love and trust others is founded on the security provided by a safe home with caring parents. Children expect to be protected by parents, especially by their fathers, and an incestuous relationship with father feels neither right nor safe. Shame and self-denigration dominate the victim's psyche, and the daughter will usually blame herself for his transgressions. Also, her obligation to obey her father compels her to participate as long as he wants her to do so. She will usually be bound to secrecy, with dad threatening something she perceives as even more devastating, should she refuse.

Relationships in an incestuous family become warped. Even if other family members suspect or know about the abuse, they deny it to maintain the family's delicate, albeit dysfunctional, balance. The mother-daughter relationship will be especially marred. Complex, often contradictory emotions—jealousy, gratitude, rage, insecurity, self-blame, fear, neediness, isolation, depression, love, dread—all stampede to paralyze family interactions. In such an environment, disordered eating may be the only control a daughter can exert over her body and the only vent she has for discharging her pent-up anger and despair. When her need to take care of her family supersedes her right for sexual self-determination, she will act in a way that does not threaten family stability. Abusing her body is a maladaptive and desperate response.

Even when the perpetrator is not the father but a family friend, relative, or boyfriend, sexual trauma awakens many feelings about the father-daughter relationship. The young woman feels let down by her dad, since he was not there to protect her and has failed to teach her how to handle such advances by men. The daughter feels abandoned, but is afraid to tell her father; she anticipates that he will blame and disappoint her once more. The more distant her father has been historically, the more overwhelming the effects of sexual abuse will be.

Sexual traumas generalize to a mistrust of all men. If the daughter's relationship with her father is already distant, it will become more so after such an incident because she will withdraw from him. Puzzled by this, he may then be more unsure how to approach her, and therefore, be unable to give her support and provide corrective experiences at a time when she needs them dearly. Again, the divergent psychologies of men and women are at work, and the father, with his tendency to separate rather than to relate, unknowingly reinforces the daughter's distrust.

When fathers do provide support, the healing process following sexual trauma can be much easier. Furthermore, fathers who have been involved in caring for young children under the age of three are less likely to sexually abuse their own or other children.[1] An early intimate relationship, therefore, seems to prevent men from becoming abusers, and may equip them with the sensitivity needed to help a daughter who experiences sexual trauma.

Father-Daughter Bond: A Prototype

Since the father-daughter bond serves as a prototype for other attachments, it is important for women with eating problems and for victims of abuse to understand more about this relationship. For example, if a daughter doesn't feel loved, she may act provocatively to try to assure herself attention from other men. Her attempt to satisfy her father hunger may increase the possibility of a later sexual trauma.

Therapists working with eating disordered patients need to be sensitive to the possibility of abuse, past or present, and need to help their patients come to terms with the physical violations they have experienced. Conversely, mental health professionals treating a woman with a history of sexual abuse should inquire about the patient's eating habits and be certain that additional help is provided if an eating problem is present. In all cases, clinicians and patients should try to comprehend how the trauma reflects and affects the father-daughter relationship.

Father hunger complicates the normal psychosexual development of a young woman. She may experience the process of maturation as unpleasant, for it juxtaposes a drive to relate to men with an acute awareness of her dad's growing distance. Hoping to understand her father and connect with him somehow, she will tend to attribute his indifference or his inappropriate interest to her new sexual characteristics. Her body becomes the explanation for his behavior.

Feelings of loss surrounding her relationship to him begin to distort logic, and the young woman reasons: "If only my body were different, I'd have a better relationship with Dad." She believes that being smaller, thinner, less or more attractive, less or more muscular, will please him and will change their interactions. If not, maybe it will please some other man somewhere. Thus, discomfort in her relationship with her father evolves into discomfort with her physical self and into changes in her eating.

This system of logic has devastating effects. Father hunger distorts her feelings about her body, and this distortion in turn leads her to reject her basic and natural appetites for sex and food. She concludes that any impulses must be controlled, because her sexuality is unacceptable. Food, the fuel for her body, is forbidden. The fundamental pleasure of eating, something most of us take for granted, vanishes from her life. This is especially true for a woman whose father hunger is intensified by sexual trauma, as you will see in the two case studies that follow.

Carol: "My anger is really with my father."

Carol's story demonstrates how sexual abuse, eating, body image, and father hunger interact, producing anger that is turned inward against the self and expressed through bulimia. Although Carol's father was not the perpetrator, she felt he was responsible because of the minimal role he had played in her family. She repeated the pattern of victimization in several subsequent relationships until she was finally able to grasp the horror of her family's experience. For years, fasting and bingeing and purging were her only methods of dealing with her rage.

One of three children, Carol grew up in an intact family, but her father was chronically ill and depressed. Family life was very unpleasant. Prior to developing her eating disorder, Carol was molested by her older brother. She blamed this on her father's passivity and lack of involvement:

> He was aloof, insensitive, unaware of our feelings and what was going on in our lives. My brother took over his role—he was a tyrant, mean, and demanded everything of me, even sex. No one protected me from him. As I got older, I kept on getting involved with

men like my brother. It was the only way I knew how to be with men. I'm sure this would have been different if my father had done more with me . . . I know I really wanted approval from men, and that was the only time my brother had shown affection. I picked a lot of men who hurt me, and I was always trying to please them, not me. By being thin I was trying to be sexier for them.

Carol grew angry when she spoke about her brother's inappropriate influence and abuse of power in the family. "He even pushed my parents around." Despite the fact that her brother was the abuser, she stated:

My anger is really with my father for not knowing me as a person and for not showing me he cared or that men can care in a noncoercive way. Until I could work this out and understand it, I ended up getting involved with men who abused me.

By adolescence, Carol's pattern of otheration had been firmly established. The desires of men always superseded her own desires, even if the result was abuse of her body or sacrifice of her own wishes.

Because the maltreatment by her brother started when she began to develop, Carol associated physical maturation with being abused. She was ashamed of her sexual feelings. Rejection of this appetite led her to also reject her hunger for food. The two became linked. She began extreme dieting. She would feel "high and virtuous" during fasting, which sometimes lasted as long as four days. This pattern alternated with periods of bingeing ("a way to eat myself to death and numb myself to the world"), followed by vomiting "to cleanse myself."

The poor self-image Carol had formed as a child was reinforced by being victimized by her brother. She became extremely depressed, and her eating disorder gave her a way to withdraw. For Carol, bleeding from vomiting represented "a slow form of suicide."

Carol's symptoms intensified when she went away to college. She got help from two counselors there, but it wasn't until she graduated and saw a therapist for long-term treatment that she began to make significant progress. In her words, seeing a male therapist helped her "form a better image of men." A healing experience with a male therapist can provide a new role model that contradicts the myths that men don't care about feelings and can't understand women and their problems.

Carol worked hard to understand the interactions that had tied together the abuse, her relationships with men, and her feelings about food and her body. During the course of her therapy, Carol's father died. Although she had been angry because her mother had ignored all the conflicts in the family, she gradually developed a better relationship with her. Carol found that she needed to recover in all these aspects of her life before she could overcome the bingeing. Her bulimia was a habit that she could only face and work on more directly after she had acknowledged her anger and developed insight into her family's problems and her responses to them.

This took years of therapy and much work on her own as well. As Carol recovered, she was able to end the pattern of negative relationships with men in which they either ignored her, as her father had, or abused her, as her brother had. Her resentment and anger about the role her father played in the family had to become conscious before she could change her life.

Carol's story suggests that there are many paths to recovery. She had been sick for a long time, and she needed to understand the family dynamics before she could get better. Others may need to control their symptoms before they can develop insight into the many factors contributing to their illness. I wonder if Carol's healing process might have been quicker or less painful if her family had entered treatment during her adolescence. Perhaps had their dynamics been identified earlier, Carol's bulimia could have been prevented, or at least would have been less deeply entrenched.

If you or a loved one are suffering from anorexia, bulimia, or both, keep in mind that full recovery can take many years. Carol was sick for 14 years. Her recovery, though slow, has been quite complete.

Carol wishes her father had been alive so she could have talked to him as she worked through issues related to him. With the help of a therapist, she found ways to process her feelings anyway. Letter writing and other ways of speaking symbolically to her father facilitated this. Later, she did confront her brother about his abuse and her mother about her denial. Gradually, she healed the wounds that had led her to bulimia.

Carol's anger subsided because she took the risky steps necessary to resolve it. She has since had positive relationships with men, in which she asserts herself and expresses anger outright rather than turning it against herself. She has chosen a single lifestyle, but feels confident and comfortable negotiating differences and communicating feelings with both men and women.

Jenna: "I could control what I ate."

Jenna's story also includes incidents of sexual trauma. Her words may help you see how an eating disorder can be a means of coping with feelings, particularly the loss of control brought on by victimization.

Refraining from eating became Jenna's language. It gave her a feeling that she was controlling her life after her father began to molest her. Food had been a very tightly managed commodity during Jenna's childhood. Money was limited, and Jenna felt that her parents dominated her through what they allowed her to eat, while blaming this on sparse resources. Food intake was an easy way of expressing herself and trying to regain control. Although it was her father who molested her, Jenna was angry with both her parents:

> My father molested us, and my mother would sit there and watch. When I asked her for help she'd say, "He is your father, he is not hurting you." I couldn't control that at all. I could control what I ate. That's how my undereating started.

Jenna's mother was passive and went along with everything Jenna's father did. Her dad appeared overly interested in sexuality, and this made her self-conscious about her own sexual development:

> My father was always talking about sex. He's the one who explained the facts of life to us. I remember thinking about all the people he would tell when I got my period and all the jokes he would make. Maybe if I had a better relationship with him, he would not have used sex—the jokes and the molestation—as a way to get close.

Because of her father's constant remarks about sexuality, Jenna had difficulty feeling comfortable about herself as her body matured. She felt guilty about her interest in sex and about all of her needs. When she was 17, her unmarried sister became pregnant and her father grew even more concerned about Jenna's sexuality. "He was always accusing me of things I didn't do."

As a response to this sexual trauma and the lack of support from her father, Jenna developed severe anorexia. By starving herself, she intended to control her anger and her body. She wanted to be more in charge of her life, no longer dominated by her father's demands, which now included sex. Food was the only thing she could control, and it served another purpose as well: it punished her for desiring a relationship other than the one her father could give, and for being unable to achieve this on her own.

Throughout her early adulthood, Jenna's father hunger and self-rejection persisted and she had many negative relationships with men. She would do anything for them, including trying to change her body or lose weight to please them. Like many women with eating disorders, she was both interested in and terrified of sex. Her father's emphasis on her sexuality and his accusations made this a highly charged issue for her. She saw herself as being at the mercy of her own curiosity and of her father's impulses, rather than being in charge of her own destiny.

Years later, Jenna was able to recover in many ways. Physically, she returned to the weight she had been before she stopped eating. She developed a positive relationship with a man, married, and now has a family. She also has a professional job, which she enjoys. She worries about her children's relationship with her husband and tries to foster an active role for him and to share responsibility with him. Jenna is a conscientious and thoughtful woman, spouse, and parent who has struggled to find comfortable ways of controlling her life without being too rigid.

Her father's criticisms, emotional distance, and inappropriate sexual behaviors remain open wounds, and Jenna's efforts to heal her relationship with him have occurred without his involvement. Her father was certainly instrumental in her life, but she has had to recover and take charge of her life without the benefit of his participation in understanding and rebuilding their relationship.

Questions and New Connections

- What influence have social expectations and myths about the roles of males and females had on the father and daughter(s) in your family?

- How have father hunger and sexuality been related in your family?

- If you are a daughter, what can you do to achieve a closer and more caring relationship with your dad?

- As a father, what do you want your daughter to believe about men?

- If you are a father, what can you do to achieve a closer and more caring relationship with your daughter and help her become more confident in herself as she becomes a young woman?

- As a father, what can you do to protect your daughter from sexual abuse and trauma? What can you teach her that would help her protect herself?

- How can you build positive aspects of your father-daughter relationship to serve as a prototype for future relationships with the opposite sex?

- Write three conversation starter statements you could use to begin a positive discussion about what daughters need from their fathers.

CHAPTER 9

The Family's Functional Dysfunction

The father hunger that pervades contemporary society results in unfulfilling, frustrating roles for all family members, who are forced to develop ways of interacting and maintaining themselves without men being actively involved at home. Fatherless families must find dysfunctional ways to be together in order to function at all. In this chapter, we will look at this "functional dysfunction," which requires families to operate in a manner that works successfully at a superficial level but is not satisfying, productive, or conducive to personal growth and deep, meaningful interpersonal relationships.

Families generally mirror the prevailing beliefs and norms of the society in which they find themselves. If families are functionally dysfunctional, then the culture is dysfunctional as well. The families portrayed in this book replicate the skewed distribution of power in our society: men have power in the wider world, so women usually have to find power elsewhere—within the family or through their bodies. When an adolescent or young woman worries about her future as an adult female, the achievement of a "perfect" body, disciplined exercise, or weight loss may emerge as goals.

Loyalty to myths about mothers' and fathers' roles may result in a lifestyle that looks good and is successful in the outer world. Yet the scene is often not as pretty on the inside. Parents may not feel supported by each other: mothers feel burdened, fathers feel excluded, and children do not receive the love, security, and acceptance they deserve from both their mother and their father. Global girls may cope with this inner emptiness by eating to fill themselves up or by starving, exercising, or obsessing about appearance or weight because they believe that external appearances are all that count, and they do not deserve to feel fulfilled at a deeper level. Almost every woman who suffers from eating problems, body image dissatisfaction, and weight preoccupation experiences these patterns of functional dysfunction.

The paradox for these individuals and families is similar to the double bind that many fathers in our culture experience: the more empty and unsatisfying their internal life is, the more successful they appear to be in the world. In fact, women with eating disorders systematically report that at times when they look their best to others, they are actually doing their worst in terms of symptoms, depression, despair, loneliness, and hopelessness. In this chapter, we examine why this functional dysfunction occurs and how some individuals will wage war with their bodies and their appetites as a result.

Common Patterns in Families with Eating Problems

When we study families whose members have developed severe eating problems, body image dissatisfaction, and weight preoccupation, we find that they do not all fall into one particular family type. In fact, the family is only one of many forces that collide in an individual's life to lead to such suffering.

Furthermore, we never study families until the problem has become deeply entrenched, so we cannot know whether a style of family interaction preceded the problem or resulted from it. Eating problems are extremely challenging for families, and parents may respond with ineffective coping mechanisms because they are so worried or overwhelmed. The stress of the eating disorder may lead to new dysfunctional interactions. Thus, the ways in which a family functions must be seen as both contributing factors and consequences.

Some common patterns of interaction have been identified in families with eating and body image problems. However, because each person and family is a unique blend of the many influences affecting them, these dynamics will express themselves in different ways and to varying degrees in each case.

One common pattern in families with functional dysfunction is that they tend to avoid conflict as much as they can. Mothers strive to keep the family running smoothly, since their role is the day-to-day maintenance of relationships. They want their husbands to see what a good job they're doing, but may define that in terms of children who achieve, express few needs, go out of their way to please adults, and never fight. Fathers, invested in how well they provide for the family, may expect gratitude and serenity at home, so children learn to tiptoe around dad. Mothers characteristically say things like, "Don't upset your father," unknowingly contributing to the distance between fathers and children. Conflicts between the parents or between parents and children are usually either not identified or ignored. Communication is stunted or minimal, and the family tends to deny and avoid problems just to keep the peace.

In these families, parental authority is often absolute and unquestionable. No disagreements or hot issues can be discussed, so children do not learn how to negotiate a position for themselves. Girls feel especially powerless as they see their parents act out these roles, because they are particularly aware of the family's emotional tone. Their brothers, conditioned to be more independent, may not be as concerned with family dynamics and can usually find ways to assert themselves outside the home.

Global girls face two major dilemmas when they recognize that their families have problems. First, they blame themselves, and second, they feel impotent because they can't make things better.

We do see some general differences between the ways in which conflicts are manifested in anorexic and bulimic families. Those afflicted by anorexia exhibit many of the patterns just described—their members are so adept at denying problems that they truly do not see or feel the tensions within the family. People get along with each other, at least superficially. In families with a bulimic child, conflicts may be more visible, and the home life is often chaotic and stressful. Despite this awareness, however, no resolution occurs and the relationships suffer.

In both family constellations, because of the peripheral position the father occupies, the parents do not share responsibilities. The frustration resulting from this failure to manage problems effectively becomes a backdrop for the family's emotional life. People cannot feel good about themselves when they avoid obstacles instead of facing and overcoming them. In these dysfunctional homes, trust and emotional support take a backseat to presenting a positive impression to the outside world. Being honest about one's own feelings is considered a betrayal of the family. Loyalty to the establishment supersedes self-disclosure. Communication is stifled.

In an anorexic or bulimic family system, members may become entangled with each other because individual identity is poorly defined. Boundaries between siblings and between generations are weak. Children may end up taking care of the adults, since they do not know how to articulate their own feelings or desires. Although they may long for more satisfying contact with mom or dad, they will be unable to express this directly. Family members have little personal space or privacy, and again, the individual's needs are sacrificed for the group. Pseudomutuality results from this pattern of conflict avoidance and constricted communication: family members pretend that everything is OK, but at great cost to themselves.

When families fail to establish well-defined intergenerational boundaries, parents have difficulty distinguishing children's needs from their own. One or both parents may become overly close to a child. This pattern is potentially disastrous, because it keeps parents from facing problems within their marriage. Marital dissatisfaction is common in eating disordered families, but the parents typically do not deal with it directly. Instead, because of the blurred boundaries, the child becomes a best friend to one of the parents or tries to bring them together through her symptoms. Losing weight, becoming unhealthy, and bingeing or purging may be unconscious attempts to get the parents' attention and keep them focused on a shared predicament.

Triangulation occurs when a child is pulled into a marriage in this way. Instead of the parents dealing with their own problems as a couple, a third party gets in the middle of their communications. The triangulated system does not allow for privacy or separateness. Dyads rarely exist—all relationships tend to be triangles. Even when an issue occurs between one parent and a child, the other parent will become involved. These interactions are unhealthy because people are not dealing directly with the problem or with each other. Conflicts are rarely resolved. Also, the more a child is triangulated into marital issues, the less she will be involved in normal childhood activities that are more satisfying and developmentally appropriate.

Triangulation severely handicaps children, and global girls may react through misuse of food and their bodies. The more a daughter caretakes her family, the less apt she is to progress normally and to separate from her parents appropriately during adolescence. An eating disorder or conflicts about body maturation and appearance may seem to be the only safe way for her to express that something is wrong with the family's functioning. In fact, most eating problems develop during adolescence, when children normally leave the family nest. They cannot easily proceed with their own lives until some of these problems are addressed.

Viewing an eating or body image conflict as a sign of functional dysfunction and an attempt to cope with outdated cultural myths and multigenerational traditions can give families the insight they need to help the suffering person as well as themselves. In fact, they can use the problem to find ways to improve their relationships rather than blaming themselves or each other. As we discussed early in this book, families are complicated systems in which no one person exclusively causes the problems. Thinking about single causes is not very helpful when we are dealing with such a complex reality as a woman's relationship to food or her body. Instead, it is helpful if families look at ways in which acceptance of the prevailing culture, beliefs, and traditions has compromised their happiness. What we find is that our culture's shared father hunger and the desire for more personally satisfying roles for men and women often underlie the family's veneer and functional dysfunction.

Parental Roles

Children are not the only ones who suffer from father hunger. Both parents are often burdened with the same sense of deep disappointment in their own fathers. Furthermore, since father hunger is a cultural tradition handed down from one generation to the next, this loss may not be a conscious one. Thus, men and women undertake parenting with a handicap that even they may not recognize.

This limitation will affect all their interactions with their spouse and children. How can a man who was not fathered himself know how to parent a child? How can a mother who also was not fathered help her husband develop a constructive, involved, emotionally attached connection to their children?

Too few couples are able to overcome the impact of father hunger when they become parents. Instead, most families adjust to a life of functional dysfunction. Mothers tend to do too much to compensate for the husband's absence. As wives, they feel overburdened, overextended, and in need of help from their husbands, but their background of father deprivation keeps them from asking or expecting to get it; they feel they have no right to request more from men. Fathers continue to underfunction and feel left out, isolated, and unimportant to the family. Each parent may want more from the other but not know how to ask. Their frustration leads to bitterness and hostility. No one finds satisfaction in such a dysfunctional system.

This is the template global girls are given for their lives. They grow up expecting to carry most of the day-to-day responsibilities for their family. Furthermore, they believe they have no control over the situation, and many feel secretly or openly angry about this heritage. They may be resentful because their mother relies on them excessively to help with the house and other family responsibilities. They may also feel guilty about being resentful because they are aware of their mother's burdens. Wanting more from dad and being angry with mom easily translate into food conflicts.

Jessica describes how such mixed emotions led to her severe eating problems and rejection of her body:

> *I felt guilty all the time—guilty because I was angry with Mom for needing me to help—guilty for wanting more time with my dad. I hated myself—I thought I was bad for having these feelings. I would punish myself by not eating. Then I'd crave food and overeat. I thought I was the problem and that there was something wrong with me. Now I know it was because my dad was just never there. My mother and I both needed more from him than he could give. But he was a "good father" by our society's standards.*

Jessica's family is a good example of functional dysfunction and the negative consequences of father hunger. From the outside, they appeared to be a perfect, successful family, a pillar of the community. They "had everything." Her father ran a business handed down in his family, and he made lots of money. Her mother was a model homemaker whose home, social, and community responsibilities left little time or energy for herself. Her parents operated in different spheres, coming together only for social purposes and for the children; they did not share responsibilities. Her mother felt overwhelmed but accepted this lifestyle as the unquestioned family tradition and cultural dictate. Unable to ask her husband for help, Jessica's mother demanded a great deal from her. In turn, Jessica spent her adolescence resenting her mother and dreading adulthood.

As an adult, Jessica came to realize how her father had contributed to her feelings. But for years she lived in anger with her mother and in conflict about being a woman. The following quote reveals her confused perceptions:

> *My father was in his own world—work and golf. My mother had too much to deal with—all of the kids and the responsibilities for the family. . . . One of the most damaging things was that we were so sheltered and protected. Our parents never let us know the pressures that were going on. My mother also made my father look like a god. It was so unfair. It was the opposite of what was really happening.*

Once she understood the role her father had played in the family's life and how his culturally endorsed script kept him from understanding and supporting her mother, Jessica was able to make peace with her mother and herself. Gradually, she was able to eat with less conflict and to accept her body and her femininity.

Jessica's experience is common among women who suffer from eating and body image conflicts. A girl who grows up seeing her mother receive little thanks or recognition can easily develop negative feelings about the prospect of being an adult woman. If some of women's greatest assets—caring for others, nurturing, and relating—are not even rewarded at home, what are the chances of their being recognized in a world based on masculine principles and power? The burdens of femininity do not look attractive, and the payoffs are few. This may lead to a rejection of the physical changes accompanying maturation or a desire to return to childhood.

Frequently, young women with eating disorders describe their desire to avoid a life like their mother's. They do not want to sacrifice so much to please others, or to be required to take care of their families with little help. They may decide to avoid men or may be unable to discover a better balance in heterosexual relationships. Many act out their ambivalence about being a woman through their bodies and food. One woman stated:

> *I didn't want a life like my mother's, so I didn't want a body like hers. I didn't want the same kind of relationships and I didn't think*

I could find any other way. So I rejected my body and retreated from the world. Maybe if my parents had had a different kind of relationship, I would have felt OK about becoming a woman. I blame my dad a lot. If he had been a different kind of husband, I probably would have had a different life. Maybe I wouldn't have had all these problems with food and my body.

A Child's Solution

Children sometimes develop problems in a subconscious attempt to get their parents to solve their differences and work together as a unit. Family therapists treating many different kinds of problems see this phenomenon repeatedly. When children develop eating problems or compromise their health in another way, parents usually rally together to address the issue. Yet much of the unhappiness is rooted in the unsatisfying roles played by the parents and the long-term consequences of father's absence from the family.

Linda's story provides a good example of this. Linda blamed herself for her parents' strained relationship and inability to communicate with each other. Linda's mother had had a breakdown during Linda's childhood, and her father tried to make family life as conflict-free as possible. Her mother tended to be very emotional and to "fly off the handle," while her stoic father rarely shared his feelings. Linda often felt confused by her parents' interactions. Although her mother said her dad was in charge, in reality her mother ran the show. Linda felt responsible for their problems and used refusing to eat as a way of punishing herself.

Mother always put father in a leadership role, but they were really playing a game. I always knew my father was just doing what she wanted. I felt I was a problem between them. I felt guilty, in the middle of them, and thought I should punish myself. I stopped eating.

Linda was anxious for her parents to work out their conflicts. She had grown up feeling insecure and unprotected because of her parents' fights and inability to share parenting. They, however, were unable to admit their problems and instead acted as if everything were fine. This confused Linda. Not only did she blame herself for their problems, but she also condemned herself for her unvalidated perceptions. She had begun to feel that there was no place for her, either in her family or out in the world. Starving herself became a way to get her father more involved in the family and to clarify who was in charge.

> *I felt if Dad had been more involved before, it might not have been as severe, may not have happened. . . . I saw my father come into my life when I got sick. Although it was presented that he was head of the household, it just wasn't so. I wanted him to be more involved because I felt he understood more than Mom did.*

Through treatment Linda was able to stop the cycle of self-blame and accept the roles her parents chose to maintain. She came to see that her eating disorder was directly related to her parents' patterns of interaction and emotional expression. Her troubles arose not only from having a perfectionist, strict, demanding mother or from having a nonexpressive, stern father, but also from the ways in which her parents interacted. Linda's example clearly shows how an eating disorder can be an urgent plea for the father to be more present and available. It is also a forceful demand for change in the family. Until the underlying family issues were addressed, starving, bingeing, overexercising, and purging were the only ways Linda could safely express pain.

Parents, Power, and Food

Food is a potentially powerful medium for self-expression in all families, but in some families it becomes a primary means of exerting power and control. Many women use food as a weapon, perceiving it as their only defense in a world they experience as unfriendly. How does eating gain such power, and how does it reflect the functional dysfunction we see in these families?

Many factors coalesce to give food such a strong influence. Food is an infant's first and most frequent demand. The way in which parents respond to an infant's hunger will affect the child's subsequent relationships. Based on her earliest experiences, she will come to expect interactions with caregivers to be either satisfying or frustrating, consistent or chaotic.

As the child grows older, parents may use food to control behavior. In response, the child may perceive eating as an arena in which to challenge parental authority. Often these interactions replicate ways in which the parents' families used food with them. For example, if the parents were raised with a great deal of parental control over eating, they may repeat this pattern without questioning it. If the parents are dieting or struggling with their own weight or body image, they may unknowingly convey negative attitudes about food. They may even underfeed young children or criticize the child's natural appetite. If the parents have opposing attitudes or behaviors surrounding food, this can be confusing to the children, who may not know when and how to eat or even whether their appetites should be satisfied.

Fathers of infants often feel very left out of the closeness and warmth of feeding a child, especially if the mother is breast-feeding. As the child grows older, the dad may become involved with feeding to strengthen his emotional connection. If he remains uninvolved until a problem surfaces and the child is not eating well, he may resort to force-feeding. This is a frequent pattern in families with eating disordered children and adolescents. Such controlling and punitive efforts rarely work, for by that time, eating has assumed tremendous importance in the young person's psyche. Food refusal has generated a welcome response from dad, and the behavior may continue in a determined attempt to maintain his attention.

Young people who compulsively overeat may also want their dads to intervene, but overeating rarely elicits the response they seek. Parents may be critical and even disgusted when children eat too much, but seldom do they examine how their family's emotional functioning, their structure around food, and their attitudes toward their children's bodies encourage these behaviors. In any case, whether children are undereating, chaotically eating, or overeating, they are expressing important needs that are not being understood or met. Often these include feelings of depression and low self-esteem stemming from the father's unavailability.

In many families, mealtime is the one occasion when everyone comes together and children see their fathers. Unfortunately, this may also be a time when punishments and criticisms are dispensed and conflicts are expressed. The more food is associated with the bad news of the day, the less enjoyable and more conflictual it becomes. When adults with eating problems are asked to describe their family's meals, they usually talk about how unpleasant these were.

Mealtime was the only opportunity to fight in front of Dad. I think
we all hoped he would jump in and solve our problems. Instead, he
yelled at us about grades and homework, about how tired he was at
the end of the day, and how horrible it was to come home to us. He
would scream about our not appreciating all he did for us.

Powerful unconscious associations emerge in these situations. Soon, food and eating come to represent tension and conflict. Instead of feeling satisfaction in gathering together for meals, the children feel disapproval, disconnection, and discomfort. If this is the only time children spend with their dads, we can see how an appetite for food and a hunger for daddy can become intertwined.

Meals may also evoke conflicts because they are the times when the husband and wife come together in their traditional roles as providers and nurturers. Mothers who continue to do most of the cooking may feel overburdened and resentful. At the same time, they may have great difficulty asking or allowing their husbands to help them in this area. After all, for centuries the kitchen has represented power and identity to women, and it's hard to give that up. As one feminist asked, "While you can take the woman out of the kitchen, can you really take the kitchen out of the woman?"[1]

Girls who grow up in a home where women are in charge of meals and men make a lesser contribution learn to assert themselves through food. They may express their resentment of the role handed down to them to cook and care for others by ignoring their own hunger and needs. Thus, food preparation becomes another dimension that reflects the damaging consequences of the traditional division of labor and the absence of father from the day-to-day operations of the family.

Laura: "My anorexia was a challenge to my father, to get him more involved."

The story of Laura, a young woman who recovered from self-starvation, illustrates many of these tensions. Her family was successful and admired by others. From the outside, they looked very happy and functional; but inside, they were miserable, emotionally disconnected, and dysfunctional. Laura's parents never shared responsibilities. Her mother was tired and angry, and her father was oblivious to this and to the damaging results of his peripheral role in their home. Laura saw no way to express her pain other than through food. Her physical emptiness reflected an emotional abyss.

To understand why she had developed such a serious eating disorder, Laura had to explore the transgenerational patterns in her family—the values, interactional styles, roles, problems, and coping mechanisms that had been handed down from one generation to the next. Fortunately, Laura's parents willingly participated in therapy with her and worked hard to open channels of communiccation in the family. This helped her to understand the family mold, gave her permission to free herself from expectations that didn't work for her, and enabled her to create new ways of being that would end the emptiness of starvation and lead to a fuller life.

Looking back on her childhood, Laura remembered nothing unusual about the way her family treated food. She had always been a good eater and enjoyed food. Mealtime, however, was the only time she saw her father and the only time the family came together.

> Food wasn't a big issue, but dinner was the focus of family life. The dinner table was an emotional cauldron where all hell broke loose. I was usually the center of that. I think my anorexia was a challenge to my father, to get him more involved. I had always expressed my conflict with my mother at the dinner table for the same reason.

Laura described her parents as being very controlling. Any expression of feelings was denied. Her father, especially, conveyed that "feelings are not allowed." The family atmosphere had been like this for generations, and Laura explained that "control simply became a part of me." This excessive control logically extended to her eating habits and her anorexia.

When Laura's father was present, usually only at dinnertime, he was always setting limits. "He'd say, 'Calm down; speak up.' I just couldn't win. He had tremendous authority and power over the family."

Laura felt ignored, unimportant, and confused. She wanted to live up to her parents' expectations but couldn't break through their defenses to tell them what she needed. And their pattern of relating prevented them from saying what Laura most longed to hear: that they were pleased with her and satisfied with her efforts, and they thought she was good enough.

Laura's family heritage included a preoccupation with physical appearances. As Laura became an adolescent, she experienced pressure not only from her peers and from the wider culture to focus on her appearance and to be thin, but she also received this message repeatedly from her family, who considered thinness a positive sign of self-control and achievement. Because Laura did not feel good about herself and did not feel her parents' acceptance and love, these cultural communiqués about the value of being thin assumed even greater power over her life.

In addition to the pressure to be thin and the family's focus on emotional control and external appearances, Laura experienced another very significant problem. Her twin sister had a physical handicap that affected her growth. This made Laura more acutely aware of her own body. When her sister received experimental medical treatments, Laura was often evaluated at the same time to provide a basis of comparison. She was never asked how she felt about this, as the family's emotional energy was directed toward helping her twin make it through the medical procedures and adjust to her handicap.

Laura's family experienced many stressors that were never discussed but that nevertheless overshadowed her needs. Moreover, her sister's most intense medical intervention coincided with their early adolescence and physical maturation. Also at this time, the family moved to a new community and Laura's mother returned to work. Laura felt ignored and controlled even more than before. Not only was she alone more of the time, but she was given increased responsibilities, which included cooking dinner.

Family life was emotionally empty. Something had to change these patterns, and that something was anorexia:

> My anorexia shocked them into knowing I had feelings. They began to talk to me more. I needed affirmation and didn't have it inside me. It came first from others and then from my parents.

Laura's eating disorder developed during her freshman year in college. In many areas in her life she had not been allowed to make her own decisions. She attended a prestigious and very competitive women's college far from home, which was chosen by her parents. When she went away to school and was on her own for the first time, she felt unsure of herself and was lonely.

For Laura, as for many others, the stresses preceding her eating problems had existed for many years, but the transition from home to college life stimulated the onset of symptoms. To make matters worse, she felt she had to handle her feelings and doubts alone because she could not express them to her family and had no other close relationships.

Laura had many new pressures to face, but her family remained focused on her sister. It is a well accepted psychological fact that an adolescent will have extra difficulty in separating from the family when there are obvious conflicts at home. Leaving for college was bound to be troublesome for Laura. She worried about her twin and felt guilty for being the "normal one." She was angry to think that her normalcy and competence had cost her the opportunity to receive her family's support.

Although Laura achieved academically, she still experienced pressure in such a competitive college environment. She did not know what to do about her unhappiness and confusion. She felt abandoned, sad, and empty emotionally. By not eating, she stayed physically empty, which distracted her from the emotional void. In her words: "Food was an instrument of what I was experiencing—things I couldn't face directly."

She isolated herself from everyone, withdrawing into her dormitory room, locking the door, and studying constantly. She started cutting out certain foods. She wanted to be more attractive but also struggled with questions about the value of her life and thoughts of death. Paradoxically, her eating disorder expressed an openness and desire for change and growth as well as a deep despair. Her anorexia became an internal battle between life and death.

> *I had these life and death forces inside me. Both sides were very active—they took me over. Till then my life had been determined by my parents. Finally I had a life of my own, and I was experiencing life and death warring inside me through the anorexia . . . . I didn't feel depressed but I had lots of thoughts about suicide—how I would do it, not that I would do it.*

When she left for college, Laura was 5'5" tall and weighed 115 pounds; in the spring she came home weighing 75 pounds. Her parents were shocked. They gradually began to talk to her and support her as she struggled with the decision about transferring to another college. She was showered with attention and concern that had previously been reserved for her sister. Unfortunately, it took this crisis for her parents to be able to reach out to her in a way that felt loving and affirming. They entered family therapy.

> *My family could finally say things to each other. Communication opened up. Therapy should involve the whole family, not focus on the anorexic. Even if done in a supportive way, it feels like the anorexic is the rotten spot. I was feeling part of the family—we were working together. Before, I was only the emotional instigator. Things started to go better.*

As Laura looked back, she realized that a major stress in her family's life and in her development had been the inability of her parents to work together and support each other. They had never shared the responsibilities of raising the children, so the weight of Laura's sister's problems had fallen on her mother exclusively. Her father was doing what he was expected to do—providing financially and staying out of the day-to-day family problems. It may never have occurred to him that he could help his wife in any way. But she, like so many women, carried the burden of the family as well as a new job outside the home. She was truly overwhelmed. The family legacy had excluded any way for the parents to discuss these feelings and problems.

By default, Laura had become the sounding board for her mother's anger and irritation. In addition, her mother expected Laura to take over any responsibilities she herself could not handle. Anger, resentment, and conflict filled the space between Laura and her mother; otherwise, their relationship was devoid of emotional connection.

Because of the way "the masculine and feminine clashed in the family," Laura was given a very difficult role, one that would compromise and confuse her development. Only through therapy did she come to see her eating disorder as a response to these family issues, especially the balance between the masculine and feminine.

> *I experienced the domination of both my parents in different ways. . . . I wasn't prepared for being on my own in college. Because they had been so domineering, I didn't know myself. But it was really because they couldn't come together and work together. My mother was in charge of the family, but my father was in charge in a different way. They both tried to be in charge, but they had a deep inability to understand each other. The masculine and feminine clashed. . . .*

When I became anorexic, I was trying to be more attractive and more sexual. I was struggling to be more feminine, but I had always been a tomboy. I was in conflict between my mother's life experience and my father's.

Laura went on to have individual treatment in addition to the earlier family therapy. She came to understand how the differences between her parents' life experiences contributed to the void she felt in her family and herself. Understanding these dynamics helped her to stop blaming herself and start to forgive them. The space between them was filled by love and caring, so she no longer needed to keep her body empty as an illustration of their functional dysfunction.

Questions and New Connections

- In what ways might power and responsibilities be more equally shared among the members of your family? How might this be beneficial to each person?

- How can the family work together to make sure each individual's needs are met?

- How would you describe any areas of functional dysfunction in your family? How would you describe a more smoothly functioning family unit? How can the family discuss this?

- What unresolved conflicts exist in your family? How could the family go about facing and resolving conflicts more openly?

- How would you describe dinnertime in your family? What is the emotional tone? What messages about food, body image, love, and control are communicated directly or indirectly at the dinner table?

- If you are a father, can you ask your daughter what she needs from you and respond to her with love and understanding? If you are a daughter, can you find a way to tell your father what you need from him? What would you say?

- What can your family do to give its daughters firsthand experience that it is wonderful to become a fully developed, strong, respected woman?

CHAPTER 10

The Legacy of Loyalty

Unquestioned loyalty to culturally accepted myths and traditions about men's and women's roles can exact great costs. As we have seen in earlier chapters, in many families it allows father hunger to flourish and brings misery to all involved. Since most of us have grown up indoctrinated by these myths, we know little about alternatives. Nor have we spent much time figuring out the lasting effects. The myths are, however, pervasive, insidious, and intangible, compromising our connections not only with dad but with other family members who also want more from him, and with relationships outside the home as well.

Many children who grow up without their dad's approval are plagued by self-doubt. A constant never-good-enough opinion of themselves affects their peer relationships, school achievement, behavior with adults, and many other aspects of their interpersonal life. Father hunger causes children to disown parts of themselves. Instead of actualizing their full potential, boys may reject their feminine side, and girls may either reject their masculine side or try to emphasize it by developing a more male body or attitude. Victims of father hunger suffer from feelings of guilt, grief, anger, loss, and alienation, but they may be completely oblivious to the origins of these feelings. This is the legacy of loyalty, the undiscerning, sentimental allegiance to past beliefs about men and families.

Compromised Connections

An essential ingredient of healthy adolescence is the development of new connections and relationships. A young woman must learn not only how to relate to her own new body, but psychosexual maturation also brings changes in interactions with parents, other authority figures and adults, peers, the social environment, and the culture as a whole.

Parents who remain faithful to the traditional demands and myths about parenting may be compromising all of these connections. Though this adherence to the old ways is usually unconscious, it nevertheless causes families to get stuck in old patterns of relating and to ignore each other's real needs and feelings without looking for effective solutions. For example, a wife who wants her children to have a closer relationship with their father may express this by nagging because she assumes she doesn't have permission to ask for more from men, so she cannot speak directly or assertively.

Taking this progression one step further, a woman who does succeed in helping her children connect with their father may feel jealous, angry, or once more deprived of a special, exclusive relationship with a man. So children, especially daughters, will suspect that a more satisfying relationship with their father carries a high price because mom will be angry. Being close to dad will mean losing mom. As a result, many daughters remain stuck and unfulfilled in their relationship to their father.

A daughter in such a situation will usually work hard to please both parents. Often her most powerful desire is to bring mother and father together. She convinces herself that if she is the perfect daughter or has a perfect body, her parents will be happy not only with her but also with each other. In this way, her parents' unhappiness becomes her unhappiness as well as her focus in life. She is now effectively cut off from her own needs and feelings because of her family's ineffective patterns of interacting.

This daughter's connections outside the family will also suffer as a result of the dysfunction at home. If she devotes so much energy to solving family problems, pleasing her parents, and maintaining family roles, she won't have time to develop herself or her friendships. She will end up feeling empty, disconnected, and depleted. Although she may have superficial relationships with peers, a global girl growing up in this type of family will suffer compromised connections in all her relationships.

Division of Labor: Division of Self

Loyalty to the old myths about parents' roles in families also contributes to a marked division of labor based on sex. Men and women grow up and survive in these systems by internally separating their masculine and feminine impulses from each other. These two dimensions do not come together in the family, so they cannot come together in the self. Men reject their feminine side—the nurturing, caring, emotive, and intimate behaviors associated with being female. Women may shun their masculine side—the striving, performing, independent, and controlling attributes. On the other hand, they may overemphasize these qualities to try to win father's approval, and reject their feminine qualities. In either case, they will have difficulty integrating their femininity and masculinity.

Loyalty to dysfunctional myths causes both sexes to disown important parts of themselves and suppress their full potential. For example, if the family believes that the home is woman's work, so fathers are not expected to be emotionally available to their children, then mothers are likely to suppress their desire for a career and feel burdened by family life. If the family believes that making money and doing things away from home is primarily men's work and women are not expected to contribute to the family's support, then fathers are likely to feel like unsupported outsiders who are not expected to develop affectionate relationships with the children. This division of labor can lead to dangerous divisions in relationships both to others and to the self.

Such fragmentation affects a girl's interpersonal world, her self-concept, and her self-acceptance. It also influences how she feels about becoming part of the culture that promotes it. Hesitating to venture out into that culture, she will be increasingly affected by the dysfunction and divisiveness at home.

Young women with eating problems often describe the impact of the split between masculine and feminine roles and the divided parenting that results: mothers nurture too much and fathers nurture too little, if at all. They frequently make comments such as, "I know my mom got too close to me. I know it hurt me in the long run, but she was only trying to make up for my dad. He was never there for either of us."

When a mother becomes overly close or enmeshed with her daughters to make up for the lack of fathering, this compromises the daughter's development; she can't develop her own individual identity because her mom is excessively involved in her life. It limits all her relationships. The daughter feels guilty when she wants to develop close connections to other people; she knows how much mom loves her, and she fears losing her or hurting her. So instead, she abandons herself. She disowns her feelings, one of which is a desire to have a personal connection with her dad. Without a relationship with him, she loses her most important opportunity to learn how to relate to men.

The following quote shows how this dynamic can lead to an eating disorder:

> I know now that it wasn't right, but back then it seemed that my mother and I didn't need my father. We were perfect without him. But then when I got to be a teenager, I had no way of dealing with men. I was petrified of losing my mother and petrified of growing up. But I knew I had to. I felt a battle between these sides of myself. I couldn't face these problems head on, so I developed an eating disorder. Eventually, we all got help and the different parts of me could come together.

Another way families exhibit this division of labor occurs when a father tries to relate to his daughter by buying her things instead of taking an active part in her life. Being the economic provider isn't a sufficient basis for a fulfilling relationship, and the daughter feels guilty for wanting more. She may then try to deny these emotional needs. One woman described how this contributed to her eating problems:

> On the outside, my dad was perfect. He bought me everything, and I went to the right schools—other kids were always jealous. I felt guilty about wanting more from him. I wanted a relationship, not just the trimmings. But I couldn't say that, so I got sick instead. That brought us into therapy, and gradually we could talk. Now we have a good relationship. But for years, I just felt bad about wanting more.

Excessive loyalty to external standards forces families to deny their own needs and divide their emotional experience into what is acceptable and what is not. When global girls have internalized the belief that dad is unimportant, they will reject their desire for a relationship with him. To control the hunger they have for him, they may try to deny their appetite for food as well.

Guilt

Part of the legacy of loyalty to the old ways is a heavy burden of guilt. Mothers experience it because they bear the responsibility for the family's emotional life, which isn't working out as well as they had hoped. Daughters encounter it because they believe they should be satisfied with what they are given, while they long for more. Fathers have it because they sense that they are failing to make themselves more available to the family. When things go wrong, they second-guess themselves, considering all the things they could or should have done.

Although men wrestle with guilt when their children are having problems, they may have borne little responsibility for the day-to-day life of the family. In this case, they may feel less accountable and have more ways to escape the problems at home. In contrast, women are likely to have more difficulty managing this emotion. A mother's culpability is based on what she has done; father's is more likely based on his absence and, therefore, on what he has not done. Mothers, held liable for the family's well-being, question, "What did I do wrong?" Fathers, removed from the inner workings of the family, think, "If only I had been there, I could have changed everything."

Absence guilt and presence guilt are very different experiences. It is helpful to understand these disparities as we address myths about parenting and try to come up with new ways for mothers and fathers to work together.

To start, let's acknowledge that mothers consistently receive bad press in contemporary popular psychology. When mothers seek help from therapists, guilt is the predominant theme. Unfortunately, they will hand down self-blame and remorse to their daughters, just as they bequeath cooking and homemaking to them. Why is guilt such a universal experience, especially for females? Again, the answer is found in the family's division of labor, where guilt and gender interact. Even feminist literature and the family systems approach overaccentuate the importance of the mother-child dyad. In the 1980s, an analysis of articles in nine major clinical journals, including those devoted to family therapy and those written by women, found that mothers were blamed for 72 forms of psychopathology![1]

The bias persists to this day, largely because research simply hasn't included fathers.[2] Despite the many changes in the modern family structure and the fact that most families today do not include a full-time mother at home, this mother bashing continues. Furthermore, women generally accept the blame for their children's problems because they consider relationships their primary function and the emotional well-being of others their responsibility.

An example of the extent to which mother bashing persists is the common view of incestuous families, in which the father is the perpetrator. Society often blames the mother for not protecting the child from the father. In fact, people often believe that the mother contributed to the molestation because of her inadequacy, distance, and failure to satisfy her husband's sexual needs. We minimize the father's role by holding the mother accountable for his behavior, blaming her for the abuse her children have endured. As a result, mothers often condemn themselves for their children's unhappiness and losses, even when they had little or no control over the events.

A father's guilt, based on his absence and the lost opportunities to protect his children or to provide emotionally, is a different phenomenon. Mothers experience regret, but fathers often feel empty, lacking, and confused about what they can contribute to their children. They react by maintaining their distance, a response that continues the pattern established by the legacy of loyalty.

As a result of these persistent myths and attitudes, we find that both mothers and fathers feel blamed, misunderstood, inadequate, and wrong. This does not lead to strong, confident parenting, nor does it help parents work out their problems together. Instead, our myths about mothers and fathers cause deep misunderstanding between men and women. In turn, this contributes to young women's confusion about their future role as adults and uncertainty about their own effectiveness and adequacy in important relationships. Such feelings lay the groundwork for eating disorders.

Other sources of guilt will fertilize the seeds of eating and body image problems as global girls look forward to adulthood. Whether they choose to focus on career or on family life, or to combine the two, they can expect to feel inadequate. To understand how this happens, consider how the opposing myths we have about motherhood feed self-doubt and self-reproach.

Modern society tends to look at mothers either as being flawless and loving, meeting all society's expectations, or as being horrible and rejecting, meeting none of our expectations. Mothers are one or the other, with nothing in between. We expect them to take perfect care of their families and to be happy and patient always. They are often required to have a job outside the home and contribute to the economic well-being of the family as well. Mothers must operate in two very different worlds and do it all in a loving and selfless manner. (Of course, they're supposed to be thin and beautiful as well, as they manage all this!)

Can anyone really be a perfect, all-loving being while anticipating and meeting all the needs of others and constantly communicating affection and support? We expect mothers to nurture us when we need it and back off when we don't; and to know the difference without our telling them directly. Could any human being, man or woman, possibly do all this? Who would be fool enough to sign up for such a job?

Even women who choose a less traditional path, perhaps a single lifestyle, lesbianism, marriage without children, or a career-centered life, are not immune to these expectations. Going against the family legacy and doing things differently from their mothers is not easy. It may be seen as a betrayal, one that endangers a young woman's connections to the family. In these scenarios, parents, especially mothers, may ask what they "did wrong" that their daughters have not followed the family tradition. Other relatives may criticize the parents as well. So guilt sets in, for both the parents and the young woman attempting to pave her own way in life—daring to follow her dreams.

Many global girls see the guilt-ridden expectations for adult females as less than enticing. They may show their ambivalence by developing eating problems and denying their body's feminine nature. Feeling guilty about rejecting their mother's lifestyle, they renounce themselves as well. They reject the myths that dictate women's roles, but they have no clear alternatives—the legacy of loyalty limits their vision and their experience. Their preoccupation with food and their bodies can distract them from this pain and emptiness.

Grief

Mothers often feel remorse for what they have done, but fathers more often reproach themselves for what they have not done. Thus, the father's emotional experience may be more similar to grief, a sharp sorrow or pained regret for having neglected his family or having been neglected himself. He grieves all his lost opportunities for loving family interactions. Thus, while guilt may be the primary area to explore in therapy with women, grief can serve as "the doorway to a man's feelings."[3] And like guilt, grief is a shared experience in families who are loyal to ill-fitting myths.

Why is grief such a common but difficult emotion for men? Once more, we can find an answer in the myths and traditions that compromise our emotional well-being. Earlier, we examined how little boys are rarely allowed to express feelings and are instead told to "keep a stiff upper lip." They grow up believing that their feelings are wrong and should be dealt with and dismissed as quickly as possible. Furthermore, boys are pushed out of the nest by mother after a comfortable and often indulgent early life. All too suddenly, they are expected to act like grown men.

Although boys accept this separation from mom, they may always long to find a similar connection. Their feelings of abandonment and repeated disappointment build to a deep undercurrent that makes them dread opening up emotionally, because they fear they will never regain control of themselves. They may know they have accumulated years of pent-up losses and disappointments, yet they avoid exploring and releasing the sadness these have caused. Thus, they leave their children vulnerable to the same painful cycle.

A man who is unable to process his own sorrow and feels inept as a parent is likely to withdraw when confronted by the strong emotions of an adolescent daughter. If his daughter develops conflicts about food or her body, he may retreat even further into his own core of grief. While on the outside he appears to be hard and unfeeling, rational and calm, internally he may be deeply affected by his daughter's problems. His accumulated losses and his poor preparation for parenting paralyze him. He is stuck in a gridlock of grief.

Daughters in these families also experience loss and grief over their desire for a connection with dad. They may develop health-impairing or life-threatening problems to create an opportunity for their fathers to come to their rescue, or at least to be more involved in the family. Thus, a daughter's eating problems may motivate the father to overcome his past withdrawal and get in touch with his unexpressed emotions. Often in therapy, families need to explore the long-term origins of the father's grief, the sorrow he has felt over incomplete attachments with both men and women, and his regrets about his life. This may be difficult for all involved because it means acknowledging that men have feelings, counter to our expectations and world view. However, the father's admission of his feelings, his despair, and his concern for his family can be pivotal to his daughter's coming to terms with her need for him and moving toward recovery.

Anger

As with guilt and grief, anger does not belong exclusively to daughters. Parents also feel it, particularly when they are forced to face the power and resiliency of eating problems and body image distortion. And anger and rage are the emotions that young women who develop eating and body image problems have the most difficulty confronting.

Throughout modern history, anger has been the most unacceptable emotion for females. Our social roles and expectations for women forbid them to express anger. As a result, many global girls handle their fury by obsessing about their bodies and food. Their preoccupation with these behaviors keeps them from feeling much of anything. Anger is numbed by the anesthesia of eating, restricting, purging, exercising, or torturing their bodies in some other way.

Rage is infrequently identified by this torrent of symptoms. The problem for these young women is that they usually don't know they are angry. Therapists may describe them as "swallowing their anger." In therapy, patients do come to see the link between feeling misunderstood, unappreciated, ignored, or hurt, and the justifiable anger that is a logical response. I sometimes tell patients that they have "angerexia" to clarify how their anorexia or bulimia is suppressing a well of anger.

The longer young women do not feed their bodies, the more their "angerexia" is fueled by the legacy of loyalty to old ways of living in families and in our culture. Rage grows when girls do not feel loved and cherished by their father, when they experience too many demands from their mother, when their own needs take second place, and when they perceive that their parents always expect them to be perfect. It is fertilized by a global village that constantly tells women how they should look, act, feel, and eat—a culture that defines these expectations to suit fashion trends and money-making motives rather than people's real needs. In this system, women's appetites for food, sex, and self-expression are censored, and bodies that are not skinny become indictments of poor character. These circumstances underlie angerexia.

Throughout the chapters of this book, you have read about many women who have succeeded in linking their eating problems and body image dissatisfaction with their accumulated anger. They have been speaking, however, from the vantage point of recovery. During the height of their illness, most were unable to identify their rage. To recover, they had to uncover these feelings. In families where connections are shaky, communication is constricted, and expressions of love and affection are lacking, members learn that talking about anger and rage (and even allowing oneself to feel such emotions privately) is either prohibited or extremely risky. During recovery, global girls must receive permission to express their anger and must learn how to do so constructively—just as mothers must manage their guilt and resentment and fathers must experience their grief and responsibility.

Loss

Families who experience extreme father hunger suffer feelings of great sorrow and loss. When their daughters develop eating problems, this may present an opportunity to explore and resolve the losses and to change relationships. Still, the emotional damage can be gut-wrenching for fathers and mothers who were only trying to do the right thing according to established cultural myths about men's and women's roles in society. They may have firmly believed that following these cultural dictates and multigenerational patterns would assure their children's adjustment and happiness. When their daughters develop conflicts about food and body image, they find themselves facing a breakdown of confidence in their parenting. They begin to question every decision they make and even to doubt their past intentions.

They also lose the shared fantasy that everything is perfect in their family. This is another severe injury to their sense of themselves as good parents. Even though they believed they were on the right path and often received praise from others for their efforts, they now realize that they must find new ways to interact with their children and to be together as a family. Both their self-esteem and their world view are shaken.

What's more, parents who spend time looking at their own families of origin may uncover pain and disappointments that they had long ago set aside out of loyalty to family traditions. Often, parents of young women with eating problems feel caught between their own families of origin and their children. They rarely feel understood by their parents and may, in fact, still feel criticized or undermined. As they begin the healing and change process, their great burden of sadness may rise to the surface and find release.

Alienation

The sum total of the legacy of loyalty—compromised connections, divisions within the self, guilt, grief, anger, and loss—is alienation. Both the young woman and her parents experience this isolation and estrangement. For the young woman, the total experience of the legacy of loyalty is one of being detached or separated from the world—both her inner reality and her interpersonal environment. She is cut off from her feelings, her body, her sense of self, her appetite, her femininity, her family, and her peers. She is also estranged from the culture into which she is supposed to assimilate.

Becoming part of the world outside the family and adopting the views, norms, and practices of the sociocultural environment are tasks of adolescent and young adult development. A global girl who perceives that she is not recognized, valued, seen, or heard by her father—in essence, is not "real" to him—anticipates the same experience with the culture, for he is its most important representative. She wonders how she will ever become part of the world if she is not a part of his life, and whether she will ever feel loved and accepted.

She may decide that the best she can do is find a limited place for herself, one prescribed by the culture, not necessarily one of her choosing. So she does things that her father or the masculine culture endorses. She expresses her femininity as prescribed and controls her impulses surrounding food, her body, and her emotional needs.

Hoping to connect to the world, she withdraws from herself; in reality she is cut off from everything. Her experience is one of alienation, and she feels estranged, alone, unaccepted, isolated, and confused.

Parents share this sense of alienation when they become involved in their daughter's recovery. They feel cut off from their own parenting: the happiness they intended for their daughter has not materialized, and they wonder what they did wrong. They question themselves endlessly, and they feel misunderstood by everyone—their daughter, friends, and extended family. They begin to question the values of a culture they have supported, and even the very lives they have lived. They ask themselves repeatedly: how could we have been so wrong?

Although the parents' alienation concerns their past, the daughter's alienation involves the future. Her life is put on hold while she wrestles with how to become part of a world that feels hostile to women and that has fueled her father hunger. In the best of situations, families are able to confront and process these issues together. When parents, especially fathers, are willing to do this, they show their love in a very important way. They help their daughters heal their father hunger and resolve their food and body image problems. With help from the most special man in her life, a daughter may discover how to become part of a dysfunctional culture without denying or destroying herself.

The Parents' Perspective

"We're still mourning all our losses, and I'm learning how to be a father. Neither of us really had one." This comment and the conversation that follows came from the parents of Mary, a young woman who had developed a serious eating disorder. They illustrate how feelings of guilt, grief, anger, loss, and alienation flow from the legacy of loyalty to myths about men's and women's roles in families. This couple was interviewed after a year of family therapy. While their daughter was on the road to recovery, they were still working hard to understand and change their patterns of interaction and to reverse the effects of father hunger in their own lives.

Mother: What we went through as a family after Mary's problems developed was really hard. We read about eating disorders, and we knew we needed to get into family therapy. But it was so scary.

Father: Our families had never been talkers. We didn't realize how that had affected us, but we had been married for 25 years and we still didn't know how to communicate. I must admit I was worse than my wife—she was scared, but I didn't even know how I felt. The therapist would ask questions and I would have no idea what to say. Here I was, very successful, I owned my own public relations firm, and I couldn't even talk to my family.

Mother: Yeah, that was probably one of the biggest blows for both of us—we had both felt very successful. Sure, we worked hard, but it had paid off—all we ever heard from other people was that we had great kids—Mary especially got good grades and excelled at everything. We had never had any problems, so we didn't know how to deal with them. When Mary got sick, I felt like my world had just been tipped upside down. Something was really wrong with us and with Mary, but I had no clue what it was.

Father: And then you started blaming yourself for everything, remember? You felt so bad about yourself—so guilty. I would try to reason with you, but it never helped. That's one thing I've learned—sometimes I'm too logical and don't give feelings enough airtime. I've gotten better, but I feel like I'm doing the opposite of what I was told to do all my life. Usually I feel better after I talk, but I must admit I'm not quite comfortable with it yet. I think I was actually depressed my entire life—I just didn't know it. So I didn't always like the feelings I started getting in touch with.

Mother: You seemed so withdrawn and cold during that time. I needed emotional support because I felt so guilty, but you couldn't be there for me. That was another really hard experience. Now I think we know how to give each other room and emotional support. Back then, I think we both felt alone. At least I did. I felt misunderstood by everyone— my daughter, my husband, my parents, my friends.

Father: I think we felt lots of losses. My wife is right—we didn't feel understood by anyone. Here we had done everything the way parents "should." My wife had read every book on child development ever written. We thought everything was perfect. Then our daughter developed this psychological problem that could kill her. Life will never be the same for me. I've lost my fantasy that we're the perfect family.

Mother: So there we were. Our daughter was in the hospital and we were in therapy trying to figure all this out. And we felt horrible about ourselves. And then, probably the biggest blow of all was how our parents handled it. We had always been very close to both sets of parents, and we felt completely let down. They couldn't deal with our not being perfect, I guess. We got no support from them, after having lived our lives trying to please them. Now I know that was part of the problem—but they couldn't understand that we needed emotional support, that we needed to talk. We felt criticized and abandoned.

Father: I guess you could say we were caught between two generations. We were trying to change to help our daughter, but all we felt were pressure and criticism from our parents. They really don't understand, and we've had to accept that. But it's caused us both a lot of sadness.

Mother: Maybe they're feeling guilty too. Maybe they're afraid to look at how they raised us. They were very traditional families. And they see us finding a new way to be together. I'm learning to speak more directly and ask my husband for help—he's much more involved as a father. Maybe it's a clash between the old and the new.

Father: What we know now is that the old ways didn't work for us, but we may never have even seen this if Mary hadn't developed these problems. One of the most important things I've learned is how Mary needs me—I can't leave all the parenting to my wife. I know I'm important to Mary. I also know how much my father missed because he was never close to me, and how much I missed as a son.

Mother: I missed a lot as a daughter too. But we're working on things now. Somehow through our guilt and our sadness we'll make Mary's life better and help her in ways our parents couldn't help us. It's a different world, so we're going to have to be different parents.

Father: Yeah, we've got to stop just trying to "do the right thing" and figure out what is right for *us*. I guess I'm still angry that although I was trying to do the right thing, to follow my family and meet their expectations, we all suffered so much. I've felt a lot of anger and frustration about things I can't control. Now I know how hard it is for girls to grow up surrounded by the media, the diet ads, the skinny bodies, and the focus on appearance. I had been oblivious to that—I just didn't know what was going on. I felt stupid for a while; now I feel outraged but I don't know what to do.

I guess you could say we're still mourning all our losses— first as children and now as parents. Anger is only part of that. I'm learning how to be a father. Neither of us really had one. Our parents don't understand that at all, but I'm convinced my kids need me and I'm going to find a way to be there for Mary—and for me.

Questions and New Connections

- Has father hunger caused you to doubt yourself and reject aspects of yourself and your feelings? How have you been affected?
- What traditional myths have compromised connections in your family?
- How would you describe the division of labor in your family? In what ways could it be more functional and allow a more balanced expression of each person's masculine and feminine talents?

- For each of the feelings in the following list, describe two important incidents in your life that left you with this feeling. What emotions need to be released? How can you release them safely so they no longer stand as barriers to fuller relationships?

  – Guilt

  – Grief

  – Anger or rage

  – Loss

  – Alienation

- What patterns or roles handed down by your family of origin need to change so your current family can be healthier and more open emotionally?

PART 3

The Solutions to Father Hunger

CHAPTER 11

How Men Can Overcome
Father Hunger

The next chapters look at what we all can do to address problems inherent in the contemporary father's role in the family. We will start in this chapter by examining what men can do to become more active parents and reverse the tradition and consequences of father hunger.

To counter the cynicism, disillusionment, and alienation of fathers in our culture, men will need to actively alter old myths and patterns of relating and become more emotionally available, expressive, and nurturing. Given paternal love, global girls can feel confident as they cope with their concerns about food, weight, body image, and self-concept. Without your love, they feel rejected by you and the culture you represent. Their resulting father hunger will cause them much agony and suffering.

Before you can become a more loving and available parent, however, you will have to face your own father hunger. For the first time you must connect to your feelings instead of denying them. In doing so, you will probably realize how you have separated from your disappointments about your dad and how this has not prepared you for being a responsive parent, spouse, or even friend.

This chapter will guide you through a psychological journey in which you will experience abandoned parts of yourself and of life that have been blocked off because of the myths and traditions established for men in contemporary society. This new intimacy will be life-transforming but frightening, because it will take you into uncharted, unfamiliar territory. It is a heroic quest that requires your firm commitment to see it through. It is likely to be gut-wrenching and to provoke anxiety, self-doubt, and questions about your self-worth, your place in the world, and the values of our society.

History and mythology are full of examples of people who dared to embark on such adventures. As described by Joseph Campbell, the renowned thinker about contemporary views of mythology, the journey involves separation, initiation, and return:

> *A hero ventures forth from the world of common day into a region of supernatural wonder: fabulous forces are there encountered and a decisive victory is won: the hero comes back from this mysterious adventure with the power to bestow boons on his fellow man.*[1]

In other words, as you take this journey to become a more loving, involved father, your personal growth will at first isolate you and turn you inward; but you will eventually return as a new, enlightened man, capable of intimacy with yourself and others. And you will be able to show your feelings, especially your love, to your daughter. This pilgrimage will teach you how to connect with others and how to feed your daughter's hunger with love.

If you have been struggling to understand your daughter's eating problems, you may have already embarked on such a mission. Your daughter's conflicts are challenging your sense of self, wrenching you from the tendency to live out old myths about families, roles, and values, and preparing you to create new ones. Her condition has threatened, maybe even shattered, your concept of yourself as a father. Panic and desperation burn in your eyes when you first bring your daughter for therapy and realize that you have been unaware of the intense pain she was experiencing. You try in vain to understand her distorted thinking about her body. The therapist senses the helplessness in your spirit when you can't make everything better for her. (After all, wasn't it always your job to solve the family problems?)

I cannot guarantee that taking this heroic journey will assure your daughter's recovery. But I know that the more you examine yourself—your strengths and weaknesses as a father, husband, and man—and the more you explore your own father hunger, the more emotionally available you will be to your daughter.

As you change, your daughter will feel your love in a new way, and as you take your journey inward to understand and heal your own wounds, you will be a great example to her of how to get to the emptiness that underlies her eating problems. She may also feel less guilty for causing you to worry if she sees that you are becoming more involved and feeling more satisfied in your relationships. Acknowledging your own father hunger—the scars from your upbringing as a male, your estrangement from your own feelings, and your isolation—will eventually lead to new and gratifying connections to yourself, your world, and your ability to father.

Face Your Own Father Hunger

You can help your daughter only if you first help yourself. To comprehend her experience as a child, you must comprehend your own. To do this, you must reverse the years of experience in which you discounted and denied your emotions, and thereby separated from the *feeling* part of yourself. Now you must acknowledge and confront the pain, hurt, disappointment, rejection, longing, and sadness you have so long ignored in order to be first a "good boy" and later a "real man."

Chances are that you, like your daughter, grew up with little intimacy in your relationship with your father—he was an elusive image, yet you desperately wanted to please and satisfy him in order to feel connected to him. As a male, you hoped to accomplish these things by trying to be like him. Unfortunately, imitating your father has resulted in repeating his patterns in your relationships with your children. To change such well-established patterns will require a strong determination to go back and *feel* what you ignored for so many years—and face your own father hunger.

Connecting with Yourself

If you are a father reading this book with the hope of helping your daughter, you may not know where to begin. The answer is simple. Start with yourself. Take time to look inward and allow yourself to have feelings—all kinds, not just the easy ones. Tell yourself it's OK for men to be sad and hurt, to feel left out, to need others, to long to be cherished, to be angry for not receiving true acceptance and unconditional love as you grew up. Recall hurtful events from your youth, and allow yourself to feel the emotions that they should have logically provoked.

Break the rules you have been taught in the past; stop separating from your inner self and start connecting with it. Bring together the different parts of yourself. Connect your underlying feelings with what you express through your behavior. This will bring you and your daughter together.

Separating from outdated myths about men is essential as you learn to develop new connections. One of the most destructive beliefs society generally holds is that men don't feel. The fact is that men experience lots of strong emotions. Most of the time, however, you are expected not to show them. Instead, you are encouraged to *do*, to achieve, to focus outward rather than acknowledging your inner life. As a result, your conditioned reflex is to tackle a problem in a concerted effort to get rid of anything that causes discomfort or anxiety, rather than to experience and deal with feelings that arise.

For your daughter's sake, and for yours, allow yourself to *feel* now, especially to be aware of the losses you have suffered. Don't fight the urge to cry or weep. Find some special trusted allies to support you through this. Some men develop informal networks of support with friends. Others form more structured men's groups that meet regularly, while still others choose to participate in organized spiritual retreats as they grapple with new means of expression.[2] By finding support in relationships with other men, you can create the bonding you missed growing up, and you will prove that the old myths that isolate men just aren't true. Most important, you can work through your own losses so they are no longer perpetuated in your daughter's life.

At this point it is important to become more conscious of the myths you have internalized about men. These may be limiting your life in many ways and keeping you from being fully conscious of your feelings about your father and your children. Most likely, you have been unaware of your own father hunger until recently. Answer the following questions, allowing any pent-up feelings to surface.

- Were you taught as a little boy not to cry, never to let anyone know you were hurt?

- Were you told to be strong and hard when you felt like crying, running away, or seeking to be comforted?

- Were you teased or humiliated for being a "sissy" or a "crybaby" or a "pansy," and did you react by resolving not to show your true feelings?

- At what age did your dad stop hugging you and expect you to stop showing affection?
- Was your dad available to you when you wanted and needed him? What experiences do you wish you could have had with him?
- What did you most long for your dad to say to you?

Now take some time to review the myths you have accepted about men and your role as a father. These might include:

- Men can't understand.
- Men are insignificant to their children's development.
- Parenting is unimportant to men.
- Men don't feel.
- Men's main role is to provide financially.
- Daughters don't need their dad to grow up.

Once you have identified your myths, you can choose to continue believing them and maintain the separateness you have been taught to develop and value, or you can challenge them and become connected. If you decide to break through the myths, your life will be fuller—attachments and connections will fill the old voids of your own hunger for closeness. Take this opportunity to actively decide which beliefs about men should guide your life, especially as a dad. Begin to pour the love you harbor into your relationships.

Questions and New Connections

- How did your father express feelings?
- How safe do you feel talking about feelings?
- What myths was your father demonstrating as you grew up?
- Of the myths about men, which ones bother you the most?
- Where can you find support and acceptance as you allow yourself to feel more?

Connecting with Your Father

In *Finding Our Fathers*, a very useful book on the obstacles to paternal intimacy, Sam Osherson wrote that connecting with your father necessitates "healing the wounded father within, an angry-sad version of ourselves that feels unloved and unlovable."[3] In other words, the scars men carry into adulthood from the distant, demanding relationship most have experienced with their fathers have to be examined, treated, and healed. Pretending they do not exist only prolongs the pain. Only with this insight and regeneration will men be able to father differently from the way they were fathered.

Gus Napier, a family therapist and author, describes the impact of fatherlessness on men who want to be more involved in their children's lives. He writes about his own deep wounds, "When men like me decide to try to be more involved fathers, we encounter this vast emptiness; we learn about the father who was not there."[4]

When you look at the relationship with your father, you will likely be shocked by your neediness. You were taught that you didn't need anything from him, other than money or "things." You may experience much pain when you realize that your life has been an attempt to cover up this emptiness and maintain the illusion that you were self-sufficient and invulnerable.

If your father is still alive, consider talking with him about the pressures he felt as a parent and the losses you felt as a son. If he is no longer living, you could instead talk to other relatives or family friends to gain insight into what motivated this mysterious man. Understanding more about his experience and why he was unavailable to you will help you avoid repeating the same mistakes.

Once you acknowledge your own father hunger, you will be more capable of understanding your daughter's experiences. Admitting how your father withheld love, affection, and acceptance and how you responded back then (through achievement, sports, workaholism, denial, isolation, etc.) will lead you to find a different way to be a father. By exploring and then departing from your past, you will be renewed, capable of giving, loving, and understanding for the first time. Separating from your old ways will allow you to connect to new ways.

Questions and New Connections

- What are some memories of your relationship with your father?
- How did he relate to you?
- What kept him from being a more loving and involved father?
- What keeps you from this?

Finding Help in Therapy

Facing your father hunger means not repeating the pattern of handling things alone and needing no one. Seeking assistance from a therapist may help you overcome the tendency to separate and teach you how to connect. Sharing your feelings in therapy can be a turning point, because it unlocks many of the doors that the limiting myths and roles have closed in your life.

Therapy, however, is a world different from the one for which most men's past socialization has prepared them. Those who have a deep commitment to the outdated myths will generally have a hard time seeking and accepting the help of a professional's perspective. The role prescribed for fathers insists that you can take care of anything (the old "Father knows best" syndrome)—but let's face it—you can't! You will probably need guidance to switch gears; to learn how to question, not to answer; to explore issues, not to quickly get rid of them. Therapy is an excellent way to start this growth.

Working together with your daughter in family therapy is an extremely effective way to get to know her and discover how to be more connected to her and the rest of the family. This closeness may not happen instantly, though. In fact, at first you may become aware of how much you haven't known about the emotional lives of other family members. You may feel uncomfortable and want life to go back to the way it was before all these emotions were being verbalized, or you may worry that all this talking is only going to cause more stress. You will probably be tempted to jump into your accustomed role of protector, wanting to eliminate the problems.

Although those old patterns may be familiar and secure, they have contributed to your daughter's turmoil. Remember the old saying, "Sometimes things have to get worse before they get better." What your global girl needs during this phase is to know that you love her, accept her, and respect her feelings, and that you will stand by her no matter how painful the issues or how long it takes to explore them together.

Your daughter may have several possible reasons for resisting your involvement in her therapy. She may perceive you as focusing too much on her symptoms instead of supporting her as a unique individual. Think about how to relate to her as a person, not just as your anorexic or bulimic daughter. She may also be afraid that you will be disappointed in her or ashamed of her if she lets you know about her conflicts or insecurities. Furthermore, she may not trust your interest or affection; she may fear that your attention is temporary and that the only way to maintain it is for her to be sick. So hang in there and you may gradually convince her of the permanence of your love.

Many fathers, once they overcome the masculine barriers to seeking help, also benefit from individual therapy. Since your daughter's problems have shattered your identity as the protector and problem solver, you need to rebuild your *self* as well. Looking back at your experience as a son, your expectations for fatherhood, and your own coping mechanisms can be an invaluable way to improve your life. By supporting yourself with the assistance of a mental health professional, you will also be supporting your daughter as you try to build a more satisfying and loving connection with her.

Although the notion and process of therapy run counter to how you were raised, you may find it helpful and even fun! Fathers often tell me afterward how much they have enjoyed and appreciated it. By working hard to uncover a greater capacity to love, you can discover how to be a more whole, happy, fulfilled person.

Questions and New Connections

- How do you feel about therapy? What would your father think about it?
- What old myths keep you from seeking help from others?
- What issues do you need to work on to be more connected to your family?

Work on Your Relationships with Women

To develop a nurturing and loving relationship with your daughter may require attention to how you relate to women in general. For years your daughter has been watching your interactions with women, searching for clues about what you like or dislike about women and how much you value them. These impressions are very important to her as she moves toward womanhood. Try to see through her eyes how she might perceive your relationship with her mother. Notice when you are repeating your father's past behaviors in your present role as a husband.

Explore your attitudes toward and expectations of women. Before you can be more present to your daughter as a positive role model, you may have to figure out how to share power and responsibility with her mother, how to find a positive role for yourself in the family, and how to work together, even if you are divorced.

Connecting with Her Mother

One of the most important ways you can help your daughter is to look critically and honestly at your relationship with her mother. Family conflicts affect females very deeply. When girls are worried about their parents' happiness or marital stability, they don't have the emotional energy necessary to face the ups and downs of adolescence. Often, in the effort to make things better for their parents, they will put themselves on hold. Addressing your relationship with your wife or ex-wife will allow your daughter to focus more appropriately on her own needs, feelings, and desires.

Accepting that you have flaws as a husband will also serve as a positive model for your daughter; your openness will convey that no one, not even the most important man in her life, can be expected to be perfect. In turn, this will help her overcome the constant struggle for perfectionism reflected in her eating and body image problems. At the same time, you will also be emphasizing the importance you place on the relationship with her mother.

Take some time alone to work on this. Be honest with yourself about what kind of husband you have been. Resist the impulse to blame all the problems on your spouse or any other single person. If you are willing to take an additional risk, ask her what she has experienced as your wife. Look for links between your family-of-origin experiences and your present style as a husband.

Many of your positive as well as negative qualities are probably direct consequences of the role your father played when you were growing up. If he was absent, aloof, or emotionally cut off, you will have missed learning how a man can express love and respect to his wife. If he didn't show you affection and didn't teach you how to love in his interactions with your mother, you may be uncomfortable with these expressions. You may not feel lovable or be able to show love. If he lacked the communication and negotiation skills to resolve conflicts peacefully, you will have to work hard to figure out how to solve problems more effectively in your marriage. By looking at how your father functioned as a husband and assessing which of his mistakes you have repeated, you will open yourself up to a new way of relating and modeling healthy interactions for your daughter.

If you are separated or divorced, it is important that you assume some of the blame for the breakdown of the marriage so that your daughter does not perceive that the responsibility for relationships belongs only to women. Try to avoid discussing her mother's shortcomings (you probably have some too!). Your daughter needs to identify with the positive and loving aspects of her mother as she becomes a woman. She probably already knows her mother's faults well enough! She may have decided she has all the same traits as her mother, or she may determine that she wants to be completely different from her mother because of what she has observed in your interactions. Either is a normal response of an adolescent working to explore and develop her unique identity. Above all, resist the temptation to place your daughter in the middle of your marriage or divorce. Allow her the freedom to concentrate on herself, not on your problems.

Whether fathers are married, separated, or divorced, the messages they give global girls about their mothers are important. If a father puts his wife down, he is also putting his daughter down by association, since the daughter's primary role model is her mother. Find out if your wife (or ex-wife) feels respected by you. If she doesn't, your daughter will not feel respected or secure either. Your relationship with her mother serves as the prototype of what your daughter expects from men. Think about this; decide what model you want her to have, and see if you can create it.

Questions and New Connections

- How am I similar to my father as a husband?
- How did my mother feel about her marriage?
- What patterns do I want to change?
- What messages has my relationship with my wife/ex-wife inadvertently or intentionally communicated to my daughter?
- How could I improve my relationship with my wife (or ex-wife)?

Exploring Your Attitudes Toward Women

Your daughter will be keenly sensitive to your interactions not just with your wife, but with all women, so it's important to be conscious of your beliefs and interactions and pay attention to what messages they convey to your daughter. Since women's roles have changed so much in recent decades, it's quite likely that your ideas about femininity are in transition. Take an inventory of your attitudes toward women: What do you consider femininity to be? What is the ideal woman? What do you want for your daughter? What qualities do you value in women? By addressing these questions, you can become more aware of what your daughter may be deducing from your words and actions. Furthermore, you may begin to notice conflicts between what you say to your daughter and what you want her to learn.

As you work on this, try to remember how your father treated women when you were growing up. You may have unknowingly internalized some of his attitudes. By understanding these influences from your childhood, you can differentiate between what you are unconsciously passing along from your family history and what you really want to convey to your daughter about being a woman.

Because of the differences between how you were raised and the nature of life today, you are probably facing experiences you did not anticipate. For example, women have gained some power in the marketplace, and men react to this in different ways. Some men resent women, while others respect them; some may have no trouble dealing with women's newfound authority, but others detest it, resist it, or try to undermine it. Many believe that women should not hold certain kinds of jobs. It will help to honestly explore these feelings, because you might be surprised how visible they are to your daughter.

Do you think that power and femininity coexist, or do you believe that one cancels out the other? Consider how you would like your daughter to integrate these qualities. Take time to think about issues raised by the women's movement and how they are affecting your global girl. Discuss with her how women's roles and power have changed in your lifetime and how these shifts have affected your ideas about women and your interactions with her.

If you do not sincerely appreciate women and their concerns, your attitudes will be evident even if you give lip service to more liberated ideas. One test of whether you really value women and take your daughter seriously as a separate young person with her own ideas and feelings is very simple: Do you sit down and really listen to her?

Fathers often discount their daughters' troubles instead of listening to them. For example, if a daughter says she is worried about her math grade, she is probably not asking for a solution from her dad. Rather, she seeks an understanding ear and a chance to work out her own dilemma with a supportive and empathetic listener. The door to her confidences is slammed shut if he dismisses her comment with a casual reassurance such as, "Don't worry, honey. You'll do fine."

Even more revealing and destructive is a stereotyping reply such as, "With your great smile, no one will ever notice if you need a calculator to balance your checkbook." Although this father may have intended to be supportive, his response cut off his daughter's attempt to communicate her feelings and showed her that he is not available to hear what she has to say. Not only that, but unaware, he has filtered the issue through his own ideas about femininity—that her smile and appearance are more important than her feelings and her sense of competence. She will wonder if she should take herself seriously, since he apparently doesn't.

Another approach to use in examining your attitudes toward women is to compare the way you speak to and treat boys and girls. You would probably clearly tell your son that math is important, and he needs to study hard. Giving your daughter the same respect and taking her concerns seriously will show her that she is important and valued. Even if your daughter is interested in areas that are not traditionally feminine and your son is interested in more traditionally feminine areas, giving both sexes equal opportunities to develop in their own way will communicate your confidence in and respect for each child's innate abilities.

In these ways, you communicate support and recognition of your daughter as a person with legitimate rights, abilities, feelings, and desires. Your actions will tell her that she is acceptable to you and worthy of your love, and that women are equal to men.

Carefully listen to yourself to detect any potentially negative attitudes toward women or toward your daughter that might be implied in your jokes, lectures, or off-hand remarks. Tuning in to your daughter's reactions to you will give you instant feedback about whether she feels you are respecting and honoring her. Your alert awareness and self-examination will help to make sure that your attitudes toward women do not unintentionally jeopardize your daughter's development and healthy sense of self.

Questions and New Connections

- In what ways are my attitudes toward women similar to my father's?

- What beliefs about women do I want to convey to my daughter?

- Do I listen to my daughter? Does she feel that I listen to her? In what three ways could I improve our communication?

Rethinking Roles in the Family

If your daughter is waging war with food and with her body, she is struggling to gain power. She has concluded that she has no other vehicle for autonomy and effectiveness in the world because she has not been able to find a more appropriate way to exert control and share authority in relationships. A global girl growing up in a culture with unhealthy, imbalanced distributions of power needs you, her father, to try to understand and correct these patterns.

You may not appreciate how confusing power is to your daughter until you examine how you own and express it at home. Although many of the cultural conflicts between men and women concerning power are not of your making, your daughter will still benefit immensely if you look at how you personally are contributing to her turmoil and her struggle to claim her share of personal power.

How do you approach family interactions? Does your family perpetuate an old internalized, dysfunctional picture of father left over from your childhood? If your dad was treated as the ultimate authority—"king of the castle," strict disciplinarian and rule enforcer but otherwise gone most of the time—you probably weren't shown how to share authority with your wife, and you may be stuck in the same old rut. Although fathers who sporadically emerge out of the shadows to take charge may have great influence in a family, this kind of authority is paradoxical because it is based on absence and fear, not presence and love. If your dad played such a role, he was probably lonely and unsatisfied. His power did not bring him love or intimacy. If you want something different, you will have to act differently.

To this day, most women maintain their power in the family by assuming most of the responsibility for taking care of the home, food, child care, and everyone's emotional and physical health. Studies show that even in families in which both parents work, mothers still spend twice as much time interacting with the children. Despite substantial changes in mothers' employment, the number of fathers who assume a significant amount of child care has not increased substantially.[5] Fathers tend to do the more pleasant child care tasks, like taking the kids to the park so mom can clean the house, do the grocery shopping, or run errands. Overall, children still get disproportionately more of mom and less of dad. As a result, families remain deprived of a father. Mothers overfunction, fathers underfunction, and their global girls learn to repeat this pattern instead of learning how to take care of themselves and balance the family's needs with their own.

Examine the day-to-day activities in your home and figure out what you can do to function more fully as a parent. Look carefully at the distribution of duties between your wife and yourself. You might keep track of who does what over a period of a few days or a week. You will probably find that she does much more than you. Try doing some of the central things your wife does and let her take over some of the peripheral tasks many fathers do. Talk to her about how you could operate more equally in the daily life of the family. This will show your daughter that men and women share responsibility for relationships.

Once you have reassigned household tasks, look at the power distribution in your family. Work with your wife (or ex-wife) to provide a model of shared parental control, decision making, and responsibility. This will assure your daughter that there are positive ways to feel capable and effective, and that she needn't deny herself food or attain a perfect body to gain your respect and feel powerful in the family.

Questions and New Connections

- What kind of power do you hold in the family?
- How does your wife (or ex-wife) hold power?
- How are decisions made in your family?
- In your daily life at home, how similar are you to your father?
- Are there some jobs at home that you absolutely view as women's work and refuse to do? What are they, and why?
- What changes could your family make to achieve a more equal distribution of power?

Coping with Divorce

Your crusade to find a more fulfilling role as a father is apt to be much more difficult if you are divorced or living separately from your daughter. In such circumstances, many factors affect the father-child relationship, including remarriage, geographic distance, custody arrangements, visitation rights, and the children's developmental issues, social lives, and preferences.

Divorce does not have to destroy your relationship with your daughter. However, to play an active role as a divorced father may mean defying a number of the myths you were taught. You may need assistance to figure out how to construct this different kind of life. Again, therapy will help, and so will talking and listening to your daughter.

The importance of parents working together and fathers being active and available in their daughters' lives does not evaporate when a marriage dissolves. Although some divorced couples do find mutually agreeable ways to share custody and time with their children, many are unable to work together to coparent their children. The myths that mothers are instinctively better parents and that fathers are inept lead many men to abdicate their parenting role, leaving mothers to assume the sole responsibility for the children. This frequently contributes to the mother's feeling bitter and resisting any involvement of the father in the children's lives. The tragic outcome is that innocent children lose the vital opportunity to have two active, caring parents.

Sadly, the majority of children in divorced families describe their relationship with their fathers as poor. As many as 34 percent of children in the United States don't live with their dads. Furthermore, 40 percent have not seen their father in the past year, and half have never visited their father's home.[6]

You can choose not to become one of these statistics. It is never too late to address and repair your relationship with your ex-wife and your children. Why not use the crisis of your divorce to reassess the roles you want to assume?

In some cases divorce actually improves a father's relationship with his children. For one thing, it may end the constant tension or fighting between parents; and for another, it may leave you more emotionally available to your children. Until you have adjusted to your new lifestyle, the transition period can be very painful, but at the same time it may give you the opportunity to develop personal relationships with your children apart from your wife.

Your children probably need to see you more, not less, if you are living apart. Planning to be available to them regularly is extremely important to assure them that one of the two most important people in their lives has not abandoned them and that they can trust you to be there for them. Although you may be tempted to work longer hours to earn more money or to provide a new structure to your life once you are no longer living with your family, keep in mind Liz's words, "All I wanted was my father's love." A divorce disrupts your lives—but it does not have to disrupt your love.

Questions and New Connections

- How can a husband divorce his wife without divorcing his children?
- How could you spend more time with your children?

- Is your children's mother always in the middle of your relationship with them? What can you do to build a personal, one-to-one relationship with each of your children? How can you build their trust in you?

Help Your Daughter Satisfy Her Father Hunger

Once you have begun to face your own losses and wounds as a son and to address your relationships with women, you are ready for the next steps in overcoming father hunger: helping your daughter manage her disappointments with you and other men, assert herself in relationships, and feel valued as a unique individual and as a woman. These are lofty goals. To reach them will require building a stronger basis for your relationship by learning to be a more fully present father and by responding supportively to her developmental needs and changes. This involves listening to her as well as assessing your own attitudes about food, weight, and body image to determine how they may have affected her. It also necessitates finding ways to cope with her eating problems and support her treatment.

Connecting with Your Daughter

Having a close relationship with someone else, especially with your own flesh and blood, should be easy, but it isn't for most men. The constant pressure to separate and handle things independently and to avoid feelings affects every aspect of a man's life. Even the most powerful human experiences and the closest attachments are filtered through this ingrained way of looking at life. For most fathers to enjoy a close relationship with their daughters will require much self-examination and willingness to change.

Since relationships, feedback, and approval are important to your daughter, try to be more involved and more present at home. Praise and reinforce her so she knows she's good enough for you, that she has pleased you and made you proud of who she is. As you talk to her, overcome the tendency to present yourself as all-knowing and all-powerful. Let her know that everyone has worries and self-doubt, that no one is perfect, and that you are human. Seeing you in these new ways may quell the perfectionistic impulses that cover up her lack of self-acceptance and compel her constant, though misguided, attempts to win your approval. If she already has your attention and affection, she won't need to use self-destructive means to get it.

If you share more of your thoughts and feelings with your daughter, you will be less of a mystery to her, and the world of men will not be so frightening. Equipped with knowledge about what motivates, bothers, or pleases you, she will feel more comfortable with the opposite sex, less anxious about whether she will be able to function or find happiness in the world outside the family, and more confident of herself overall. She will be relieved from the insecurity and self-doubt that can overwhelm young women and result in their denying or destroying their bodies through disordered eating. The more you reveal yourself to her and share your vulnerabilities as well as your enthusiasm, the more your masculine adult world will appear inviting rather than intimidating.

Similarly, the more interest you show in your daughter, the more she will believe in herself and come to know that men respect and value women. If she is struggling with her body image and with eating, she needs to see that you are interested in her as a whole person. Avoid the tendency to focus on your worries about her symptoms, as this reinforces her beliefs that weight and food intake are the most important parts of herself. Build a broader basis for your relationship, so she in turn will become aware of her other precious and lovable qualities and the important contributions she has to make in a world where her talents are needed and valued.

Be sure to discuss values, beliefs, community issues, relationships, emotions, and problems in a give-and-take manner. Express your ideas, and ask to hear hers in return. Show tolerance and acceptance where you differ, showing her that you respect her freedom to form her own opinions even when you don't agree with them. Most of all, convey respect and caring for her as a person, not just as an obedient daughter.

Questions and New Connections

- How well do you know your daughter as a person? Make a list of 20 of her most endearing qualities, and share it with her.

- How well does she know you? Begin sharing your experiences and thoughts with her. Invite her to ask you about your life and your feelings and opinions, or anything else she wants to know about you.

- How could you get to know her better? Plan opportunities for the two of you to be together, enjoying shared interests and activities. Show your interest by listening to her express her thoughts and feelings, without trying to solve her problems or minimize her concerns. Offer yourself as a sounding board for her to bounce her ideas off of. Without pushing, gently ask questions that express your interest and help her to develop her thoughts and draw her own conclusions.

Learning to Listen

Finding a more positive role for yourself in the family and helping your daughter define herself can only happen if you first learn how to listen. This may sound elementary, but it is not. As a male you were raised to be independent and separate. Now you are being called to master a new set of skills: those for developing connections and *inter*dependence.

Not only does listening foster connection, but it also is one of the most important gifts you can give your daughter, because it empowers her by conveying trust and faith in her ideas and opinions. These are pivotal building blocks to her self-esteem and self-concept.

Listening is very different from lecturing, but in families the two are often confused. As a man, you may occupy a position of authority at work and believe that you are supposed to be the expert at home as well. Lecturing may be second nature to you; it's just part of your role as manager and problem solver. Being lectured, on the other hand, is an experience that hardly anyone enjoys.

One way to check the quality of your communication with your daughter is to consider how it resembles the way you approach subordinates at work. The more similar it is, the less appropriate it is in your relationship with your daughter. Keep in mind that she is not an employee; she's your daughter, and she's struggling to grow from her childhood relationship with you into the position of an independent adult.

That's her job now. She needs your respect and support, not your domination. As you switch from your public role in the community and workplace to your private role as father, you need to communicate in a different way. Your daughter desperately wants you to be more personally involved with her. You can break through barriers by disclosing more of yourself emotionally and listening more.

Listening empowers, while pep talks, lectures, and judgments disempower. To your daughter, they may just be further indications of how out of sync the two of you are. To help her, you must connect with her pain and accept her where she is emotionally.

You can probably remember the frequent dismissal you heard from your parents as a child: "That doesn't hurt." In fact, your toothache, bee sting, or scraped knee *did* hurt, didn't it? In their attempt to console you, they added insult to injury by denying the reality of your experience! You probably felt misunderstood and angry, left to yourself to suppress your pain. In contrast, have you ever noticed a child's response when you say, "Does that hurt—a lot?" and offer a comforting hug? Given permission to experience the pain, the child feels the reassurance of being understood, cries to release the hurt, and moves on.

To your daughter, pep talks may feel a lot like "That doesn't hurt." They can do more harm than good, showing her you don't understand her pain. So leave the lectures at the office and switch to real communication at home—disclosing yourself and listening to others. Admit your vulnerability, and acknowledge the possibility that you could be saying or doing the wrong thing. Express how much you care and want to understand.

Family therapy can help. You may learn a great deal by watching how the therapist communicates with your daughter and with you. Gradually you will come to recognize when your daughter would welcome a pep talk and when she just wants someone to hear her out. On your own, it may be very difficult to know what she needs from you from one moment to the next.

Fathers often convey a strong belief that any obstacle can be overcome by sheer willpower. These well-intended positive messages may inadvertently communicate to your daughter that she is a failure because she lacks willpower, or that recovery is another arena where she must perform to earn your love. Quite likely, she will feel increased pressure to please you, a pattern she is trying to change. But fearing she can't recover "perfectly," she may give up.

Being lectured also activates the conflicts she has about whether she is living her own life or living only to please others. Recovery, therefore, becomes one more task to do for others—an extension of her selflessness. In reality, recovery must be based on desires that come from within her: she has to feel she is worthwhile and that she alone owns and is responsible for her body and her life. Encouraging your daughter to articulate how she really feels and to recognize the disappointments she has suffered will be far more valuable than any lecture or pep talk.

Believe me, you will not regret this change. It will enrich your life as much as it enriches hers. You have a lot to gain from learning more about your daughter!

Questions and New Connections

- Remember an occasion when you felt truly heard. What was this like? What did the other person say or do to encourage you to express yourself?

- As a boy, what was it like to talk to your father?

- How do you want your daughter's experience to be different from your own experience as a child? How do you want your daughter to see herself?

- What are your daughter's reactions to you really communicating?

- What anxiety do you have about really listening to your daughter? How will you handle whatever she might say to you in a loving, caring, fatherly manner?

Redefining Fathering

A realistic concept of being a father in today's world should be an adaptable, flexible one that adjusts to meet the changing needs and realities of the family. More than likely, this is not the model your father's life demonstrated to you. What you needed as a male of your generation and what children, especially global girls, need today are not the same. Furthermore, your daughter's desires will be different from yours because of the unique experiences children of each sex have as they grow up. Also, what your daughter needed from you when she was five is not the same as what she requires at the age of 15 or 30. So you must commit yourself not to specific behaviors, but to a way of being a father that responds to your daughter's development and to the differences between her feminine urge to maintain connections and your masculine emphasis on separateness.

One way to begin to redefine fatherhood is to invent new myths for fathers that can replace the old ones we have discussed throughout this book. Look at your day-to-day interactions at home, paying close attention to how available you are on a feeling level. You might write your new myths in a journal and use it to track your emotional experience, your progress sharing feelings with your daughter, and your successes with shedding the old myths and following your new ones. Analyze how well you listened to your daughter that day as well, since that's also going to require time and practice.

As you work to establish a closer relationship with your daughter, be sure to honor her need to gradually grow away from you and the security of home. You may want to re-create experiences you both have missed as she was growing up. You may actually want more closeness with her than she can deliver, because of her natural developmental progression away from the family, toward other relationships. Consciously try to let go of the little girl you cherished and allow her to become a woman. For her to feel comfortable as an adult, she needs you to accept her as one.

As an adult, you can discuss this with her and show her that you accept her growing need for independence, even as you welcome her desire to maintain closeness to you. Talking with other fathers will give you insights into how they have dealt with their feelings as their daughters matured. In the end, you will have enjoyed a much fuller life if you allow your definition of fathering to be dynamic and adaptable.

Questions and New Connections

- What is the ideal father like today? What does your definition include?

- What new myths do you choose to help define your role as a father in today's world?
- What does your daughter need from you now?
- How can you be a flexible and adaptable father as your daughter grows up?
- What kind of relationship would you like to have with your daughter when she becomes an independent adult? What can you do now to foster her independence while maintaining a loving relationship?

Assessing Your Own Beliefs About Food, Weight, and Body Image

Fathers of daughters who are conflicted about food and body image may also need to examine their own beliefs and behaviors related to food, weight management, and exercise. Earlier we examined how troubling these subjects are for women, but today men are also becoming concerned about them. Messages directed to men, however, stress being strong and healthy, living a long life, and avoiding cardiovascular disease. Messages directed to women, on the other hand, concentrate mostly on appearance. In response to these contrasting messages, men believe that being thin will prolong their lives, while women *endanger their lives to be thin*, courting disaster after internalizing so much erroneous information.

Part of your work as a father will require that you look more objectively at your own beliefs and behaviors concerning food and body image. You may need to educate yourself about the connections between nutrition, weight maintenance, and health. In media messages to men, the food, dieting and exercise industries promote the concept that lower weight leads to a longer life. They often distort or exaggerate the potential negative effects of higher weights.

For example, despite the frequent headlines about the health risks of weight gain, the research is quite mixed, and conclusions are often flawed and biased. The most reliable studies base major conclusions on correlation rather than causation, but still the results reported by the media and promoted by the diet, drug, and fitness industries make many fearful of any weight gain. Yet, comprehensive research from the National Institute of Aging indicates that a gradual increase in weight over the years is associated with the lowest mortality rate.[7]

Because men want to be productive and take care of their families, however, the messages that link weight to health and longevity are very powerful. As a result, many men reading this book may have their own hang-ups or misguided ideas about weight and food, and these may have affected their daughters' beliefs.

In many families I have treated, the fathers were dissatisfied with their bodies and wanted to lose weight or control their weight. Their daughters were keenly aware of the fathers' concerns and often tried to help them by developing exercise programs, working out with them, and cooking low-calorie meals. These young women attempted to become ideal models for their dad or to please him through their own successful weight-loss or exercise programs.

Educating yourself about our culturally accepted biases concerning weight and body size can help. You may catch yourself sharing the bias of *weightism*, a prevalent prejudice against larger people in our society. If you have said negative things about fat people to your daughter, she may be trying to assure your love by controlling her appetite and being thin.

Think about what you have communicated to her about the connection between love and people's bodies. Examine how important a person's size and appearance are to you. Be honest with yourself about whether you approve of, trust, like, and respect thin people more than fat people. Think about how weight and sex appeal affect your reactions to women. You may believe that you could never love a fat woman. Consider what this attitude expresses to your daughter about her mother's body and her own: that thinness is the all-important criterion for being lovable.

These are important issues because your daughter treasures and respects your opinions and wants to please you. Conceptualize how ideas about eating, weight, body shape, and fat may have become entangled in her perceptions of your love for her. Take time to figure out how you feel about these issues and what you really want to convey to her.

Questions and New Connections

- How important are appearance and weight to you?
- How do you feel about your own weight and physical appearance?
- What is your opinion about messages from the media pressuring people to be thin?
- How are your feelings about a woman affected by her weight?
- What do you say when you see a heavy person on the street or at the beach? How might your words have affected your daughter?
- How do you feel about your daughter's weight? Would you stop loving her and lose respect for her if she had a large body?

Coping with Eating Problems

Anorexia, bulimia, yo-yo dieting, and compulsive overeating are especially difficult issues because food is an absolute necessity of life. The person with conflicts about eating must face the problematic substance many times daily, every time food is planned, prepared, consumed, and cleared away. The family must find a way to manage food in the home while structuring meals to help the person who has difficulty with eating. Deciding who shops, who cooks, who cleans up, who eats together can all become major issues. It's important for the father to participate in the planning and handling of all these chores— they should not become the mother's sole burden.

Here again, your own childhood experiences may affect how you handle your daughter's eating behaviors. You may believe that since you're the father, she should just do what you say in all things, including eating. So, instead of tuning in to how she thinks and feels about food and trying to comprehend her pain, you simply tell her, "Sit down here and eat your dinner like everyone else. Just eat." However, she will not feel loved if you try to dominate her. If you nag about her eating, she will feel misunderstood, let down, and alone. If she experiences a twinge of anger, she will soon feel guilty and then will have even more trouble with food. The more you try to take over, the more havoc you will wreak.

Take a minute right now to imagine what it must be like to be so petrified of food, so worried about every mouthful, and so dominated by this fear. Imagine the pain and agony that your daughter suffers. Let her know that she can talk to you about it and that you will support her and love her, no matter what. Ask her if you can help in any way. Most important, accept that these odd behaviors around food are actually symptoms of her illness. Don't take it personally if she refuses your logic or willingness to help.

If you find yourself getting angry, again remind yourself that she has an illness—her rational mind is not in complete control. You can help your daughter simply by trying to get to know her as a person and by showing her respect. Her symptoms, especially her eating behaviors, may be distracting, so you will have to work hard to keep your focus on loving and trying to understand her.

The more you focus on her symptoms, the more you will reinforce the message that her body image and eating are the most important things about her. Questions such as What is your weight? or Did you throw up today? only reinforce her single-minded preoccupation with her eating problem. Furthermore, if you talk to her only about her problems, she may conclude that her symptoms are the only way to get your attention. This will make her more reluctant to give them up.

This doesn't mean that you should go to the other extreme and ignore her problems. That's even more dangerous; either she may think you don't care at all, or your denial could intensify her own. She may believe she can never get your love or attention, or she might resort to still more drastic measures to get it (losing more weight, vomiting more, or hurting herself in another way).

You might want to solve her problems by taking over, or you may be tempted to succumb to the tendency to disconnect from difficult emotional situations. Try to find a middle ground. Let her know that you care, that you will help if she wants, and that you love her despite these problems, no matter how long her recovery may take. Building a bigger base to the relationship between you and your global girl is critical. Think of ways to expand your relationship to include real, open conversation and shared interests.

Questions and New Connections

- What would your father do if his daughter had eating problems? How did he respond to problems in general? How are
your responses similar to or different from his?
- In what ways does your daughter need you as she works to
recover?
- What can you do to encourage your daughter to trust you
and open up to you?

Supporting Your Daughter in Treatment

Treatment for eating problems is a long-term process, characterized by slow, small steps. Even after the individual has changed her
behaviors concerning food and her body, she needs help to understand
how to deal with life's disappointments and challenges without hurting herself. This is best accomplished through relationships with a
therapist, dietitian, and other health-care professionals. These connections promote recovery.

Fathers who have listened for years to masculine messages such as,
"You can do it on your own," "Keep a stiff upper lip," or "Beat it" may
not instinctively understand the nature of the treatment or recovery
process. It is important to accept that both you and your daughter
need guidance and direction from others. If you admit this for yourself, it will be easier for your daughter to engage in treatment. Otherwise, she will feel that you disapprove of her and see her as weak or
disloyal to you. So abandon your old "macho" convictions and replace
those "I don't need anybody" and "I can do anything I put my mind
to" beliefs with ones that will allow your daughter to connect to the
people who can help her.

Once you have taken the major step of seeking help and allowing
professionals to become part of your life, the next challenge will be to
reign in your impatience and desire for instant results and develop a
sensitivity for the individual pace of your daughter's recovery. Without
an intuitive understanding of everything involved in recovery, you may
feel that no progress is being made. You may not see her internal changes
and the small adjustments she is making with her eating. While it is

certainly OK to share your doubts, be careful how you do this. Otherwise, she will feel once more that she is disappointing you, that you can't accept or love her, that you will never understand.

Remember that recovery is a more feminine process, based on gradually uncovering and releasing the burden of pain your daughter has accumulated over years of being disconnected from you, her mom, the rest of the family, her peers, and the world. It also requires making fuller, healthier new connections. So allow her the time to make these new connections, and give her the opportunity to connect with you.

Patience is the quality most fathers have to work hardest to develop. Sometimes a father is more ready than his daughter to rebuild their relationship. Because she is working hard to recover in so many areas, and because she is at a different developmental point than you, she may need to address many other issues or attachments first. She will gradually get to you, if you can wait. If you pressure her to work out your relationship before she's ready, she may feel scared by the intensity of your needs or she may, once more, feel out of control of her life. Be patient—nurturing a close connection with your daughter will be worth it!

Questions and New Connections

- What messages have you been giving your daughter about treatment?
- What do you hope will result from her treatment? Beyond her eating problems, what underlying issues need to be resolved?
- What recovery timetable is comfortable for you?
- What do you think your daughter's timetable is?

Summing Up: What Fathers Need to Know About Recovery

Recovery is a long and difficult process. Because most young women with eating disorders are perfectionists and are quite demanding of themselves, they have difficulty with the slow pace of their own change. Unrealistic parental expectations are counterproductive and inhibit progress.

Let's look at some common pitfalls, so you can be prepared to avoid them. First, it's important to realize that some words have different meanings for you than for someone with an eating disorder. While words like *healthy* and comments such as "You're looking better" or "You've gained weight" may seem neutral or positive to you, they are very frightening to your daughter. Having an eating disorder or being sick have become a central part of her identity, often making her feel special or unique. Any change in her body, even if she is eager to recover, represents a change in her identity—and a personal loss.

Compliments on her progress may make her more uncertain of herself, raising anxiety that others will see her as less important. Your daughter has relied on the eating disorder for a long time, seeking comfort and stability through her relationship to food and rituals related to her body. These habits are hard to give up, and she has to develop other coping mechanisms and ways to self-soothe. This takes time. Once she has developed other support systems and a stronger sense of identity, she will be able to let go of her symptoms. Be patient, and you can help her to be patient with herself.

Your daughter's perceptions of her body and of hunger and satiety are deeply affected by her eating disorder. As such, they are quite different from yours. Her fluctuations in nutritional intake and frequent attempts to significantly restrict food intake have slowed down the gastric secretions in her stomach and intestines. Food is likely to take longer to move through her system. This causes a distorted sense of fullness and distress about her stomach when she does eat. As one patient aptly explained, "You don't understand: every meal feels like Thanksgiving."

Both psychological and physical factors contribute to this. Be understanding when she complains about these feelings. They are real. Offer to do things together after meals to distract her from the discomfort. Reassure her that working with her therapist and dietitian will help her find ways to handle the discomfort, and her system will gradually function more normally.

You have heard about "phantom limb pain." It is a common phenomenon in the experience of amputees. Your daughter experiences "phantom fat." She truly sees her body as much larger than it is. You can't talk her out of this perception, since her feelings about her body actually contain a great deal of unexpressed emotional pain, which she may not yet have the words to express. Arguing with her about whether or not she is fat will only make the problem worse, as she will feel misunderstood and maligned. Therapy can help her identify the sources of emotional distress, verbalize her emotions, and decide how to handle them. This will help her cope with the phantom fat phenomenon and negative body image. Gradually, she will no longer need to translate all her emotions into the language of fat.

When your daughter begins to eat more normally and seems visibly better to you, she will actually be in more emotional pain. Eating disorder symptoms are great distractions; like alcohol and drugs, they numb pain and allow a person to avoid difficult issues. In fact, for that very reason, **relapse is a normal part of recovery**, and she will have a strong pull to regress. Your opinion is very important to your daughter, so resist the temptation to see her recovery in black-and-white terms and react to setbacks with disapproval, rejection, or anger. You can help her most by accepting that recovery is an imperfect process, filled with the challenge of acknowledging and working through difficult feelings.

Similarly, plateaus are part of the recovery process. During recovery, people with eating disorders often get to a point where their visible progress seems to slow down and come to a halt. Inside, they may be experiencing many feelings of loss as they give up parts of their eating disorder and develop new ways to look at themselves. They are also being challenged to deal with emotions and relationships without falling back on the comfort of their symptoms. In many ways, they are consolidating the changes they have made before they regroup to climb the next mountain. To other people, this inner work is not apparent. Realizing what's going on will help your efforts to slow down your expectations and be patient with the process.

Throughout your daughter's life, she needs to be showered with love and acceptance—whether she is 5 years old and totally healthy or

25 and in the midst of recovering from an eating disorder. "There's only one answer to those questions your daughter asks about how she looks," one father said. "You must give your total approval, tell her that she is beautiful inside and out, and that you love her *as is.*" If you can't say those words, you need to ask yourself why, and examine your own issues about weight, appearance, and women's bodies.

Your journey has just begun. I hope that it will be full of fabulous forces and that your decisive victory will be one of love—that both you and your daughter will be able to love more freely because you have healed the wounds left by father hunger. The changes necessary to overcome your separateness and become connected to yourself and to other men, to women, and especially to your daughter may seem daunting. However, with support from your family, friends, and therapists—you can discover ways to help your daughter and fill her father hunger with your love.

What Fathers Can and Can't Do for a Daughter with Eating Disorders

1. You can't make her want to get better. You can help her find a therapist and other treatment resources, provide economic support, and fight for insurance coverage for her, as this is frequently a problem. Let her know that you will be her advocate.

2. You can't force her to explore underlying issues or to change. You can set an example by being in therapy yourself and by participating in family therapy if it is recommended, talking openly about your feelings, and demonstrating your willingness to identify and resolve problems.

3. You can't understand how she feels about her body, as you do not see what she sees when she looks in the mirror. You can respect how deep and painful this is for her and appreciate how men and women in today's global culture have such different body experiences. Raise your consciousness by reading and asking women about the pressures they feel regarding weight, eating, and appearance.

4. You can't make her love herself. You can provide unconditional positive regard and a loving, supportive, and consistent relationship with

her. Let her know that you care and always will. Be patient with her and let her know you don't expect her or her recovery to be perfect.

5. You can't convince her to ignore pop culture and all its compelling messages to girls about beauty, appearance, and weight. You can help her become media literate by discussing how women's bodies are treated in the media and encouraging her to think more critically about this when you pass billboards on the highway or watch TV together. You can find a helpful "Active Advertising Acknowledgment" exercise in my book *Body Wars: Making Peace with Women's Bodies*.[8]

6. You can't change her response to cultural images and standards for beauty and thinness. You can work to change the culture by becoming an activist. Read *Body Wars* for ideas about activism and join the organization Dads and Daughters[9] to become part of their advocacy network. A very effective e-mail system is available on this site to identify ads and marketing campaigns that contribute to negative self-esteem in girls. Throw your weight around as a man and a consumer. You can make a difference.

7. You can't take away the dangers, risks, and challenges she experiences as a female in this culture. You can become a feminist man by supporting any and all efforts to achieve gender equity, end all forms of violence against women, and recognize the contributions women make to the world. This will enhance the status of women and help your daughter feel stronger and safer as a woman. In addition to becoming part of DADS, join organizations like the National Organization for Men Against Sexism[10] and use your influence as a man to make the world safer for girls and women.

8. You can't take away the feelings of shame, guilt, and embarrassment she has about having an eating disorder. You can, by learning about eating disorders and the many factors that contribute to them, help her to accept that her condition is truly an illness. As with most illnesses, the individual is not to blame, and recovery is a process that takes time.

9. You can't solve her problems. You can tell her you believe in her and know she will find the answers she needs. As Joe Kelly of Dads and

Daughters advises: "Don't just do something, stand there." It can be hard for fathers, but, more than anything else, she needs you to do just that.

10. You can't speak for her. You can listen to her. She will feel respected and confident if you do, and her positive feelings will generalize beyond your relationship. After all, whether you believe it or not, you are the most important man in her life. Listening is the greatest gift a father can give his daughter.

CHAPTER 12

How Mothers Can Help

Men and women must share the challenge of overcoming father hunger, supporting their global girls, and transforming family roles to adjust to the realities of 21st-century life. Many women reading this may think, "Why do I have to change again? I've been changing for the last 20 years!" They have been working hard to expand their lives and pursue new opportunities brought on by the feminist movement. However, this next series of changes can bring a much more satisfying balance between the sexes. Because of the private power women hold in families, they can do a great deal to help daughters connect with fathers and men overcome their separateness.

Just as men are challenged to take a journey inward to become more active, loving, and available fathers, women are also called to engage in a process of transformation that includes exploring the ways in which father hunger has affected their personal development, identity, and skills as a wife and parent. Fathers have to learn how to connect, and mothers have to learn how to separate, feel less responsible for everyone else and more responsible for themselves, and find balance between self and other. Working on these issues for yourself will equip you to support your daughter through recovery.

Facing Your Own Father Hunger

Father hunger is not unique to your daughter and her generation; more than likely, you have suffered it as well. The two of you may be on parallel tracks; and she will handle her struggle better if you pave the way by understanding and managing your own. The first step is to acknowledge and feel your own father hunger.

Until now, you may have denied these feelings and been unaware of their effects on your self-esteem, identity, goals, values, relationships, marriage, parenting, and life decisions. Get ready to be shocked by the power of the new discoveries you are about to make. Ideas and feelings avoided for so long can be scary and disruptive. Your father may have played out his prescribed cultural role quite well, even to the extent of being a model or prototype, but you will probably find that he wasn't very available to you emotionally. That realization will hurt. Facing reality can be painful.

Your Family Legacy

To understand the residual effects of your father hunger, begin by tracing the outline of your father's imprint on your life. Think back to your earliest memories of him and the feelings between the two of you. Be honest about how much you tried to please him and whether you ever felt you accomplished this. Recall how your relationship changed as you grew older. You may have felt connected to him at some points more than others. Remember what you did to try to develop a closer bond between the two of you. Jot down a list of events and occasions that stand out in your memories of your experiences with your father. What conclusions did you draw from each experience? The most basic issue is how satisfied you felt in the relationship. Take time to ponder that.

You may have limited your life to win your father's approval, or you may have surpassed his expectations for the same reason. Consider how his values and beliefs affected your decisions. He may have viewed certain jobs, hobbies, or activities as appropriate only for men. Figure out how these attitudes affected your participation in school, sports, and hobbies, as well as your career aspirations. Are there ways in which they still affect your decisions? It is likely that your father hunger has also influenced your choices in relationships, especially the types of men you are attracted to and the way you act around them. Take an inventory of ways in which your behavior and expectations as a woman, wife, and mother reflect the interpersonal history between your father and you.

Once you have explored these patterns, you will understand first-hand how a father can affect a daughter's feelings about herself. It's natural to feel sad, let down, even bewildered that you haven't recognized this before. The pain will eventually subside—but only after you have faced it. Healing your own father hunger requires learning to separate from his expectations and lessen the influence he still has on your behavior and emotions. The reward is learning that you can survive and thrive in a healthier, more balanced, and more self-generated style than you have known up to this point. In turn, your daughter will learn to address her issues with her father.

As you discover more about the lingering effects of your relationship with your father, first on you as a woman and now on you as a parent, you may want to share this new understanding with your daughter. Be sure to acknowledge that your experiences are different from hers and that you each have to find your own solutions. Give her the message that you believe in her, so she will feel confident about solving the dilemmas she confronts in life, beginning with the relationship with her dad.

Questions and New Connections

- Have you ever felt comfortable and satisfied in your relationship with your father? Describe occasions when you felt comfortable and satisfied, and other occasions when you did not.

- How have you tried to get your father's approval? Describe times when you were successful, and times when you were not. What conclusions did you draw from these experiences?

- In what ways do your adult interactions, especially with men, reflect your relationship with your dad?

The Delicate Balance: Self Versus Other

For you to feel entitled to a mature, loving relationship with your dad will require first strengthening and developing your own sense of self. Your work is different from that prescribed for fathers, which is to connect more closely with the family. As a woman, you are probably already good at that. Instead, you can achieve a better balance by focusing more on yourself and being more independent and separate, both from your father's needs and expectations and from your daughter's disappointments with her dad. This new attention to self will mean departing from the emotional aftermath of your father hunger and discovering new ways to function in all your relationships.

Think about the frequent conflicts you experience between pleasing others and expressing your own needs. More than likely, you often feel forced to choose between yourself and your relationships. And because your upbringing emphasized devotion to caretaking and nurturing, especially of men, your characteristic choice is self-sacrifice. Just like stockbrokers handle other people's money, you handle other people's feelings—and suppress your own. These patterns can leave you devoid of a connection with yourself, or *de-selfed*.[1] Quite simply, most women report to far too many people, and lose themselves in the process.

Think back to your early relationship with your father and honestly assess how much room it allowed for your needs. More than likely, in many of those interactions you were de-selfed, trying to connect any way you could, hoping to win his love and attention by allowing his needs and feelings to take priority over your own. Now is the time to start reporting to yourself first and setting a better example for your daughter.

For women, de-selfing results in a dangerous pattern in which too much of the self is negotiable. "We" and "you" become far more important than "I." Thus, the early relationship with dad can establish a standard of selflessness that lasts a lifetime and serves as an unhealthy model for your daughter. You can reverse the years of de-selfing and reclaim your inner self, but only by departing from the past. Once you do this, you will have a stronger identity. You will be less resentful and better able to assert yourself and get your own needs met. You will be able to deal with your own father hunger and your daughter's with a fresh perspective. And you will shift the balance of your marital relationship toward greater equality.

Questions and New Connections

- What or who comes first in your life? How many people do you report to?

- How many people do you want your daughter to report to? How can you help her change this family pattern?

- How can you achieve a better balance between your needs and those of others?

- What aspects of your *self* do you want to reclaim? How can you find more room for yourself in your life?

Learning How to Be Angry

Many women expend tremendous amounts of energy riding waves of anger. Unexpressed rage comes out in many ways, contributing to depression, illness, and marital problems. The inability to deal with this emotion emanates from a cultural expectation that was learned as a child: girls are not supposed to be angry. Expressing anger, especially to or about your father, was forbidden.

While men can express anger more openly, a woman's expression of anger, annoyance, or irritation is seen as "a real turnoff," unattractive, and masculine. Most women are aware of this unwritten rule, and they occasionally question its legitimacy. Still, they fear the consequences of showing anger. In many instances, the only time women express anger is when their emotions have built to an exploding point and they are extremely irate or even hysterical. Needless to say, this is not the ideal climate for working through feelings or understanding what needs to change.

The very first step in helping your daughter release her emotions is to reconsider your own beliefs about anger. Instead of viewing it as disturbing and destructive, begin to look at it as a valuable temperature gauge that signals the need for preventive attention or action. Acknowledging and accepting your anger will enhance your self and your relationships. Begin to put your anger into words.

Harriet Lerner's masterful book *The Dance of Anger: A Woman's Guide to Changing the Patterns of Intimate Relationships* shows how unresolved anger can create deep, dark shadows and how working through it can bring about important changes in your life. Anger can be a positive force, according to her profound statement: "Anger is a tool for change when it challenges us to become more of an expert on the self and less of an expert on others."[2]

This does not mean that venting anger will solve everything. In fact, just expressing your rage may serve to maintain the old patterns. A new, more effective approach is necessary. It involves working to understand why you're angry and figuring out what you can do to effect change. Trace your anger back to your relationship with your father. Look at how you handled anger with him and whether you ever expressed yourself directly. Think about how anger has surfaced in other areas of your life. For example, ask yourself how much you deny angry feelings to maintain connections with the opposite sex. Honestly assess how your problems with anger reflect your tendency to please everyone else and deny yourself.

Women with eating problems express their rage and struggles with self-worth through their bodies. Compulsive eaters are said to be swallowing their feelings, bulimics throw them up, and anorexics completely deny them. Feeling worthy of anger and strong enough about yourself to express it are major steps toward recovery because they rebalance the tensions on the self. Your work in this area will demonstrate to your daughter that she is also entitled to her anger and will help her find symmetry and equality in her relationships.

Questions and New Connections

- Did you ever express anger to your father? How? What happened? How did he react?
- What happened when you openly disagreed with your father?
- In what situations have you denied angry feelings to maintain family connections?
- How can you express and constructively deal with your anger about a particular family situation?
- What are you teaching your daughter about anger?
- What are you teaching her about negotiating conflicts with men?

Using Your I-Voice

Paying attention to your communication style may help you become more assertive and expressive. One of the most effective communication techniques you can learn is to use your "I-voice" to speak directly from your self. Replace the old blaming refrains that begin with "You" or "You *never* . . ." by messages that begin with "I" and give straightforward information about your feelings. The I-voice is assertive and powerful. It can move you closer to resolving problems in a way that blaming never does. For example, your husband is more likely to listen if you say, "I really feel insecure about our relationship when we spend so little time together" than if you say, "You don't love me. You're never home. You'd rather work than be with me."

Think about how your relationship with your dad would have been different if you had been able to use your I-voice as a little girl. You might have said, "Daddy, I need you to tell me you love me" instead of guessing how to make him happy and hoping he would notice. This would have affected your relationships with men throughout your lifetime. You would have learned to connect with men without giving up yourself. It's not too late to learn this, if you are willing to work at it.

As you develop your I-voice, you may find that some of those old myths about men get in the way—especially the beliefs that men don't feel and just can't understand women. They must be challenged and discarded, for they keep you from speaking directly and getting your needs met in relationships. They feed your de-selfing tendencies, making you give up too easily on your attempts to use your I-voice. You'll be able to leave your father hunger behind only when you are more grounded in yourself. So practice using your I-voice to express your disappointments and needs, especially to men. Don't let the eternal desire to please and to be connected to your father keep you disconnected from your own self.

Questions and New Connections

- How did your parents discourage your I-voice?
- What important I-voice statements would you like to have made during your childhood? What conclusions did you draw when you were unable to make them?

- Write a list of I-voice statements you would like to make to family members today. See if you can remove any hint of blame to deliver a pure message about your feelings.

- How are you encouraging or discouraging your daughter's I-voice?

Formulating Goals

To achieve equanimity between self and other, between separateness and connectedness, women must formulate their personal goals and then stick to them. By bringing your father hunger into your conscious awareness, you can now decide how much you will allow it to continue to dominate you. You can assess whether trying to please men to make up for your dad's indifference should continue to rule your life.

Once you grapple with this, many other decisions become easier. You may, for instance, decide that you no longer have to dress a certain way or diet to maintain a weight that pleases some men but starves your spirit. Perhaps you'll set more realistic goals for yourself in terms of work, community involvement, or even housekeeping. Whatever the area, dealing with your father hunger will free you to set your own priorities and follow them. This will be an extremely effective model for your daughter.

Take some time to think about what you want out of life right now. List the feelings and experiences you want to have. Write down the things you want to achieve, and set realistic dates for completing them. These may be either personal or professional goals, as long as they are truly *your* desires. Look at the ways in which your tendency to focus on others, your self-denial, and your longing to please men have gotten in the way of meeting your own needs and expressing yourself. Then stop worrying so much about everyone else's happiness and start concentrating on your own. This will gradually allow you to separate from the demands of others and connect to yourself. Initially, just thinking about your own desires may seem foreign, but breaking this new ground will create new opportunities for your daughter as well. Instead of obsessing about how to please her father and other men, she may follow your lead and develop goals of her own.

Questions and New Connections

- How do your goals reflect or contradict your father's goals for you?

- What obstacles have kept you from reaching your goals? What new options do you see now for overcoming those obstacles?

- What are your current life goals? What experiences and feelings do you want to have? What do you want to accomplish? What new aspects of yourself do you want to express?

- In what ways can you encourage your daughter to develop and pursue her own goals?

Dealing with Guilt, Feelings of Failure, and Perfectionism

Guilt and perfectionism seem to come with the territory of motherhood and are reinforced by the countless articles and books devoted to the mother-child relationship. They are also fueled by father hunger, so that always trying to do more, attain perfection, and please others become habitual responses—accompanied by the acute awareness that one has failed to achieve perfection and is thus to blame for the family's problems.

Mothers of children with eating problems feel more than their share of these agonizing emotions. Many have worked hard all their lives to become the perfect, overfunctioning supermoms that their families and culture taught them to be. Subconsciously, they believed this would satisfy the men in their life and win their approval. Now they are tormented by the question, What went wrong?

Usually by the time I first meet the mother of a new patient, that mother has read at least five books about eating disorders and has internalized every negative idea about the mother-daughter relationship. The fact that fathers were hardly mentioned does not seem odd to her since, according to the prevailing myths, families are supposed to get along without fathers anyway. This just intensifies the mother's guilt, as she feels solely responsible for her daughter's problem. I often suggest that mothers stop reading this material, since it keeps them stuck in self-blame.

If you have been following other people's rules, remaining loyal to the old myths about women's roles and how unimportant men are to children rather than figuring out what is right for you and for your family, your daughter has probably absorbed the same values. Unsure and unaware of herself, she will try to follow tradition, be perfect, and please everyone, especially her elusive father. Your ability to help her will depend on coming to terms with your own drive for perfection and your feelings of guilt and failure. You can begin by looking at the origins of these emotions to determine how much they reflect your unresolved yearning for connection to your father.

Questions and New Connections

- Did you ever feel good enough for your father? List some times when you were poignantly disappointed by his responses to your attempts to please or impress him.
- How has this affected your relationship with your husband? How has it affected your parenting?
- What are you teaching your daughter about guilt? About perfectionism? About placing others' needs before her own? About the importance of pleasing men?

Seeking Help

One step toward a better balance between self and others is deciding to seek professional help not just for your daughter, but for yourself as well. This action asserts that your needs and feelings are also important and that you are willing to "re-self." Many mothers hesitate to enter treatment because of the sense of responsibility and failure that has resulted from years of skewed roles in families—they expect that, once more, they alone will be blamed for whatever has gone wrong.

However, the door to a therapist's office is actually the door to liberation from guilt and self-blame. *Family therapy* can help you and your husband or ex-husband achieve a better balance of responsibilities in managing the family's life. As you examine how father hunger has affected the parenting roles, division of duties, and emotional environment in your home, you can adjust the energy you devote to others. You can learn how to advance beyond guilt and feel free to give more to yourself. *Individual therapy* allows a more in-depth look at how your father hunger continues to resonate in your adult life. Your new understanding will enhance all your relationships. *Parent groups, mothers' groups*, and *family support groups* can also provide valuable new ideas and insights.

Questions and New Connections

- What are the biggest obstacles to your becoming involved in therapy? Are your goals strong enough to overcome these obstacles?
- How would your father feel about your seeking help? How do your feelings about therapy reflect his?
- What aspects of your deepest self have you sacrificed for your family? What price have you and the family paid for this?
- What preferences, choices, experiences, feelings, and lost parts of your identity would you like to reclaim?
- What benefits do you hope that your being in therapy will have for your daughter?

Working with Her Father

Now that you are aware of your own father hunger and its persistence well into your adult life, it is time to look at your current family structure and relationships. It is so easy to unknowingly repeat the patterns of the past; both men and women readily fall back into those old familiar roles at home. There are many things you can do, however, to break the pattern. Separating yourself from your old ways, particularly from the tendency to monopolize all the family responsibility, allows your husband to connect with his children. You can do this even if you are divorced or separated, and it may help to spare them from the father hunger you have suffered.

Redistributing Power and Roles

Start by assessing how you balance the male-female seesaw of underfunctioning and overfunctioning. Is it true that your only sure power comes from overfunctioning at home? Are you, like so many other women, gaining influence by doing everything for everyone, exhausting yourself so there's no time or energy left for you? That's not real power—it's slavery. Even if you didn't see this until now, your daughter has, and her eating problems and dissatisfaction with her body are her ways of rejecting that role. She desperately needs you to find more real, satisfying, self-affirming authority.

To do this, you will have to stop mothering your husband, learn to ask for help, and determine your goals for yourself and your family. Until you alter the established patterns, he won't have to assume more responsibility at home because you're treating him like another child. He can then be aloof and irresponsible, you can be angry and overwhelmed, and your children can experience father hunger first-hand.

Both of you will need to change. If possible, discuss the ideas in this book with him. Talk together about the interpersonal dynamics of father hunger and how a new balance between the two of you can help your daughter. Make a list of changes you can make to arrive at a better balance of responsibilities and power in the home.

Sharing responsibilities more equally will mean that when he starts doing more in the home, he will do things in his own way. He may not pay attention to the details you think are important. Allow him to grow into his new role, while you are letting let go of your demands that everything in the house has to be perfect—for these indirectly perpetuate father hunger. It may be difficult to be patient and give your husband time to learn new tasks, but with sufficient time the two of you can work out a way to share responsibilities. So be creative as you make new adjustments. His increased participation will make him more important to the children, and your daughter will learn that men and women can support each other, work together, and share family burdens.

Questions and New Connections

- How were the responsibilities and power distributed in your family when you were growing up? Is your marriage replicating this?

- In what areas of family relationships is a better balance needed?

- What are you afraid of losing if you start doing less and letting your husband do more? What kinds of support can you ask your husband to give you?

- How can you begin to alter your roles and encourage your husband to participate more fully in the family? What can the two of you do to overcome the obstacles?

Escaping the Superwoman Syndrome

Since World War II and the entry of women into the workplace, women have increasingly taken on more multidimensional roles, with many conflicting priorities to juggle. To their traditional roles of cooking and cleaning, managing a house and family schedule, coaching and emotionally supporting their families, they added working in the business world or community. While men were traditionally assigned a focused role of working outside the home and being the economic provider, women learned to constantly transform themselves, moving from role to role in the various chapters of their lives.

To make the switch from homemaker to career professional, many women even today feel they have to prove themselves by showing that the family's welfare will not suffer because of their added responsibilities outside the home. Having learned not to expect much from men, they feel they should need little help from their husbands. They are supposed to be able to do everything a man can do, in addition to everything a woman can do. While working very aggressively in the traditional male world, they also strain to be supermom, superwife, and super household manager. They pressure themselves to perform perfectly in all arenas. In doing so, they become victims of a self-imposed "Superwoman Syndrome."[3]

Do you see yourself in this description? The superwoman does it all, has it all, and needs no one. Theirs is a very powerful—but very lonely and precarious—position.

The Superwoman Syndrome myth has a severe impact on female self-esteem. Some studies have shown that the women most at risk for eating disorders are those who believe they should be totally independent, competitive, and successful in the world, denying their own need for relationships and the connectedness that is a central part of femininity.[4] If you can begin to revise the roles in your family so that your children see two interdependent adults sharing responsibilities, each needing the other and meeting the other's needs, you can do much to counter these destructive cultural images that contribute to the overfunctioning superwoman ideal.

Questions and New Connections

- Describe your ideal woman. Is she a superwoman? How does your ideal fit with your parents' ideals?
- Are you satisfied with yourself as a woman?
- What are you modeling for your daughter? Is she trying to be a superwoman? Have you pushed her to be one?
- With your husband, make a list of all the roles each of you fills. Discuss possible solutions for the superwoman syndrome problem and how they could benefit each person.

Making Room for Daddy

Daughters need their dads. Helping your daughter develop a strong connection with her father should be one of your primary goals as a mother. It requires that you separate your own needs, losses, disappointments, and anger with your father, from hers. At some point, did you unconsciously decide that your daughter doesn't need her father because yours was not available to you and your other relationships with men have not satisfied your longing for him? Work on distinguishing your needs and desires from hers. You can survive your father hunger without sentencing your daughter to a life with it. She is entitled to a relationship with her dad.

To make room for daddy, you must stop protecting him from

day-to-day concerns. Make a new agreement with him that honors his importance in the family. Involve him in what's going on—both the good and the bad. Share the burdens of getting to appointments and lessons and handling the many other tasks you've been managing alone. Ask him to take care of some of the extended family business also, like buying birthday cards or presents.

You may need to be very direct in telling your husband exactly what help you need. When it comes to housework and child care especially, you can't expect him to read your mind. Most men have never been expected to do these things before, and unlike you, your husband was probably not brought up to see day-to-day family life as his business. So talk this out with him and enlist his support. Then give him some leeway. Don't expect him to be perfect. The outcome you want is probably within reach if you both define it as satisfying your children's father hunger, rather than as having a perfectly clean house.

As your husband becomes more actively involved in the life and responsibilities of the family, you may be tempted to jump into the middle of the relationships he is establishing in the family. You read earlier about women whose mothers did too much with them because their fathers were unavailable. Although the mothers meant well, their overinvolvement sometimes served to maintain the distance between father and daughter. Moreover, their interference certainly did not address the problems that kept these fathers so peripheral. From their mistakes you can learn to stand by, watch, and do less interfering. Have faith that your spouse can work out his relationship with the kids and other family members, and that he'll ask for your input when he wants it.

Your new cooperative relationship with your husband will redefine both your roles. Rather than viewing your husband as a helper or babysitter, think of him as a peer or co-captain instead. Stop seeing him as a second-string quarterback who gets called into the game only if you're injured. Just remember, the differences between men and women have been accentuated by years of socialization. Let him find his own way of interacting with the kids. It may be different from yours, but that's OK. As you stop supervising and interfering with his attempts to be involved in the family, he will feel more comfortable about doing more.

Questions and New Connections

- When you were a child, what was your father's role in the family? How is your husband's role now similar or different? What myths about men have been perpetuated in your family today?

- What habits do you have that exclude your husband from the family's daily life and emotions? Would you feel insecure if he started doing more at home? Work together with him to come up with alternative strategies that give him a more central role.

- Take an inventory of all the small ways you may be blocking the father-daughter relationship. How can you foster an environment full of opportunities that will strengthen your daughter's connection to her dad?

Coping with Divorce

Sharing responsibility, coparenting, and finding balance are more difficult to manage after a divorce. Despite your desire that your children will not be hurt by your divorce, it is almost inevitable that they will be. But you can repair some of the damage if you work hard to understand the connections between your own father hunger and the breakdown of your marriage. When a marriage ends, you lose the man you may have thought would take your father's place and satisfy all your unmet needs. This raises many complicated emotions that must be processed as you struggle to cope with the aftermath.

To minimize your children's father hunger, it will be critical to resist the urge to draw your children into your conflicts with your ex-spouse. Make a joint decision to work through your anger with each other so that it doesn't affect them. You should also resist the tendency to protect your children from disappointments with their father because in doing this, you will come between them and interfere with their direct relationship with each other.

Unresolved rage causes many divorced mothers to limit or control the relationship between their husband and the kids. Already burdened by daily responsibilities for the family, they feel resentful or jealous of the children's affection for their father. This is further aggravated when the father's time with the children is devoted to fun weekend outings, while the mother is left to handle all the drudgery of household chores and setting limits.

In summary, situations of divorce can make it difficult to resist the urge to misuse your power and restrict the children's time with their father or make them choose between their two parents. A man who believes all the myths about fathers' insignificance may too easily accept a reduced role. If this happens, the children lose one of the most important people in their lives, and you and your ex-husband lose the possibility of sharing the responsibility for parenting—which your children deeply need you to do.

Questions and New Connections

- How do your feelings about your husband reflect residual issues between you and your own dad? What can you do to resolve these issues?
- In what ways are you and your husband acting out your anger with each other through the children? What effects does this have on them? How can the two of you work through your anger for the sake of the children?
- What can you do to support and encourage your daughter's relationship with her father?

Helping Your Daughter to Let Go—and Let Grow

In addition to working on your self-development and your relationship with your daughter's father, there is another important way you can help your global girl deal with her father hunger. She needs to separate from you in order to connect with him. So your goal must be to let her go and let her grow.

Your words and actions must communicate to your daughter that you will survive if she grows up, and that being an adult woman who eats healthfully and accepts her size and shape is desirable. Show her that women can negotiate satisfying relationships with men and with a society that can feel foreign and scary at times because of its masculine power and value system. Your daughter needs to feel that you and her father see her as a separate, important person with legitimate rights, needs, feelings, and ideas—someone who will be able to make it in the world.

Global girls who develop eating problems are struggling to find a personal identity—to differentiate themselves, and yet still feel attached and fulfilled in their relationships. Because female development is usually characterized by an ongoing connection with mother, in contrast to the male experience of separation, a daughter's identity formation will involve finding a way to be independent but still close to her mother, and to connect to the adult world without completely losing her childhood. Your efforts to do this yourself will help her be less frightened of adulthood.

Letting your daughter grow up can be a challenge. Without realizing it, you may want to keep her close and may undermine or reject her natural movement toward independence. This may sound malevolent, but it's really not. You love her; in fact, you love her so much you don't want to let her go. She fears that if she tries to be herself, she will lose you. Since she already feels she lost her father, she can't risk losing you too, so she chooses to give up her *self* instead. Unless you give her clear permission to grow and separate from you, and demonstrate that you will still be there for her, she may not be able to take these steps.

Mothers show their ambivalence about a daughter's growth in various ways. An overfunctioning mother unknowingly keeps her daughter dependent on her, while an underfunctioning mother requires her daughter to overfunction and take care of *her*. The daughter can't move away from her mother because the mother needs her too much. In either case, both mother and daughter have underdeveloped selves and must strive to develop mature adult identities. Both will have to work equally hard to find a new way of relating that replaces the old, overly close, needy way that led to these problems. Then they will be able to let go and let grow.

Questions and New Connections

- In what ways are you dependent on your daughter?
- How have you encouraged her to be dependent on you?

- How did your own parents react to your needs for more independence? What was your response? As an adult looking back on these experiences, how could they have been handled differently?
- What messages do you want to give your daughter about growing up and becoming an independent adult?

Know Her As a Person

To grow, your daughter must differentiate herself from you. You can help by choosing to see her as someone you would like to get to know, instead of someone who is just like you. Even though you may feel confident that you have known her intimately all her life, there is probably much you don't know about her. This is understandable: within every person lies a world of feelings and thoughts that aren't freely shared, and almost everyone screens their behavior and responses to fit the expectations of different relationships. So stop assuming that your daughter feels and thinks exactly as you do. Instead of feeling cut off and rejected by her individuality, practice enjoying the many ways she is different from you.

Be very clear to her about your own thoughts and feelings—use your I-voice. The more you work on your own self-development and on speaking in your I-voice, the more you will be able to help your daughter find hers.

When you talk with your daughter, make it a two-way conversation. Help her share what she thinks and how she feels. Encourage her to define her own thoughts, feelings, and self, separately from yours. It may be useful for her to hear how you would handle a situation she's facing, but you should avoid giving advice, or worse yet, telling her what to do.

If you pressure her to follow your suggestions, she may feel angry that you're not allowing her independence and respecting her ability to make her own decisions. She will probably also feel guilty about not following the path you prescribe.

Guilt is like quicksand for people with eating problems. There's nothing like guilt to convince them they should not eat, or should not stop eating, or should not keep the food in, or should exercise more, or that they are not worthy of life. So it's important for you to become more aware of the things you say and do that might provoke guilt. This is a good topic to work on in therapy. The solution is to take responsibility for your own feelings, accept that the two of you are separate individuals, and allow your connection to build in a new, adult way.

If I could suggest just one rule to guide you in supporting your daughter through her recovery, it would be to learn to know her as a full person, not just as an anorexic, a bulimic, a dieter, or an overeater. Mothers often worry so much about their daughters that their interactions begin to focus on problems and symptoms rather than on the person. Consequently, women in recovery often report that friends are more helpful than family. Instead of reacting only to symptoms, friends often convey appreciation for the many other dimensions of the individual. As a loving mother, your task is to achieve a balance between confronting and acknowledging symptoms and getting past them to know the real person who is your daughter.

Questions and New Connections

- How well do your father and mother know you? Can you truly be yourself with them?
- How well would your daughter say you know her? Does she feel permission to be different from you? Ask her if she is willing to allow you to get to know more about her thoughts and feelings.

Let Her Reject You

Recovering from any personal problem requires taking responsibility for it. To achieve recovery, your daughter will have to take responsibility for her eating problem. You can't do it for her, and your efforts to relieve her of responsibilities she needs to handle are likely to backfire.

That doesn't mean that as a mother, you should abandon your daughter, withhold assistance, and never tell her what you think. You should be talking about many things, including her eating difficulties and her relationship with her dad, and you should offer to help. But wait for your offer to be accepted, and listen to her answer instead of forging ahead on your own. When she says, "No, I don't need you," respect that and let her know you still love her. Don't make your love contingent on her doing things your way or even listening to you. That's another quick road to disaster.

If she rejects you, some of your own pain about being rejected by your father may surface. Get ready for feelings that you may not completely understand. You may also feel abandoned if she develops a closer relationship with her dad. These are natural events. Let them happen. Work on understanding your feelings and how they relate to your father hunger. Remember that to make better connections in the future, both of you need to separate from the way you have interacted in the past.

Questions and New Connections

- Did you ever reject your mother? How and why? How important was this in your development? What did you need from your mother at that time?

- How do you feel when your daughter disagrees with you? What are some good ways to respond?

First Steps Toward Change

A positive first step to help your daughter overcome her eating and body image conflicts is to simply accept that you and the family environment need to change, even though you may not yet know how or why. This may be scary, but it is absolutely essential. Rest assured that you are not totally responsible for her difficulties—her father shared in creating the family dynamics. Knowing this, you will be better able to survive the crisis and support her through recovery. Look at this as an opportunity to establish a better balance for everyone between self and others, and between separation and connectedness. Why is this an opportunity? When you succeed, you will all function more fully and more lovingly as a family.

Also keep in mind that the problem is more than just your daughter's eating or body image. Her issues with food and her body are her way of coping with pain about many issues, including her father hunger. She has been unable to connect with her dad, so she has become disconnected from herself and will do anything to please others. She needs help to figure out how to relate to the masculine world and how to accept her feminine self. Until she solves these problems, she will act out her conflicts through her body.

Your job is to resist the temptation to simplify the problem, and to help her deal with the bigger issues head on. Stop looking for "A causes B" solutions and open yourself up to the larger screen of her life and yours. Tune in to your father hunger and see how it has affected both you and your daughter. Involve her father in the recovery process.

In summary, your daughter's recovery will be supported by your willingness to accept the following new ways of thinking and relating.

1. Accept that she needs help from others.

Although your daughter's father may be saying that she can "do it on her own," work with him to arrange professional help as soon as possible. Your daughter may need dietary counseling, medical assessment and follow-up, individual therapy, family therapy, and possibly group therapy or hospitalization. Ask for direction from these professionals regarding how to handle eating at home. Let her work on her issues with food and her body individually while you make changes within the family, support the building of a relationship between her and her dad, and encourage her development.

Be sure to address your own reactions to her new relationships. Sometimes mothers feel replaced by their daughter's therapists or rejected if she reaches out to others. The attachment to her dad may especially bring up issues for you. Remind yourself that she needs to separate from you in order to connect with herself.

2. Accept that it is necessary for you to change.

Unknowingly, you have brought your father hunger to your marriage and your parenting. Your daughter needs you to change so she can have a different kind of relationship with you, with her dad, with

herself, with food, and with the world—and learn to establish relationships that are free from father hunger. If she sees you addressing
emotional issues, she'll feel safer as she figures out what she should do
to improve her life. She will be less scared that you will reject her if she
alters her relationship with you and becomes more connected to her dad.

As you address your own disappointments with your father, your
marriage, and your life, you will model for her that change is desirable
and beneficial. She will believe that if you can overcome problems, she
can too.

3. Accept that you may have some unhealthy attitudes toward food or weight.

Your attitudes, self-esteem, and body image all reflect your reactions to your own father hunger. If you have tried to please your father
or other men through your appearance, by losing weight, eating less,
or pursuing the "perfect" body, you will have to work hard to change
your own beliefs and practices to help your daughter.

The children most at risk for developing eating problems come
from families that stress appearance and believe that weight is voli-
tional and represents self-control and personal achievement. The more
preoccupied a mother is with weight, diet, and appearance, the more
at risk her daughter is for eating disorders. Criticizing a daughter's
body, encouraging her to diet, and competing with her regarding
weight loss or management all contribute to eating problems.

Supporting your daughter's recovery will mean facing these issues
yourself. You will need to be honest about the meaning and importance you give to weight and body image and how these reflect your
desire to please men. Like your daughter, you have grown up in a culture that is not friendly or accepting of the range of female body sizes.
By figuring out how you have responded to that, you will help your
daughter find peace with her physical needs.

4. Accept that her father may need to be more involved in her life.

By now you probably realize that you can't wave a magic wand and
make everything all better. I hope you also see that you did not cause

all your daughter's problems and that casting blame is a futile game. The next step is to encourage a better connection between her and her father. You may need to work through your own feelings about him and acknowledge any jealousy of their relationship. Your goal is to foster love, openness, and personal development—to let your global girl go and grow.

CHAPTER 13

How Daughters Can Cope with Father Hunger

For too many global girls, father hunger skews the balance between self and others. Craving a relationship with this special man, they will do anything to please him. Failing that, they go to extremes to win approval from other men and authority figures. Although their intention is to connect with dad, the result is separation from themselves and a general sense of disconnection from life.

The road to healing passes through a winding course of self-discovery and resolution of this father hunger. It emerges into a clearing where you discover the tools for forging your own path in the world as a strong, assertive young woman, able to withstand the unrelenting messages you receive about weight, beauty, dieting, slimness, fashion, and appearance. Along the way, you also learn to manage your doubts about how to please men.

This chapter examines how you can readjust the balance between yourself and others—first by focusing on yourself, next by connecting to your dad, and then by concentrating on your family, social relationships, and culture.

Connecting with Yourself

Let's begin with the basic Three R's: **Recovery Requires Reconnection.** To heal your father hunger, overcome your eating disorder, and get your life back on track, you must first reconnect with yourself. The only way to do this is by slowly separating from your eating disorder. You can start this process by learning about the *function* of your symptoms: discovering the pain they have covered up and the objectives they are trying to accomplish. Gradually you will understand their true meaning—how they expressed the hunger for father and for other connections that you couldn't put into words. Then you can begin to face the facts of your eating disorder by admitting, confronting, and changing your behaviors toward food and your body. In this way, separating from your eating disorder will allow you to reconnect with yourself.

Your attitudes and behaviors related to food are very important to you, or you would not continue them. In some complex, unconscious way, you started them hoping they would help you deal with life.

When I ask patients why they think they developed their eating problems, they usually say, "I just stopped eating," or "I just wanted to lose weight," or other simple "I just . . ." statements. Only later do they come to understand the deeper meaning of their symptoms. Like each of them, you will have to find out for yourself how your eating problems have helped you cope with your life. You might as well start by accepting that eating problems are not "just" anything. Instead, they are complicated cover-ups of other conflicts.

One woman who struggled with an eating disorder for many years said, "*Just* is a four-letter word." Whenever she hears herself say, "I just . . . ," she knows she has to dig deeper into her inner self. She's right. It can take a long time to figure out the function of your symptoms and their relationship to your father hunger.

As you begin connecting with yourself and understanding how you ended up with these problems, you may be searching for one experience or one person to blame. But human behavior doesn't fit into a simple cause-and-effect model, so allow yourself to see the bigger picture of feelings, relationships, and interconnections. Resist simplifications such as, "I only wanted . . ." or "It's just that . . ."—they're misleading.

No one is to blame for your problems with food—not your father, not your mother, not your family, your siblings, or your friends, and not yourself, either. Your symptoms took hold because they were the only way you knew to express your pain. Although your family has been hurt by your problems, that was not your intention. You are not to blame—you were doing the best you could at the time. So start by resolving to forgive yourself and your family—no one is to blame, and blame offers no solutions.

Once you acknowledge that your symptoms are more than "just" one thing or another, think about the ways in which symptoms similar to yours have functioned for the women we discussed in earlier chapters. Many thought they could gain power or control over their lives by limiting their appetites, overeating, or hurting their bodies through purging or excessive exercise. For some it was a way to achieve, please others, and prove their self-worth.

However, despite your initial intention that your symptoms would connect you to your dad, to other people, and to positive feelings about yourself, they have not accomplished any of these goals. Instead, they have separated you from yourself. Look carefully at what your obsession with food allows you to avoid. To reconnect with yourself, you must face those disappointments, losses, conflicts, and painful feelings. It won't be easy, and you will probably need some help—but you can do it, and you will be glad you did.

Discovering the Hidden Meaning

Your symptoms have meaning. They represent your inner wishes and feelings, but at the same time they shield you and insidiously separate you from them. Overtly, they communicate to others that you want to be left alone, that you need no one, that you will get through life with your eating disorder as your best friend. Underneath, however, you desperately want a connection, especially to your dad.

So let's take some time to discern what your eating problems say to others and what they really mean to you. You may discover they are loaded with hidden contradictions. Consider the following examples.

1. Not Loving Yourself—Feeling Unloved by Dad

One statement that your eating problems make to other people is that you don't value yourself. The true meaning of your behavior, though, is that you have not felt loved by others, especially by your dad. You can't fully love and accept yourself because, for whatever reasons, you haven't felt consistently and unconditionally loved by key people in your life. Gradually, you will need to explore your experiences of love within your family and in your relationship to your father. To get better, you must face this honestly instead of eating, starving, overexercising, or purging the feelings away. As you expand your vocabulary of words and ways of thinking about your past experiences, you will discover new tools that give you the power to do this.

2. Being Successful in the Male World—Feeling Unappreciated by Dad

Your behaviors toward food and your body express an acceptance of many cultural values that you might not have thought to question before. Self-control, excessive exercise, denial of feelings and needs, and a lean, hard body—which you may have pursued heartily—are signs of achievement for many men. Yet they can represent a deep feeling that your dad does not appreciate or value *you*, apart from these external expectations. You need him to acknowledge you as a female, but the only way you have found to pursue this is by being more male. You must reconnect to your femininity and become aware of how the superficial things you have done to please men can never succeed in winning love and approval for the *inner* you, for who you truly are inside. Instead, they have effectively separated you from important parts of yourself as a woman.

3. Behaving Rigidly—Covering Up Inner Turmoil

Others may see you as someone who appears driven and self-confident. What they don't know is that inside, you are horribly confused about your feelings, decisions, beliefs, values, relationships, and future. The rigidity of your eating problems covers up this insecurity. It provides a temporary sense of safety and predictability and seems to shield you from the chaos of your world. Once again, however, the real meaning of your behavior is an unsatisfied desire for connection. Your symptoms mask your confusion about how to be a real person and how to be accepted by your dad and others. The only way to discover a real, self-based identity is to separate from these dysfunctional patterns of avoidance, admit how cut off you have been from yourself, and begin to build a life free from your symptoms.

4. Maintaining Distance—Wanting Closeness

The conflicts about body image and food that accompany eating problems instantly and pervasively create distance between yourself and others. When you refuse invitations because of your fear of eating in public or being seen as fat, people naturally conclude that you don't want a relationship with them. Gradually, you exclude yourself from social activities, family events, and relationships—but this all started because people were so important to you! In fact, you want to please them and be liked, while many of your actions tell them to leave you alone.

Again, although the desire is for closeness, your symptoms are separating you. Your dad, like other people in your life, doesn't know the hidden meaning of your behavior, and, with all his masculine beliefs about separation, he will easily be convinced to leave you alone. You must learn more about how you subconsciously convert your desire for closeness into behavior that distances others.

5. Denying All Feelings—Being Overwhelmed by Your Emotions

When others look at you, they probably see a well-defended fortress—someone who admits to no feelings, maybe even someone who "can deal with anything." Your inner reality is different from this. You, in fact, have very few ways to cope, and thus, you rely on your eating disordered behaviors to avoid anger and pain. Your feelings about your dad are among the most difficult. The only way you are sure to maintain equilibrium is by denying your discomfort with him and with everything else. The result is an agonizing separation.

Your only solution is to slowly confront your inner life. In fact, you have powerful, frightening feelings and an emptiness that gnaws at you. Satisfying your hunger for connection, especially with your father, will begin to fill the void and will provide support as you learn how to cope with feelings more directly.

Questions and New Connections

- How do your eating and body image problems keep you from knowing yourself?

- What did your dad teach you about feelings? What are your memories of times when you wished you could share your feelings with him?

- What feelings about your father have you been trying to avoid? What will happen if you express these feelings directly?

- How do your eating problems reflect your father's messages about emotional expression?

Getting Support

The most difficult fact to face is that to connect with yourself and in relationships, you must separate from your eating disorder. When you are actively symptomatic, you focus on food, calories, your body, and weight. These become obsessions—nothing else seems important. Your symptoms keep you from recognizing feelings and numb you from the pain in your relationships. You must acknowledge that you have used food to avoid other issues.

Confronting your problems honestly will enable you to gradually normalize your eating. This takes hard work, but it will pay off. You will begin to replace your conflicted ideas about food and your negative obsession about your body with more positive experiences. Opening the door to painful feelings allows you to have good feelings as well! Being honest with yourself allows you to have real and satisfying interactions with other people—perhaps even with your dad. For the first time, you will learn to balance the tension between yourself and others, and between being separate and being connected.

Start by agreeing that you could use some help. Entering treatment will challenge those old notions that therapy is for everyone else, not for you. You may have said you don't need it—but you have a problem that could kill you. You're sad, lonely, overwhelmed. Friends and family don't seem to know how to help. You feel terrified and out of control. But entering therapy means admitting you can't take care of everything yourself. It means giving up the masculine mindset of not needing anyone, and this frightens you.

As in other addictive behaviors, you may have to "hit bottom" before you can admit to needing help. Each person experiences this in a different way. For Karen, hitting bottom occurred when she could no longer deny her physical symptoms:

> *I finally realized I had a problem when I wanted to eat but couldn't, and I started falling apart in school. Friends had tried to tell me; doctors had tried too; but I was the one who had to convince myself. The day I couldn't walk I was scared—I woke up and couldn't feel my legs. The doctors couldn't find anything wrong with them. The two hospitalizations hadn't convinced me, but this did. I finally realized I was hurting me. Then I started eating and talking to my therapist.*

For others, hitting bottom is a more spiritual or abstract experience. Suzanne reported this encounter with herself:

> *I remember the turning point—it was almost mystical. I couldn't sleep and would be awake very early. One morning I got up and went for a walk around 6 o'clock. It was going to be a beautiful summer day. I felt the sun and leaned against a tree. Then I realized that I had actually felt good for a second. I hadn't felt happy in so long—it felt so good. I decided right then that I deserved it, that it wasn't worth it to keep going the way I was. I remember walking into the house and making a peanut butter and jelly sandwich. I still thank God for sunny days. I needed therapy but I wasn't ready until then.*

Even after hitting bottom, you may have misgivings about therapy. You might still believe you should try to be strong to please your dad or try to be superwoman like your mom. In either case, you're not supposed to need anyone. In relationships, you've been the giver; it's humbling to think about becoming the receiver in a relationship in which the self/other balance would be so different.

You probably also worry about what your therapist is going to expect and whether you'll be able to measure up, since you have desperately wanted approval from your dad and haven't been able to get it. Your past relationships have felt like constant demands and disappointments, so you may be skeptical about the benefits of treatment. It's hard to imagine a relationship that's there just for you.

If your approach to recovery replays the masculine myth—that you need no one, you must try to do everything yourself, and you should be able to control your life by thinking away your problems and never admitting you're sad—it's probably not going to work. Even if you can manage to change your eating and start treating your body better, that may not be enough, because it doesn't resolve the underlying causes. You need to understand *why* your conflicts with food and your body developed. You need to see your problems and emotions not as demons or enemies but as agents for change. Your feelings need to be aired, not buried, and therapy is the best way to accomplish all this.

In therapy, you have to stop wearing a mask. It is the one place where you are expected just to be yourself. You may not know who you are under the anorexic mask, bulimic mask, compulsive eater mask, or "perfect little girl" mask, and a therapist can help you along this scary road of self-discovery. Therapists are guides, trained to help others identify, understand, and express their feelings. In this safe arena, you can examine your disappointments with your dad and understand how your father hunger still affects you. Working with a therapist will show you how to express yourself and get your needs met, how to balance self and other, and how to be both separate and connected in more satisfying relationships.

A therapist who has had training and experience in treating eating disorders can be especially valuable. A specialist will know when you need additional professional support and what local experts are available to help with the medical complications that accompany eating problems. This is especially important if you have been symptomatic for a long time.

Regardless of the length of time, however, anyone with these unhealthy behaviors is at risk for serious medical complications, especially those related to cardiac functioning, hormone production, fertility, bone formation, and digestive problems. Because each of us is biochemically unique, people can have medical complications at any point. Be sure to discuss these concerns early in your treatment.

A specialist can also help you make sense of the feelings about your body associated with changes in your eating patterns. He or she can help you see how these experiences fit into your long-term recovery. When you feel hopeless, weird, or stuck, an experienced therapist can help you identify positive signs of progress.

Specialists can also identify problematic patterns of interaction in your family, and they will work with you to understand your family of origin, your place within it, and the unhealthy interactions you have replicated in other relationships. A therapist can help you distinguish the people from the patterns, so you will feel less guilty about exploring family issues. You will surely feel sad as you give up your illusions about your childhood and recognize the pain and problems that existed there. Therapy will support you through this as well.

One woman compared the experience of therapy to climbing a mountain. She saw me, her therapist, as someone she could lean on when she felt lonely, scared, helpless, or tired. She knew I would hold her up, and she wouldn't fall backward. As she worked through her fears and her self-confidence grew, she gradually found ways to support herself so that she no longer needed me as much.

Formal therapy is not the only road to recovery, although it may be the safest one for most people. In addition, you can find help by participating in support groups, attending lectures, reading books, doing new things, exploring religious or other spiritual beliefs, and just talking to people. The important thing is to open up to a new approach and leave behind the thoughts and actions that are compromising your life.

Facing the facts includes admitting that you probably don't even know what you like and don't like, what is *real*, or how to be a "real" person—because you have been so absorbed by your body and your problems with food. No matter how old you are, I recommend that you read the profound children's story *The Velveteen Rabbit*.[1] Here's my favorite excerpt:

> *"What is real?" asked the Rabbit one day. "Does it mean having things that buzz inside you and a stick-out handle?"*
>
> *"Real isn't how you are made," said the Skin Horse. "It's a thing that happens to you. When a child loves you for a long, long time, not just to play with, but really loves you, then you become Real. It doesn't happen all at once. You become. It takes a long time. Generally by the time you are Real, most of your hair has been loved off, and your eyes drop out and you get loose in the joints and very shabby. But these things don't matter at all, because once you are Real you can't be ugly, except to people who don't understand."*

Recovery is becoming real in just this way. When you are real, you value relationships and love over your appearance, your weight, or food. You no longer expend all your energy trying to look or be "perfect." You accept yourself for who you are, and you accept others for who they are. You no longer wear a mask to please others; you act from your heart. You're honest and open, and you allow others to truly know you.

To be real and to love yourself, you must give up the expectation that you should be "practically perfect in every way." You can't be daddy's little girl anymore. That unrealistic ideal cuts you off from real love. Even if your father's love is unconditional, you will never know it as long as you believe he loves the "perfect" little girl—not the real you. Just as you have to let go of the Superman myth for your father, let go of your self-imposed superwoman or perfect little girl image. The resulting reconnection with yourself will gradually lead to recovery.

Questions and New Connections

- Have you ever been real, just yourself, with anyone? Describe what that felt like.

- What masks do you wear to keep yourself from being real with your dad and other people? What if you stopped wearing these?

- Do you think your father can accept you for who you really are? Can you talk with him about this?

- What frightens you about getting better and being real? What can you do to start facing these fears?

- What kinds of support are you ready and willing to seek out? If entering therapy is scary, do you think you can do it anyway?

Connecting to Your Father

You have the right to two parents. And fathers have the right to be involved in their family's emotional lives. Try conceptualizing a new myth for your future relationship with your father and with men in general. Use what you have learned from the bad times with food to improve your relationship with your dad and build more good times into your life script. At best, you and your father can meet for the first time as two open, caring people. At least, you can understand the cycle of father hunger and its consequences in your life.

The time you devote to this will be well invested because your relationship with your dad is a blueprint for all interactions with men. Remember, history will repeat itself unless you work hard to change the painful family patterns and father hunger in your life. The anxiety you felt about whether you were doing enough for him has diminished your self-esteem, your self-confidence, your identity, and your acceptance of your body and sexuality.

Your dad may live too far away, or his own problems may make him incapable of having a healthy relationship with you. He may be unavailable, ill, or no longer living. Even if you can't change any of this, it is important for you to understand your connection with him. The insights you gain will help prevent your past anxiety, disappointments, losses, and unfulfilled expectations from compromising your future connections with boyfriends, spouses, friends, bosses, and men in general. Not only do you have the right to two parents, you also have rights in relationships with men. You will be better able to assert them if you have worked on your connection to your dad.

Give Your Dad a Chance

Just as you are unique and have developed your symptoms for your own very individual reasons, your father also deserves individual understanding. You may have angrily accused him of being less than the perfect dad you wanted. However, he was probably doing the best he could within the constraints of a very limited social role, an impossible mythic image, and the limits of his knowledge at the time. He hasn't learned how to connect with you. Give the two of you a chance. Forgive him for his imperfections and awkwardness.

Even if your dad is not available, you still have the right to know about him. Try talking to relatives or family friends to get the information he can't give you directly. Remind yourself that a complex combination of circumstances affected your father's personality and functioning as a parent, in the same way that many factors contributed to your eating disorder. Learn whatever you can about these circumstances.

For example, if one of his parents was an alcoholic, you can read literature from Alcoholics Anonymous or Adult Children of Alcoholics to gain a better understanding of what his life may have been like. If he grew up during a time of social change or political unrest, read about these events. Nonfiction will give you facts, but fiction may give you more of a feeling for how the events may have affected someone like him personally. In fact, instead of reading one more book about eating disorders, consider reading a book that will help you understand your father. Understanding his life will make it easier to forgive him for his limitations as a father.

With this understanding, you can develop more realistic expectations for your relationship. You may also be able to help him work through some of the long-standing barriers to his participation in the family. For example, asking a father to be more emotionally open and involved at home can place him in a double-bind by making two mutually exclusive demands on him. That is, society has required him to take care of his family, to protect them, and to be brave, strong, powerful, and invulnerable in the world—while now he is also being asked to be emotionally aware, to disclose his feelings, and to be vulnerable and intimate. It's especially unfair because the requirements have changed so suddenly, and society offers little help to make these changes.

Use Your I-Voice

You can enhance both your self-development and your relationship with your dad by working through your own conflict of having feelings but not expressing them. People usually hold back their feelings because they haven't learned to express them safely and responsibly. In the last chapter we considered the need for mothers to develop an "I-voice." Let's look at how valuable this will be for you too.

Imagine your father's response if you say accusingly, "You were *never* there for me when I needed you, Dad!" A blaming message like this is likely to make him feel attacked and misunderstood. He may cover up his feelings of inadequacy or guilt by an angry counterattack, and he will feel baffled or helpless about how to connect with you. He will probably stop listening, cutting off the possibility of further meaningful communication.

On the other hand, you can prevent such misunderstandings by being specific and using your I-voice: "I felt so alone and sad when you spent so much time at work. I needed to know you cared for me and were there for me." Instead of communicating blame, your I-voice takes responsibility for your own feelings. It gives you a way to share your feelings without alienating the other person. Your dad is human too; and contrary to the old myths, he has feelings. So, like the rest of us, he'll respond better to I-messages than to accusations.

As you speak in your I-voice about your experience as a daughter, you can be a model of communication for your dad. You may be ahead of him in this area, but be patient and give him a chance to learn.

Communicating and connecting with your dad doesn't mean, however, that you always have to agree. In fact, you should be disagreeing! If your parents aren't complaining about the "generation gap," you probably haven't developed enough of your *self* yet. Maybe you're protecting them from what's new and different, when you should be challenging them to understand how the world has changed since they were your age.

Let Go of the Old and Connect with the New

As you learn about the real person your father is and forgive him for his imperfections, you will be able to let go of that mythic father who was magically supposed to meet all your needs and protect you from all problems. In discarding this image, you will probably feel a loss of something that used to seem very important—maybe the security blanket of childhood or the comfort of being "daddy's little girl." However, you stand to gain something far more satisfying than an empty and outdated myth: an honest, mature relationship with your father.

You might be frightened of taking these steps. If your fear is based on the reality of an explosive or abusive father, you will have to decide carefully how, when, and whether to be more emotionally involved with him. Look to your therapist for guidance as you make these decisions. Your fear of getting to know your father might be based on the myths about men's lack of emotions and apathy about parenting. These beliefs may come tumbling down as you open up and talk with your dad.

If you are really lucky, you will be able to address your father hunger and work on your recovery with the active support and involvement of your dad. But unfortunately, many fathers have neither the interest nor the willingness to understand and improve their relationships. Although it's worth the effort to approach your dad on these issues, you may have to accept that he cannot deal with your father hunger, or with his own.

Keep working on your recovery anyway. Look for other men who can be emotionally available, safe, nurturing, and loving. They will never replace your father, but you may still be able to enjoy close relationships. Think about uncles, grandfathers, family friends, teachers, or clergymen as potential resources. A male therapist might be helpful as well. His understanding can validate your feelings. Be sure to process your father hunger as much as possible so that it doesn't continue to color every interaction you have with men.

Questions and New Connections

- How much do you know about your dad's life? How could you find out more? What are some of the circumstances that influenced him to become the person he is?

- What have you blamed your dad for? What mythical images of your dad is it time to let go of now?

- How could you take more responsibility and communicate your feelings in your I-voice? Write some conversation starters you can try using.

- If your father is no longer part of your life, or if healing your relationship with him is not a possibility, try writing your I-messages to him in an unsent letter. Who else can you share your feelings with?

Connecting to Your Family

Establishing a new relationship with your father or reconciling yourself to the old one is not the end of your work. That relationship does not exist in a vacuum. It is part of a larger family and social context. It has affected all of your interactions. Any work you do to connect with yourself or with your father will raise ripples through the whole system. Everyone in this system has suffered and needs healing in some way, although not everyone is willing or able to recognize this.

Even though your family may refuse to face the fact that your eating problems reflect underlying family issues, you need to face this. As one woman said:

> *To recover, I had to recognize all the pain in my life. I also had to accept that I could only change me, not my family. They were not interested in therapy or in talking about our problems. I had felt so deprived, but I just had to accept that and learn how to fill my own needs. Once I did, I was able to eat a cookie without eating the whole box, and I didn't have to starve myself any more.*

Once you have uncovered your pain, relieved your guilt, and said good-bye to your idyllic view of a "perfect" family, your protective armor is gone. Give yourself time to accept this loss. This will be more difficult if your family is unable to support you. You might feel stuck in anger, sadness, misunderstanding, and disappointment for a while, but with the help of therapy you should be able to move on with your life.

Liz (Chapter 7) was caught for a long time in her rage with her parents and her dream that they would change. Gradually, her therapist helped her to separate from the pain and fantasies of her childhood and form stronger connections with her future. This is how she described one of her individual therapy sessions:

> *My doctor said, "Your parents will win either way. If you die, they get lots of sympathy. If you gain weight, they'll be able to brag about their daughter who got through all this and recovered from this disease." I realized he was right. I was wasting my life because of all the horror in my family, and only I could change the result.*

Like Liz, you must accept that your needs and disappointments are real. Talk about them, mourn them, and release them, but stop wasting time fantasizing about how things could have been different. Acknowledging your losses and your pain is an essential step toward healing. Gradually letting go is another crucial step.

Revise Your Relationships

Now that you recognize how much your father's distance and unavailability have affected you, consider how this colored your relationship with your mother. Growing up, you probably had no idea what her life was really like as she carried the burdens of the family's day-to-day routine. Take another look at your childhood and your family's life. Talk to your mother about how disappointments with your father contributed to a shared unhappiness and how prescribed family roles got in the way of your relationship with her. Discuss the trouble you've had balancing self with other. If she isn't available or willing to talk in this way, it's still worthwhile for you to figure out how your disconnection with your father affected your connection with her.

Now translate how your father's role affected your connections with your siblings. Quite likely you have wounds to heal in your relationships with them. You may have competed for his attention and affection, so that you never felt comfortable with each other. You may feel slighted and misunderstood because your siblings don't understand your problems or won't discuss the family's emotional patterns. Again, it is worth your time to try to process these issues with them. With or without their self-disclosure, try to understand what was happening as you all grew up. The more pieces of the puzzle you find, the more you'll comprehend why your eating problems emerged.

Part of becoming a whole person is developing your own separate relationships with members of the extended family. While growing up, children usually relate to other relatives through their parents (often their mothers), but this limits their interactions. These relatives know you based on your family's prescribed script for you, and you are similarly acquainted with them. By meeting them on a more individual basis, you will learn a lot about your family, for you'll see things from another perspective. In turn, you will discover new things about yourself, and more of the pieces of your life's puzzle will fit together. You may even find needed support and caring in these relationships to help you weather the challenges of recovery.

Find a New Role

Separating from your old ways of interacting, finding balance between your needs and those of others, and expressing your feelings directly instead of through your body and eating necessitate a new role for you in your family. You'll want to assert yourself, instead of caving in to every demand or subtle hint at home. You will become more grounded in yourself and more aware of *why you do what you do* in these relationships. Others may be unwilling to change, but you can still alter your role in the family, and they will have to adjust. Gradually, the system will change to make more room for you and your needs. However, the burden is on you to educate the family about who you really are and what you want from them.

In your family, quite likely you have been pegged as "the sick one," "the anorexic," "the bulimic," "the black sheep," or some other limiting label. It's hard work to extract yourself from such an image, because families get stuck with labels and scripts and often resist change. Your symptoms have created a barrier that you must dismantle.

If other members are willing to participate, family therapy can be useful in this process of reconnection. There you can work on asserting yourself more openly in a safe and supportive atmosphere. The whole family can learn to show love and caring and to communicate more directly with each other.

Questions and New Connections

- How did your father's role at home influence your relationship with your mother? Your siblings?

- Which family members can support you as you address your father hunger and work toward recovery? How can you ask them for help?

- Think of a few times when you asserted yourself with your family on an issue other than your eating or your body. What did it feel like?

- Write a short paragraph or story to describe the new role you intend to play in your family.

Connecting to Your World

The transformation you have been experiencing in your relationship to yourself, your father, and your family will not stop there. Once you separate from your old method of avoiding feelings through your eating problems and you reconnect to yourself, anything is possible. Resolving your father hunger and handling issues with your family represent important steps toward translating your internal changes into external behaviors.

Gradually, all your relationships will come to reflect your newfound self-esteem. Other people—parents, siblings, relatives, friends, lovers, acquaintances, peers, co-workers, bosses, teachers—will see a stronger, more connected person negotiating interactions and giving both self and others compassion and validation. Once you discover your personal power, you can more effectively balance your needs with those of others. Your old father hunger and self-doubt retreat into the past, and you no longer need to starve, overeat, or exercise them away.

This sense of inner strength will also be evident in your relationship to the culture at large. You will be able to tolerate and withstand the negative forces that overwhelm women and exclude men in families—forces that invalidate females by reducing their worth to weight, appearance, and restraint of their eating and other appetites. You may even begin to challenge these cultural mores. You will encourage others to defy these limitations and standards and to be themselves. You will use your connection to yourself to help others separate from unhealthy ways of coping with their father hunger.

Through your recovery, you will inadvertently and unconsciously help others. Because you are different, the world is also going to be different. "The Three R's"—**Recovery Requires Reconnection**—may even expand to **Reconnection Results in Revolution**, as your new way of being in relationships empowers others to also reconnect with themselves, resolve their father hunger, and find a place in the world. The individual changes you make can eventually lead to a transformed society where men and women complement and understand each other and global girls grow up feeling valued, accepted, and loved by both parents. Father hunger will gradually fade, and women, now able to balance self and other, will no longer endanger their health to win approval from men. What a revolution!

Questions and New Connections

- How can resolving your father hunger change your life? What will be different for you?

- How is your life changing since you read this book? Give some examples of your newfound self-esteem in action.

- What is your place in the world? Can your father help you get there? How? What contributions do you hope to make to the world?

CHAPTER 14

Impasses in the Treatment of Eating Disorders

For most people with eating disorders, the road to recovery is a rocky one. Over the years, I have observed a number of impasses that present common roadblocks in the treatment of the father-daughter relationship. Facing these difficulties effectively is instrumental to therapeutic progress and the healing process.

Impasses occur when the therapy becomes stuck and static. Change seems impossible as the participants, feeling hopeless, pull away from each other and retreat into themselves. The therapist's job is to help them see what is happening that keeps them so stuck. Although the natural tendency for family members, especially fathers, is to distance themselves when they come up against these impasses, therapy must focus on helping them stay connected. Impasses are part and parcel of the therapeutic process; they are inevitable. They need to be identified, understood, and explored. An experienced therapist will look beyond them to find the keys to change, which they invariably present.

Impasses can also result from issues the therapist brings to the process of working with father-daughter issues. This type of impasse is also common. Psychiatry, psychology, social work, and family therapy have paid far too little attention to how to work effectively with fathers. In their training and personal counseling, therapists of all disciplines are encouraged to dissect and understand their issues with their mothers, while they are generally allowed to ignore or minimize issues involving their fathers. Without the necessary skills and awareness, the therapeutic community continues to emphasize the mother's role and discount the father's, contributing to obstacles rather than to change.

When Progress Seems Impossible

Therapeutic impasses occur frequently when working with fathers and daughters. Stephen Bergman and Janet Surrey, experts in the psychology of gender, have written that "male relational dread" is a major contributor to such problems. Men experience this dread when they feel inadequate or "not enough," and a common response is to either withdraw or attack.[1] Differences of opinion are often experienced as conflicts, and conflicts make most people uncomfortable. Rather than confront them directly, men will frequently attempt to evade, eliminate, or destroy conflicts as quickly as possible.

Bergman and Surrey believe that a deep fear of the potential to become violent is at the core of male relational dread and prompts this strong aversion. They identify three common impasses between men and women. The first is *dread vs. anger.* In this scenario the man retreats because of his dread of feeling inadequate and his discomfort with conflict, and the woman becomes angry. The second type of impasse is *product vs. process.* Men tend to approach emotional issues as projects or problems to be solved quickly, whereas women value the process of exploring, discussing, and processing feelings. The third type of impasse is *power over vs. power with.* When men experience conflicts or threats, they often react by wanting to gain control (take power over the situation)—while women want all voices to be heard and respected (to share power with others), so they may avoid definitive or premature resolutions.

These gender-based patterns explain many of the impasses that arise in treating families with eating disorders. The way to overcome them is to identify and deal with the conflict, keeping the family connected with one another. Fathers need to be encouraged to stay in contact rather than retreating or attacking. Mothers and daughters need to understand what drives the father's behavior, rather than automatically retreating into their anger. All need to commit to connection rather than disconnection, to speak about their own experience, and to be aware of their influence on the relationship. Instead of blaming each other for what is wrong, they can be helped to see the problems as solvable through their willingness to engage in the therapeutic process and learn to relate in new ways.

Many impasses in eating disorder treatment reflect the impact of relational dread in fathers and daughters who are struggling with their relationship. The list of impasses that follows is not exhaustive, but it gives an overview of the most common themes. Nor are these impasses mutually exclusive; most father-daughter pairs will experience a combination. However, working through one impasse can help a family identify and overcome others more readily.

Impasse: This is women's work.

A man who defines his parenting role in strictly traditional terms may not feel that he is responsible for helping his daughter overcome her eating disorder. He has been so busy being the breadwinner that he has little concept of what else he might have to offer his family. He may appear unemotional and absent to his daughter, blaming his wife for the problems and holding her responsible for finding solutions. This "women's work" attitude is sometimes articulated out loud, with much arguing, accusing, and undermining by the father. More often, however, it is more covert, with the father showing reluctance to participate in therapy, provide emotional support, or show much interest in understanding the situation. The father may simply "check out" of the family dynamic.

A daughter caught in this impasse feels insignificant and invisible to the father who doesn't seem to care about her. A feeling of worthlessness, combined with guilt over causing a problem for the family, may sink her further into depression and eating disorder symptoms. She may "up the ante," becoming even more symptomatic (losing more weight, purging more often or more openly) to get her father involved.

In this scenario, no one feels appreciated. The father feels criticized for not doing enough, the mother feels criticized for either doing too much or doing things wrong, and the daughter feels guilty for not being perfect. Such an emotional environment is not conducive to recovery. Let's look at some ways of resolving this impasse.

Some Solutions

Give credit where credit is due. More often than not, both parents have been doing their best, and each needs to recognize the contributions the other is making to their daughter's life. Helping daughters see that fathers often show they care in indirect ways is important. A father may feel he has amply demonstrated his love by working hard to assure financial stability and provide resources such as insurance and money for college. If the daughter comes to see that both parents love her but show it differently, this may help her feel more worthy of love and life.

Specific actions. A man may need very specific ideas about how to become involved in order to feel good enough as a parent and avoid his relational dread. Both mother and daughter can be encouraged to identify some specific things that dad can do to be constructively involved in the daughter's recovery and in the family in general. Helping with the grocery shopping or preparing meals might relieve mom if those burdens have all been hers to bear. Spending time together, playing a game, going for a drive, or watching a movie together after a meal might help the daughter cope with the discomfort she feels after eating. Just by spending more time with her, dad can help her feel more important and more worthy of life.

Encourage the parents to reexamine their roles. Working through this impasse requires a father to develop a new job description for himself. Being a provider can no longer be about money and financial stability alone. A father also needs to provide emotional security and attention to his daughter and family. Finding ways for the couple to alter their stereotypical behavior is critical. The daughter's eating disorder presents an opportunity for every family member to find a more satisfying balance of responsibilities. Even if they are unable to make major changes because of extenuating circumstances, talking about this will help each person feel more involved, respected, responsible, and appreciated. It will also decrease the tension at home.

Impasse: "Just eat!"

Men are taught to simplify problems so they can find a quick answer and move on. Consequently, fathers tend to have difficulty with the complex process of recovery from an eating disorder. In their male culture, relationships to food and to their bodies are usually far less complicated, and they may have little idea about the loaded meanings that food and weight have assumed for their daughter. A father who feels anxious and "over his head" or out of his comfort zone may avoid his relational dread by simplifying the problem and ignoring the underlying meaning of his daughter's eating and body image issues.

"Just eat" will definitely be seen as an attack, a premature resolution, and a dismissal of her personhood. A daughter with an eating disorder already feels misunderstood, weird, hopeless, out of control, and alone. Hearing "Just eat" only makes her feel worse. Since the eating disorder developed to give her a sense of control and effectiveness that she couldn't find otherwise, forceful orders to eat make her frightened, anxious, and unlikely to respond.

Some Solutions

Developing insight. A therapist can help a father become more aware of the tendency to try to exert power over eating disorder-related impulses instead of making the effort to understand them. Individual therapy can help a man contain and redirect this tendency, learn to express his feelings and manage his anxiety, and develop respect for the process of insight and change necessary to his daughter's recovery. Therapy can also help him understand how complex food and eating can be for women. Reading, attending a parents' group, and listening to women talk about food and weight issues are also valuable. Repeating a key phrase of self-intervention (similar to a mantra) every time he begins to say "Just eat" may help a father subdue his controlling tendencies. Some suggested examples are "Just love her" and "I can't control. I can understand."

Shared feelings. When a father learns to share his feelings of desperation and anxiety in a less threatening way, his daughter may actually feel cared about instead of attacked. Both father and daughter need to discuss how out of control they feel. No one does well when attacked, but we thrive when we feel cared for, listened to, and understood.

Anger is OK. Encourage daughters to express the anger they feel when fathers don't understand or try to simplify their problems. Hearing the words "Just eat" will make most women with an eating disorder feel angry and misunderstood. This is a great opportunity to validate a daughter's anger and help her express it directly to its source instead of through her body.

Impasse: Whose life is it, anyway?

Fathers can become very controlling when they are anxious about their daughter's problems. Feeling inadequate and overwhelmed, some men will go beyond misguided commands such as "Just eat" and engage in inappropriate aggressive attacks and authoritarian behavior. A father may try to force his daughter to eat or even physically punish her for her symptoms. This is disastrous, as the eating disorder represents her flawed attempt to gain control when she feels totally ineffective and incapable of dealing with life. In this context, punitive or authoritative behavior is completely counterproductive. The daughter will become more entrenched in her symptoms, which only get worse and worse.

This does not mean that a father should do nothing to help—but *what* he does is critical. Fathers of younger daughters need to take a more active approach than those with older daughters, but even adult women benefit from a concerned and engaged dad. Paternal involvement should respect the daughter's developmental needs because, regardless of her age, a daughter cannot get better and stay well unless she feels that she is in control of her life. It's as simple as that.

Some Solutions

Teamwork. Work with a therapist can help a father define appropriate limit-setting behaviors and contain his tendency to attack. For example, there are times when external control of activities such as exercise can be very useful. Interrupting periods of excessive exercise, not allowing new exercise equipment into the house, and withdrawing a gym membership are all within reason if recommended by the therapists involved. Any restrictions like this must be joint efforts by both parents, however, not just edicts from dad. A father needs to convey his reasons for taking such actions in a calm, nonhostile manner. Since his eating disordered daughter is already overly punitive with herself, the father will want to be very careful about the messages he conveys when attempting to limit or control her activities.

Accountability. If a father does react punitively, harshly, or angrily, he must take responsibility for his actions, apologize, and commit to handling his feelings more constructively in the future. Individual therapy or a men's support group can be quite helpful. Aggressive behavior, no matter how stressful the illness is for the family, must be addressed and stopped.

Talk about it. Daughters need to explore and articulate family patterns that contribute to their feeling out of control. The family may have other problems they are not addressing, which create anxiety and stress. Rigidly prescribed family roles and expectations may lead the daughter to feel that the only thing she can control is her food intake. Once these issues are brought out into the open, it will be easier for the daughter to develop a sense of personal effectiveness apart from food and weight.

Impasse: Progress takes patience.

Fathers frequently have great difficulty accepting the slow pace of recovery that is necessary to overcome a serious eating disorder. While mothers may also be impatient, they generally express less frustration and anger. This dichotomy exemplifies the *process vs. product* impasse: men are eager to finish a job and arrive at closure in order to avoid feeling inadequate or not "man enough," while women want to discuss the feelings and process of change, accepting that issues related to weight, body image, and food can be very deep and complicated.

When a father expresses impatience or frustration, his daughter feels responsible but becomes immobilized because if she *could* change any faster, she would. She simply has to be allowed to progress at her own pace. Her dad's impatience makes her sink further into despair and self-hatred, feeling unable to please him or gain control of her life. Black-and-white or dichotomous reasoning is a common characteristic of people who develop eating disorders, making it difficult for them to see the shades of progress they have achieved.

Some Solutions

Self-inventory. Therapy can help a father recognize that his impatience reflects feelings of inadequacy and fear. To avoid these uncomfortable emotions, he resorts to an urgent drive to solve the problem and finish the job. Fathers can be encouraged to examine the roots of their impatience and its impact on their relationships in the family.

The man in the mirror. Recovery requires patience from everyone involved. A father's pressure for a timetable for recovery is understandable in light of his role as the problem solver. Yet this demand truly slows the progress of therapy. His daughter will gradually become more positive about herself if she is allowed time to recover. Instead of pressuring his daughter, a father can be asked to identify something he wants to change about himself and be challenged to work on it—this will help him understand how difficult it is to modify one's behavior.

Get smarter. Education about the course of eating disorder illnesses and the recovery process will be helpful in understanding the timing and pace of recovery. Fathers need to realize that eating disorders are illnesses of the psyche and soul, not just obsessive weight loss techniques. Recovery is a spiritual journey that cannot be rushed. In fact, when treatment is too aggressive and rapid, the likelihood of relapse is very high. In recovery, slow and steady wins the race.

Impasse: Separate the person from the illness.

Another example of *product vs. process* is the tendency of parents to turn their daughter's illness into a problem to be solved. When parents focus mostly on their daughter's eating disorder, this reinforces her despairing belief that she has no other identity. Feeling that her family relates to her only as a bulimic or an anorexic will make her feel disgusted with herself, as if the illness completely defines her.

Women who develop eating disorders are usually struggling with their identity. No matter how many positive attributes others see in them, they are convinced that their only strength or unique quality is their illness. Thus, a father's attempt to avoid personal issues by making his daughter's eating problem into a project will actually reinforce her conviction and slow down her recovery. Furthermore, the daughter will feel disrespected and diminished, believing that her father cares only about her problem—and not about her as a person.

Some Solutions

Be important. A father should not underestimate his importance to his daughter. Although it may seem that the eating disorder is more important to her than anything else, a father must remember that this stems from her lack of identity and deep feelings of worthlessness. The illness is a symptom, not the underlying cause of her problem. Fathers offer the greatest help when they relate to their daughters as people, not as a depersonalized "anorexic," "bulimic," or "binger." This is especially challenging when they are worried about their daughter's health and are feeling out of control, but fathers can have a very important influence on a daughter's identity simply by recognizing her as a whole person and acknowledging her strengths and positive qualities.

Be interested. Fathers should be encouraged to ask their daughters less about their illness and more about their lives, feelings, interests, opinions, and activities. Most men have a lot to learn because they haven't been paying enough attention. A dad's sincere interest will help his daughter immeasurably with her need to find other aspects of herself and of life with which to replace the eating disorder.

Ask how to help. A father who turns his daughter's illness into a project is also exhibiting a *power over vs. power with* tendency. He is trying to control the problem rather than find ways to cooperate in addressing it. This disempowers his daughter. Fathers need to be encouraged to resist the tendency to objectify and attack the eating disorder and instead, actively ask how they can help.

Impasse: The Superman phenomenon

In taking on the role of Superman, ever poised and ready to save the day, fathers subliminally suggest that women cannot solve their own problems—only powerful men can. This reinforces residual gender inequities in modern culture, which contribute to eating disorders. Too often, global girls still see strong women mocked, ridiculed, and belittled, as the global culture has yet to accept true female power. Their reaction to this systematic cultural subordination is to employ their bodies and appearance in the effort to feel more powerful and respected.

When a father takes on the Superman role, he strengthens the core reasons for which the eating disorder developed in the first place. For example, by vigorously attacking the problem and taking over, he implies distrust that his daughter will be able to recover on her own. A father may also undermine or usurp a role the mother had held, provoking the daughter to see her mother as overruled and powerless. This, in turn, reinforces the feelings of inadequacy she experiences when she sees men enjoying more power and respect than women. This impasse exemplifies the *power over vs. power with* dynamic so frequently found in the father-daughter relationship.

Some Solutions

Self-assessment. Men who do not see women as equals will have great difficulty helping their daughters establish power, autonomy, and self-confidence. A rigorous personal inventory may be in order, as painful as that may be. Once a father understands the ramifications of his gender-based attitudes, he will be better prepared to see how these play out in his relationship with his daughter and to support her in resolving her conflicts about assuming power and taking charge of her life.

Honest opinions. People are often unaware of their own gender-based attitudes and beliefs. The safe confines of family therapy can allow a father to explore these and expand his awareness by asking the women in his life—especially his wife and daughters—for honest feedback about his attitudes and behaviors. Most men today do not want to convey such biases to their growing daughters. But they may do so anyway when they are unaware of them.

Lose the Superman costume. A little feminism can go a long way toward helping girls and women overcome eating disorders. Fathers can take a stand to embrace feminism and fight for gender equity. To do this, they will have to shed the Superman costume, believe that their daughters are capable of recovery, and support the process—without trying to take over.

Impasse: Too little, too late

Confronted with the crisis of a daughter's illness, a father may genuinely come to see the importance of being involved in her life and recovery. Suddenly he is eager to get to know his daughter, spend time with her, and help her in any way he can. He realizes what he has missed as a father, and perhaps he understands that his daughter has also missed a great deal. He may reassess his priorities and become much more involved in family life.

These changes, however, aren't always welcomed or trusted by his daughter, who is still struggling with the hurt from years of distance and misunderstanding. The emotional damage of the past will need to be acknowledged and worked through before she can open the closed doors.

A father who has learned to focus more on the product than on the process may not see the importance of exploring these issues, and he may resist. He may be eager to make a fresh start, while his daughter needs to go back and reflect on the past and her backlog of emotions. Or she may have reached a point in her own development when she wants more separateness from the family and is not willing to invest the time needed to rebuild this relationship. Resulting feelings of inadequacy can provoke a father to attack or quickly retreat if his daughter is unresponsive to his well-intentioned efforts.

Some Solutions

Emotional leadership. A daughter's anger does not have to signify the end of the world. Strong emotions can be frightening, but they are best managed by listening with an attitude of fatherly love and a sincere desire to understand. A daughter may have accumulated a large store of anger over many years when her father was uninvolved or only superficially involved in her life. Fathers need to move beyond their initial reaction of feeling attacked and threatened, and instead respect their daughter's feelings of anger. A father may have to accept that his daughter does not trust him despite his good intentions.

To heal this relationship, the father must overcome his own dread of inadequacy and be willing to delve into the past and to process feelings. If his daughter chooses not to be involved in family therapy with him, he needs to explore these issues anyway. This alone will show the commitment he has made to real change. Ultimately, his daughter may be willing to reengage if she sees her father working on emotional issues.

Respect her needs. A daughter who has been deeply hurt by her father needs to be in charge of how and when to involve him in her treatment. Attempts to force the relationship won't be therapeutic. If the timing is not right for in-depth father-daughter work, a dad may benefit from parent counseling, psychoeducation about the disease process, and group or individual therapy.

Staying focused on the client. Therapists naturally have their own reactions and agendas in relation to reuniting a father and daughter (more on this in the following section). The important key is to be aware of this countertransference and moderate its influence. A therapist may be overly responsive to the father's desire for involvement and insufficiently responsive to the daughter's pace and needs. This may arise out of the therapist's own unresolved issues, beliefs, or feelings. Keep in mind that successful treatment of eating disorders requires that girls and women be listened to and respected fully.

Impasse: Father vs. mother—unresolved issues

In this impasse, the father is genuinely trying to get to know and help his daughter. The daughter is responsive, feeling positive about her father's interest and efforts. Things are going well. But then the mother begins to interfere, perhaps suggesting that the father cannot be trusted or is not going to stay involved.

When this occurs, the relationship between the parents needs attention. Long-standing or ignored marital or parental conflicts must be identified and explored. A mother may feel that her role has been unappreciated and is now being usurped. She may also experience a loss of the exclusive closeness she previously felt with her daughter, or she may be angry or jealous that the daughter is getting attention and she is not. Changes in a family system tend to disrupt the equilibrium so that roles and relationships need to be revisited and revised. This impasse is an opportunity for positive change for everyone.

Some Solutions

Minding connections. Fathers can take a leadership role by being sensitive to the feelings mothers may have when a closer father-daughter relationship emerges. Therapists also need to be aware of how they may inadvertently have contributed to this impasse. Their eagerness to involve a father might undermine the efforts of the mother who may have been carrying the full burden of childcare and the family's emotional well-being. When things go wrong for a child, especially when a daughter develops an eating disorder, a mother tends to feel guilty. If the father then steps in and takes over, the mother may feel even worse, getting caught up in a cycle of self-blame and anger.

This impasse can be avoided or alleviated if the parents talk openly about how the father's involvement affects the mother-daughter relationship and other family dynamics. Rather than a narrow focus on the *product* of the father's relationship with his daughter, a broader focus needs to include the *process* and how the new insights and adjustments are affecting the entire family.

Mending the spousal relationship. If marital issues have been swept under the rug for years, this impasse will be complicated and recovery will be more difficult. A daughter may be easily triangulated into a couple's problems because she is generally so eager to please both parents and keep them happy. This keeps her focused on others' needs instead of her own. Couple therapy is the best solution.

Acting as one. No child should have to choose a relationship with one parent over the other. A mother can find ways to stay close to her daughter despite feeling somewhat displaced by the father. The father can contribute by supporting the mother's importance while he builds his own relationship with their daughter. Both parents should be aware that competing with each other for a starring role in her life will only undermine her recovery. Defining how each can help and developing feelings of partnership instead of competition will facilitate it.

Impasse: High stakes: how long will he stay?

This is a very common impasse. Recognizing the crisis, many fathers step up to the plate, become very appropriately involved in the family, in therapy, and in their daughter's life. They are doing all the right things, everything a therapist asks and more, but the daughter seems stuck and is not making progress. Quite possibly, she does not believe he will stay involved if she gets better. The cost of recovery may seem too high if her illness is the only thing that has ever been able to catch her father's attention.

Some Solutions

Clarity from the start. Discussing this impasse at the initiation of therapy can be very helpful. Fathers must be challenged to take their children's needs seriously and make a lasting commitment to them. A father needs to understand and accept that his daughter has solid reasons to distrust him if he has been emotionally absent, and that more than a guest appearance in her life will be necessary. A father who sees his daughter's recovery as a *process vs. a product* is less likely to encounter this impasse, as his focus will be on the relationship rather than on how her symptoms are changing.

Staying power. A daughter who believes that her father is going to stay involved in her life is more likely to take steps toward getting better. To prove his staying power, a father will be challenged to pass many tests. He will need to be patient with the time it takes to recover and accept that his daughter may express difficult feelings and explore tough issues in the process.

Unconditional positive regard. The bond of trust is strengthened when a father is able to stay present and convey unconditional positive regard while his daughter grows into herself as a young adult and develops her own personal identity—even to the extent of daring to challenge him. If dad can do this, his daughter will gradually believe she can get better without losing him.

Impasse: Logic doesn't work—love does.

This is the most important message in this book. Believe me, no one has ever been *talked* out of an eating disorder, no matter who does the talking or how convincing or knowledgeable she or he is. Eating disorders are not logical, so logic cannot undo them. Very often, fathers believe that they can convince their daughter to simply change her behavior and give up her symptoms. They work hard to become experts, reading everything they can, visiting websites, talking to others—then they begin to lecture their daughter.

It's no secret that lectures are disempowering. But many fathers adopt this approach to stave off relational dread: attacking, turning their fear into a solvable problem, and assuming a *power over vs. power with* approach. A daughter again comes to believe that her father cares only about understanding her illness, not about *her*. She feels reduced to the old depersonalized feeling that she is nothing more than her anorexic or bulimic symptoms. This can be a special challenge to fathers who are physicians. With their knowledge and tendency to take charge, they can have great difficulty accepting that the cure is not logic, but love.

Some Solutions

Just feel it. No matter how chaotic feelings may seem, they are a very basic and essential part of human nature. The alienation of a father from feelings erects an impenetrable barrier between him and the females in his family, as well as between vital aspects of his own identity. How can a father understand his daughter's feelings if he doesn't allow himself to experience his own and is uncomfortable talking about them? Crossing into his daughter's emotional world will seem like venturing into a foreign land!

To reach into the heart of a daughter with an eating disorder, a father must commit to exploring the unfamiliar territory of emotions. This requires risk and practice. The therapist can offer valuable assistance in facilitating the exploration of feelings, teaching and modeling the language used to release and talk about feelings, and interpreting their meaning and message. Everyone benefits when fathers confront their fears and become more in touch with their emotions.

Stop the lecture. While being educated about the illness is very important for fathers, lecturing their daughter based on this information is actually harmful. Lectures put distance between people and create an unhealthy power dynamic. Furthermore, quite often daughters already know everything their fathers are saying, as they have read about eating disorders and have been counseled by teachers, nurses, dietitians, therapists, doctors, and friends. In the many years I have treated women of all ages, a lecture has never been the turning point in eating disorder recovery.

So every time a father catches himself launching into a lecture, he should remind himself that this ineffective approach is a sign of his own underlying issues. The louder his logic gets, the more out of control he actually feels. An awareness of this dynamic will help him switch to a more fruitful approach of open and loving receptiveness. He can try repeating this mantra: "Logic doesn't work. Love does." Or, "Love, not logic."

Give it time. Fathers often do not understand how unlovable their daughters feel. This impasse may take a long time to work through. No matter how difficult it is, fathers must persist and resist the impulse to retreat, even if they feel they are not being heard or having any effect. A wise woman once said to me, "The tincture of time is the best medicine." Time heals many wounds. A daughter's healing takes time. A father's love needs time to grow and be felt by his daughter. Give it all the time it needs.

Countertransference Impasses

Impasses such as those just described could be considered necessary to the therapeutic process because they are the reason people come for help. When they realize they are stuck in their lives and relationships, and when symptoms develop, this provides the essential impetus to begin therapy.

On the other hand, the type of impasses we will discuss next, clinically defined as *countertransference*, are issues the therapist brings into the therapeutic process. It would seem that these are entirely unnecessary. Therapists should not bring unresolved conflicts or issues from their childhood and personal life into their clinical work—but they do. And these can wreak havoc when treating serious problems such as eating disorders.

Having trained and supervised many clinicians, I have observed four common types of contertransference impasses in therapists' approach to the father-daughter relationship: insufficient awareness, residual anger and unresolved issues with the therapist's own father, inadequate training, and apathy. All eating disorder specialists need to become aware of these impasses, determine if they are present in their work, and commit to addressing them personally and professionally.

One of the wonderful aspects of clinical work is that therapists are constantly challenged to grow, develop insight, and improve themselves. The downside is that this effort can be tiring and draining. Nevertheless, a dedicated clinician will make a commitment to career-long personal and professional growth. The dividends are felt in our work with clients as well as in our own lives.

Impasse: Insufficient Awareness

An important prerequisite for working effectively in the arena of eating disorders is for therapists to build awareness of their relationship to their own father. Start by reviewing the myths in Chapter 3. Identify which ones reflect your family of origin, and consider other myths that may have subliminally affected your family. Explore the primary myths about fathers that dominated your experience growing up and how they have affected you personally. If you now have a family of your own, you may have hoped to create very different myths and relationships. Have you been able to do so?

Once you have grasped how your relationship with your father has influenced you personally, you can begin to examine how it affects your clinical work, especially with fathers and daughters. This awareness is central to working effectively with men in general, and it is especially critical in working with families. Without it, clinicians are rarely able to address issues of power, authority, and gender roles in the family. Trainees, young therapists, and many female clinicians may be challenged by fathers who demonstrate little respect for their authority. Those who have developed insight and resolved their own issues with paternal figures and male authority will be much better prepared to weather these storms.

Some Solutions

Guided introspection. To further build awareness, take the time to do the following guided introspection. (This is also a great exercise for a supervision group or a men's group.)

Commit yourself to a quiet hour or two with no distractions, dedicated to building your awareness about the role your father has played in your life. Choose a comfortable place to sit and reflect. Do some stretching and deep breathing to relax before you begin. Place a pen and paper or journal nearby to record your responses and feelings when you finish. Make this a special experience. Take your time as you consider the following questions.

- When you were growing up, what role did your father play in your family?
- How did your father interact with your mother? With your brothers and sisters? With you?
- What feelings did he express? How?
- How did he influence your ability to express feelings?
- How close did you feel to him as a small child?
- How did the relationship change as you grew up?
- How would you describe your ideal father?
- How close to the ideal was your dad?
- Did you get enough from your father? Other than material things, what did he give you?
- What is the one thing you cherish above all the other things he gave you?
- How did he disappoint you?
- Were you hungry for more contact with your father? Are you still?
- Do you feel loved by your father? Respected? Accepted?
- Did you feel unconditional positive regard from your dad?
- How much have you allowed your father to know you?
- Does he know the real you?
- What were your father's expectations of you?
- Did you meet these?
- Have you disappointed him?
- Have you felt close to him? When? Under what circumstances?
- Do you have to perform to earn his love?
- Are you still trying to make your father proud?
- How open and honest can you be with him?
- What relationships with other people have you formed to fill your unmet needs for a loving father?
- How has your relationship with your father affected your choice of professions?

- What does your father think about your work? How does that affect you?
- What are you trying to prove to your father at this point in your life?
- How are you trying to connect to your father through your work?
- What is the most secret thing you never said to your father but wish you had?
- What is the one thing you most wish your dad had said to you or done?
- To more fully grasp the interface of the personal and professional issues that stem from your relationship with your father, discuss your new insights in supervision or with a trusted colleague or friend.

Impasse: Residual anger and unresolved issues with dad

Many therapists avoid addressing the father-daughter relationship because of their own residual anger with their father. To work effectively with families, they must first release their anger and make peace with their father. When clinicians consciously or subconsciously hang on to their anger or disappointment, they can't help families to resolve theirs and move through therapeutic impasses. Instead of engaging in a game of blame and shame in their clinical work, which only maintains fathers and daughters in their old impasses and stalemates, they need to understand how factors such as prescribed roles and economic pressures affected their father's ability to parent.

Some Solutions

Take time to inventory how cultural expectations for boys and men and relational dread may have affected your father's parenting. Consider how the gender-related impasses of *dread vs. anger, product vs. process*, and *power over vs. power with* were played out in your family. Try to comprehend all the factors that constrained your father and kept him stuck. Find your own therapeutic resources and go to work with them. Accept your anger and do not let it paralyze you as it did your dad. Put it into words, and see what can be learned from it. Commit to let it go and to help prevent other families from suffering in the same way.

Joe Kelly's "Five Hurdles for Fathers"[2] can serve as a good reminder of the major issues that interfere with positive father-daughter relationships. Briefly, these are:

1. Men grew up as boys, with a whole different cultural experience. Girls are typically a mystery to them.

2. Most fathers have no one to talk to. They are not encouraged to talk about parenting the way women are and have few if any forums where it is safe to do this.

3. Society stereotypes men as either incompetent bumblers or superheroes. Confused by such divergent and unrealistic roles, they have little guidance about how to relate.

4. The father's role as provider has been defined as his earning power. That places a great deal of pressure on him and limits other ways for him to contact and know his kids.

5. Most men had fathers who generally were not great examples of emotionally available men and did not talk about their experience or desires as parents.

These constraints have paralyzed men in their roles, even when they do have a strong desire for closeness and connection. Understanding these hurdles can help therapists to resolve their own residual anger, develop empathy for fathers, and work effectively with families.

Impasse: Inadequate Training

Since clinical training does not emphasize understanding of the father's importance and influence, it's not surprising that it does little to teach or promote fathering skills. While men and women are not from different planets as has been alleged, they do have some different needs and propensities in treatment.

The world of therapy is much easier for women than for men. While women are often encouraged to talk about feelings and value relationships, men are consistently discouraged from doing so. This has serious implications for therapy, as most men don't have the vocabulary of emotions or the comfort in expressing feelings that women have. They also fear being accused and blamed. Despite a sometimes tough exterior, they often feel inadequate and not enough. No matter how much a man loves his children, it can be frightening to walk into a therapist's office. Realizing this, the therapist can help to make it easier for him. Clinical training for therapists needs to include better preparation for understanding the male perspective.

Some Solutions

Clinicians who have worked through their own issues with their fathers will be much better prepared to engage fathers and make the therapeutic experience more welcoming. That's a great start, but it's not enough. The therapist also needs to work with the father's individual strengths and weaknesses.

One common weakness is the father's lack of intuition and understanding about what the women in their lives need. Clinicians can be most effective by being very specific and concrete in their counsel, especially at first. Fathers require factual information about the illness process, about the many contributing factors, and, most of all, about the stressors of growing up as a girl in contemporary culture. They also need specific lessons about how they can help and how they can't, as well as information about the experience of recovery. (See "What Fathers Need to Know About Recovery" and "What Fathers Can and Can't Do for a Daughter with Eating Disorders" in Chapter 11.)

Clinicians should also examine what they can do logistically to involve fathers more. The reality is that most men have little flexibility in their jobs because, as a culture, we have not yet accepted the importance of fathers in the family. Furthermore, men still significantly out-earn women, and dads feel very pressured economically, as the family is often dependent on their income and job security. Therapists can work to encourage agencies, employers, and policy makers to understand the importance and benefits of allowing fathers time to be fully engaged in their families. Scheduling therapy appointments on evenings and Saturdays and using a speaker phone when fathers are unable to be physically present can help make it easier for them to participate.

More than anything else, letting fathers know how important they are will help many to make the commitment needed to begin healing the father-daughter relationship. After all, being important is an idea that men are accustomed to recognizing as an affirmation of their power. The challenge is to help them utilize that importance in a new and constructive way.

Impasse: Apathy

Apathy is a disguise for avoidance. Apathy concerning father-daughter issues should serve as a strong indicator that the therapist is actively avoiding difficult emotions and unresolved issues from his or her own experience. Therapists who minimize the importance of the father-daughter relationship and do not allow a daughter to express the grief she feels have probably also been ignoring or denying their own loss, often for years and years. To be of any help to women with eating disorders, they must confront this.

Some clinicians encourage a daughter's expression of her needs but cannot allow a father time for his. This reflects a deep fear of male emotions that is shared by many in our global culture. Clinicians may wonder if they will be able to deal with men's feelings at both a personal and a professional level. If Humpty Dumpty falls, will they be able to put him back together again?

Finally, some clinicians do not believe that men will be able to step up to the therapeutic challenge, so they don't create the opportunity for a father and daughter to try. They may be trying to protect the daughter from pain, or they may be avoiding their own feelings of disappointment and anger.

Some Solutions

Supervision, introspection, open discussions with colleagues and friends, and individual therapy are all positive avenues for addressing apathy and ending avoidance. The payoff is that the therapist's clinical skills will improve, as will his or her comfort and confidence in both personal and professional relationships.

Summary of Ways Therapists Can Make a Difference

Clinicians are taught to be objective, impartial, and dispassionate. But we are human. Ultimately, we bring our own emotional realities to our work. By recognizing our own issues and the prism through which we see our clients, we become more effective therapists.

The following list provides a summary of approaches therapists can take to advance the therapeutic understanding and treatment of eating disorders.

- Explore the culture's impact on your experiences and attitudes by examining your expectations of men in families and your attitudes toward women, weight, food, appearance, and sex roles. Use this knowledge to guide your clinical work.

- Educate yourself about the psychological and physiological consequences of eating disordered behaviors.

- Explore and understand the patient's family dynamics and compare them to your own. This will help to change patterns instead of duplicating past dynamics in the therapeutic relationship.

- Assess each case individually. Listen acutely to help patients follow their own inner wisdom. Resist any impulse to generalize or stereotype. Although symptoms are similar, the underlying reasons are always unique.

- Help patients gain control of their symptoms by involving other professionals, such as dietitians and medical doctors, as needed, so the long-term work of therapy can take place.

- Move from apathy to activism. Convert your anger into positive actions. To overcome eating disorders, we need major social change, but this only happens when we are fed up with the past. In 1955 Rosa Parks was tired of giving up her seat on the bus in Montgomery, Alabama. Her angry reaction and refusal to comply with socially accepted injustice helped to ignite the civil rights movement that has transformed

American culture. Start a movement of your own—take action to help fathers and daughters enjoy a closer, more satisfying relationship. Encourage changes in families and in the culture that will allow more equitable sharing of power and responsibility between the sexes, so fathers can be more involved in the family and the world becomes friendlier and fairer to women.

Why We All Must Prevent Father Hunger

We have covered much territory as we have explored father hunger—its origins, manifestations, and solutions. I hope this has enabled you to see that men do not necessarily choose to be uninvolved, nor are they physiologically or psychologically destined to be remote fathers. The role we have assigned to them too often results in their feeling unappreciated and left out of the family. Given the opportunity, however, men can be positively and wonderfully involved with their children. Now that we know fathers can do it, our challenge is to create a system that will allow it to occur more frequently.

These changes in men's roles and family life are no longer an option or a choice: they are a necessity! As we discussed in the chapter "Getting to Know Your Global Girl," life is becoming more and more complex for each generation. A girl who has not felt loved and accepted by her dad is likely to develop conflicts about her self-worth, body image, and place in this world. Father hunger contributes to many other mental health and behavior problems in children and adolescents, including juvenile delinquency, conduct disorder, school failure, and impulsive behaviors. Teachers, counselors, school administrators, and therapists often conclude that children's problems could be greatly reduced if their fathers were more actively involved in their lives. So, for the sake of all children—the girls who will internalize their hurt, disappointment, and rejection and will endanger their health by battling their bodies, and the boys who will externalize their anger and act out in a manner that is both self-destructive and destructive to others—we must end father hunger now.

The Appendixes to this book conceptualize how people in various roles can work to reverse father hunger. They also suggest strategies to stimulate your thinking about what you can do to bring about changes. We must make men a more integral part of the family, give women more security and respect in their role in the world, and help children to grow up with the resources they need to survive in a culture that promotes unhealthy eating, emphasizes appearance and weight, and sets masculinity and femininity up as opposing forces. Use these ideas as a springboard for your own creative thinking and planning. They are only a beginning, but they may point you in the right direction.

I hope that you will use the information, ideas, and suggestions from this book to effect change in your own relationships, as well as to work toward systemic changes that will improve all of our lives. When we think about major social issues such as father hunger, we may be tempted to conclude that the problems are beyond our control. They seem so huge and insurmountable, we feel helpless and powerless to do anything about them. However, there is always something we can do. Margaret Mead once said, "Never underestimate the power of a small, dedicated group of people to change the world; indeed, that is the only thing that ever has."[1]

And Gandhi said, "You must *be* the change you wish to see in the world."[2] All transformation begins with the self. When we change ourselves, we affect many other people. So the best way to begin is by changing your old, archaic beliefs: get rid of those old myths about men and how their daughters don't need them. Recognize how you have needed your father and why he was not able to meet your needs. After you have faced your own wounds or scars from your relationship with your dad, you'll be able to help the men in your life have fuller, more emotionally connected lives. You will help to reverse father hunger as you personally work to pave a more positive role for fathers in which men and women share power and responsibility in the family.

It is time to rewrite the old myths and scripts. Remember: "If you're not part of the solution, you're part of the problem."[3] Think of new scripts that empower both men and women to achieve their potential as individuals, partners, and parents. Each us must figure out how to combine the pain of the past with our hopes for the future and how to separate from the old ways of being together and connect to the new. With your hard work, commitment, and creativity, life will be better for everyone.

Imagine a world where both men and women feel comfortable, powerful, supported, valued, loved, and loving. Imagine what would happen if we could raise children in an environment with men and women equally sharing responsibility and caretaking. Imagine global girls feeling welcomed into the adult world and knowing they don't have to prove their worth through their appearance or weight. Imagine fathers feeling satisfied, included, and connected. Imagine both men and women finding balance between self and other, between separateness and connectedness. Imagine a way to be part of the solution and no longer part of the problem. Just imagine . . . then take action.

APPENDIXES

Appendix A

Suggested Strategies for Educators

The educational environment is rich with valuable resources for teaching and encouraging family and cultural change. Most families with children are involved in some public or private school setting. In fact, increasing numbers of children are enrolled in formal day care from infancy on, making it possible for education professionals to recognize and prevent eating problems at an early age.

If you question whether schools should be involved in family problems or cultural change, consider the derivation of the word educate. Its Latin origin, educare, means "to lead out of." The educational system can help lead us out of the dilemma of father hunger by offering insight and solutions. Already, many male educators play important roles in children's lives. Male teachers, coaches, guidance counselors, and principals often find themselves spending extra time with boys who show the need for paternal attention. Unfortunately, because of our myths about girls' development, many caring male educators have not yet realized how important their influence can be to female students.

Schools are already facing the consequences of our long legacy of dysfunctional family systems. Involving them in prevention and intervention makes good sense.

Promote a Constructive Role for Men in Families

Educators should get to know the fathers of their students. Schedule meetings or phone conversations before work or in the evening for men who are unable to leave their jobs during the day. Reinforce the importance of fathers' participation in their children's education. Discuss the value of a father's encouragement, support, and praise. Be sure to share information equally with both parents; avoid using the mother as the primary link to the family.

Schools can also involve fathers by setting up opportunities that invite them to introduce and apply their special skills, knowledge, interests, and hobbies within educational programs. Community-based programs can do this too. Male staff members can be made aware of their special role of modeling ways in which men can provide emotional support, nurturing, and concerned interest in children.

Both schools and community groups can sponsor stimulating discussions on parenting, with a special focus on the importance of fathering and ways parents can work together effectively even when they are stressed by divorce, dual careers, and other problems. It can be particularly useful to educate parents about how much the world, the educational system, and our social environment have changed since they grew up.

Encourage Healthy Attitudes About Food, Weight, and Body Image

Day-care centers, preschools, and schools should sponsor programs to teach parents about nutrition, as well as about managing children's eccentric tastes and dealing with food refusal. Your State Department of Health or Department of Education may be able to provide personnel, ideas, and materials for such programs.

Child-care centers and schools should make meals and snack times pleasant, calm periods and should avoid using food as a reward or punishment for certain behaviors. By paying attention to the quality of food and the structure of mealtimes, they can be certain that children receive appetizing and nutritious food, enough time to eat, and an environment that is conducive to the digestion and enjoyment of food.

Nutrition should be incorporated into science, home economics, and health curricula. Educators should teach not just *what* young people should eat but *why* they should eat it. Let students know that their nutritional needs change as they grow and that they can expect a natural increase in their appetite during times when their bodies are growing and changing more rapidly. Be sure to teach both sexes about nutrition: it's important to point out that food is not the female's exclusive domain.

Coaches and physical educators should both endorse and model a healthy lifestyle, with stable nutrition and exercise habits. Their discussions with athletes should include the topic of good nutrition. They should be especially cautious about advising students to lose weight. If they believe that weight loss is absolutely necessary, they should provide guidance about how to do this safely and should be sure that the young person does not lose too much.

All educators and coaches should be aware of and prepared to recognize the warning signs and symptoms of eating disorders. They should be alert and watchful for these signs and should intervene early if a student engages in self-destructive behaviors such as excessive dieting, vomiting, fasting, or abusing laxatives, diuretics, or other medications to change body weight.

Educators in all content areas and grades can influence children's emerging body image. See the suggestions for pediatricians and other family care physicians in Appendix B. They can also intervene and educate to prevent bullying, put-downs, mockery, shaming, and ostracism based on appearance or body shape.

All schools should end the recent practice of measuring and posting students' weight, body fat composition, and body mass index (BMI). In many cases, these measurements are inaccurate anyway, and the harmful result is that children are teased by their peers and chastised by adults about their weight. Even for normal-weight children, this may contribute to body image dissatisfaction and destructive eating habits. Concerns about weight and pediatric obesity are best managed individually by pediatric health care providers.

Address Self-Esteem, Communication Skills, and Problem Solving

Day-care personnel and educators should ask parents to count the number of compliments and criticisms they give their children each day. Suggest a minimum ratio of five compliments to each criticism. If parents reveal that their leftover issues from childhood are getting in the way, suggest some reading or counseling to amend these patterns.

Help fathers, especially, to understand the effects that off-handed remarks can have on their children.

Educational approaches and other child-oriented activities should emphasize good communication skills and give children opportunities to say what they think. Building communication does not happen only in English classes. Encourage art, music, and other modalities of self-expression. Convey appreciation for the child's efforts no matter how the finished product turns out.

Schools should also teach children about decision making. Help them learn how to get information that will enable them to make informed choices. Encourage them to differentiate between opinions and facts and between emotion and logic. Give them experiences in finding ways to balance both sides when making a decision. Ask them to describe a problem they face, consider and evaluate possible solutions, and choose the one that fits them best, even if none of the options is absolutely perfect. Everyday issues that arise in the classroom can serve as the impetus for group discussion. Special projects in subjects such as drama and health education provide opportunities to make considered responses to difficult problems. Through role play, encourage young people to find alternative ways to solve conflicts and to cope with peer pressure, anxiety about achievement, and threats to their self-esteem.

Provide Resources on Eating Disorders

Through presenting a variety of programs and messages to students and their families, schools should work to demystify therapy and mental health problems. Convey that everyone needs help from time to time. Explain how and why therapy can help family members understand each other, talk about difficult feelings, resolve crises, and better meet their varied needs. Let fathers know how important their support is in both preventing and overcoming problems.

Schools and other organizations involved with children, adolescents, and young adults should train all staff members to recognize the warning signs and symptoms of eating disorders. They should also advise staff of the procedures to follow if they are concerned about a child. Having a team in place within the school to assess these problems and plan intervention is essential. The team should decide what person can best approach the student and family. Usually it is advantageous to share concerns with the student directly and then contact the family. Remember to include the father in your discussions. Professionals should be direct and honest about the information they have. They must also be sensitive to the student and parents. Help the parents to take charge and make decisions.

School personnel should know the resources available in their area for treating eating disorders and should give this information to parents. Advise that the young person be seen as soon as possible by a primary physician to assess his or her medical status. Ask for permission to call the doctor and discuss the school's observations. Also, let the family know that you will be monitoring the situation and calling them often to follow through and coordinate your efforts.

In all communications to the student and family, be supportive. They may have difficulty facing the problem and may suffer from guilt and self-doubt. Try not to be judgmental or blaming; remember how complicated the causes of eating problems are and realize that no one wanted this to happen. Aim at developing a working alliance between the school and family.

If the family refuses help and the situation appears severe (for instance, the student faints or falls at school), treat it as you would any other life-threatening situation. Bring your team together and consider referring the case to your State Department of Protective Services if the student is under 18. If the person is over 18, you may need legal and medical advice to help you plan other approaches. It is important to continue your efforts to get the student and family to agree to treatment.

Programs and Resources

*Friedman, S. S. *Body Thieves: Help Girls Reclaim Their Natural Bodies and Become Physically Active.* Salal Books: Vancouver, B.C., Canada, 2002. Call (604) 689-8399 or visit *www.salal.com*.

*_____. *Just For Girls.* Salal Books: Vancouver, B.C., Canada, 2003.

*_____. *Nurturing Girlpower: Integrating Eating Disorder Prevention-Intervention Skills into Your Practice.* Salal Books: Vancouver, B.C., Canada, 2003.

*_____. *When Girls Feel Fat: Helping Girls through Adolescence*. Salal Books: Vancouver, B.C., Canada, 2000.

Girl Power. Resources to educate, encourage, and empower girls as they move from childhood into puberty. Sponsored by the U.S. Department of Health and Human Services. Call 1-800-729-6686 or visit *www.girlpower.gov*.

*Kater, K. J. *Healthy Body Image: Teaching Kids to Eat and Love their Bodies Too*, 1997. A comprehensive resource manual and curriculum for grades 4–6. Available from the National Eating Disorders Association (NEDA), 603 Stewart Street, Seattle, WA, or call (206) 382-3587, or visit *www.nationaleatingdisorders.org* for this and other materials including the *GOGIRLS (Giving Our Girls Information and Resources for Lasting Self-Esteem)* media advocacy program for high school girls.

*Levine, M.P., and L. Hill. *A 5–Day Lesson Plan Book on Eating Disorders: Grades 7–12*. Carlsbad, CA: Gürze Books, 1991. Available through NEDA (above) and Gürze Books (below).

*Maine, M. *Body Wars: Making Peace with Women's Bodies: An Activist's Guide*. Carlsbad, CA: Gürze Books, 2000. (Includes a chapter on the school's role in promoting healthy body image and preventing eating disorders.)

*Mills, Andy and Becky Osborn. *Shapesville*. Carlsbad, CA: Gürze Books, 2003. Picture book for ages 3–8 about a fictional place "where it doesn't matter what size, shape, or color you are."

Partnership for Women's Health. *Helping Girls Become Strong Women*. New York: Columbia University, 2003. Call (212) 326-8860 to find out about this program.

*Piran, N., M.P. Levine, and C. Steiner-Adair (Eds.) *Preventing Eating Disorders: A Handbook of Interventions and Special Challenges*. Philadelphia: Taylor and Francis, 1999.

*Pryor, T., and J. Konek. *RSVP: Respect Self, Value People: Middle School Student Lesson and Activity Guide*. Wichita, Kansas: Healing Path Foundation, 2002.

WINS (We Insist on Natural Shapes) has a video and curriculum materials for elementary through high school students. Call 1-800-600-9467 or visit *www.winsnews.org.*

*Available from:
Gürze Books
P.O. Box 2238
Carlsbad, CA 92018
Phone: (760) 434-7533
www.gurze.com

Appendix B

Suggested Strategies for Physicians

A doctor's words and prescriptions are usually highly valued by families. Physicians can use this position of trust and authority to encourage the changes in family structure that will expand men's roles and promote children's emotional well-being and security. A child's health and development include more than just physiological factors. Pediatricians should also pay attention to psychological issues. Male physicians can model nurturing, supportive interaction with children and can discuss with fathers how to be involved and comfortable in managing their children's emotional and physical care.

Both male and female physicians should pay attention to the messages they give about parental roles and duties and should try to equalize the responsibilities and attention they give to both parents. Asking parents to share the responsibility of bringing their children to routine medical appointments and of nursing a sick or injured child will communicate to fathers that their involvement is important and that regular contact with the doctor is essential to understanding their children. This can have a positive and lasting effect on the reduction of father hunger.

Since pediatricians become involved with a family soon after a child is born, they can play a special role in fostering the parent-child relationship. Set aside time for an initial parenting "orientation" in which you invite both parents to discuss how their family life affected them and how they may want to do some things differently from their parents. Spend time talking about how to overcome hardships and allow fathers to be involved directly in child care. Give suggestions to guide them. Explain that most people automatically repeat the child-rearing techniques of their own parents; however, new information and new skills can be learned. Refer them to good books and parenting classes available in your area.

At each new developmental stage—infancy, toddlerhood, preschool, elementary school, preteen, adolescence—physicians can give dads suggestions about how their children's needs for fathering will change. Similarly, encourage couples to discuss how mothers can help fathers be involved.

If parents express excessive concern that their children eat too much or too little, are too skinny or too fat, physicians should reassure them and advise that excessive interference may cause eating or weight problems. Also, they should see the child and parents more frequently to monitor the situation. If either or both parents continue to be overly worried or have a history of eating or weight problems themselves, a referral to a therapist who can help with these problems is in order.

Physicians should also educate themselves about nutrition and examine their own views about weight to be sure they are not contributing to dangerous dieting and body image dissatisfaction in their young patients. Even a casual comment such as "You could stand to lose some weight" without direction and guidance about why, how, and what amount, can have disastrous effects on a child who is suffering from self-doubt or low self-esteem. Physicians should spend time alone with their young patients to get to know them more directly and convey interest in them individually.

If a child does develop an eating or body image problem, physicians should be sure to work closely with the other involved professionals to develop an integrated therapeutic approach. Coordinating efforts with the school and giving consistent messages will help the parents address the problem. (See the sections titled "Provide Resources on Eating Disorders" and "Programs and Resources" in Appendix A: Suggested Strategies for Educators regarding how to approach and help families when an eating disorder is evident.)

Pediatricians and other health care providers can help parents convey healthy attitudes about weight, eating, and body image by paying attention to these issues early in a child's life. They should encourage both parents to:

- Set a positive example by trusting and accepting their own bodies.
- Understand their attitudes toward weight and dieting.

- Learn about the dangers of dieting.
- Become sensitive to the relentless messages from the dieting industry and the glorification of thinness by the fashion industry.
- Talk to their children about the pressures they may feel to have the "perfect" body.
- Discuss the changes adolescent bodies go through naturally as they develop, including weight gain.
- Help their children to accept their bodies instead of constantly trying to change them.
- Praise their child's inner qualities, value, and contributions and minimize the importance of physical beauty.
- Help their child find constructive ways of expressing feelings so that difficult emotions are not converted into restrictive eating habits.
- Let their children make mistakes and learn without trying to make them perfect.

Resources for Physicians

The American Academy of Pediatrics has published a detailed policy statement on the role of pediatricians in the prevention and treatment of eating disorders. See "AAP: Identifying and Treating Eating Disorders," in *Pediatrics*, Jan 2003; 111,1, p. 204-11, or go to *www.aap.org/policy/02003.html*.

The Society for Adolescent Medicine has also prepared a position paper. See "Eating Disorders in Adolescents: A Position Paper of the Society for Adolescent Medicine," in the *Journal of Adolescent Health*, 2003; 33, p. 496–503, or go to *www.adolescenthealth.org*.

For other relevant information and treatment resources, the following websites are recommended:

Academy for Eating Disorders: *www.aedweb.org*

Eating Disorders Coalition for Research, Policy, and Action: *www.eatingdisorderscoalition.org*

National Eating Disorders Association: *www.nationaleatingdisorders.org*

Appendix C

Books and Internet Resources

An abundance of excellent information about fathering and eating disorders is readily available in books and on the Internet. Following are some recommended books and websites.

Books

Glennon, W. *Fathering: Strengthening Connection with Your Children, No Matter Where You Are*. Berkeley, CA: Conari Press, 1995.

_____. *200 Ways to Raise a Girl's Self-Esteem*. Berkeley, CA: Conari Press, 1999.

Gordon, J. *Parenting Our Daughters: For Parents and Other Caring Adults*. Denver, CO: Girls Count, 1999.

Harrison, H. H. *Father to Daughter: Life Lessons on Raising a Girl*. New York: Workman Publishing, 2003.

Henry, D. and J. McPherson. *Fathering Daughters: Reflections by Men*. Boston, MA: Beacon Press, 1999.

Kelly, J. *Dads and Daughters: How to Inspire, Understand, and Support Your Daughter When She's Growing Up So Fast*. New York: Broadway Books, 2002.

Lang, G. E. and Lankford-Moran. *Why a Daughter Needs a Dad*. Nashville, TN: Cumberland House Publishing, 2002.

MacKoff, B. *Growing a Girl: Seven Strategies for Raising a Strong, Spirited Daughter*. New York: Dell, 1996.

Maine, M. *Body Wars: Making Peace with Women's Bodies: An Activist's Guide.* Carlsbad, CA: Gürze Books, 2000.

Petrash, J. *Covering Home: Lessons on the Art of Fathering from the Game of Baseball.* Beltsville, MD: Robins Lane Press, 2001.

Pipher, M. *Reviving Ophelia: Saving the Selves of Adolescent Girls.* New York: Ballantine, 1994.

Pruett, K. *Fatherneed: Why Father Care Is As Essential As Mother Care for Your Child.* New York: Broadway Books, 2001.

Richardson, B. L. and E. Rehr. *101 Ways to Help Your Daughter Love Her Body.* New York: Quill/HarperCollins, 2001.

Websites for or About Fathers

At Home Dad is an organization that produces a newsletter for full-time dads: *www.AtHomeDad.com*.

The Center for Fathers, Families, and Public Policy conducts research, training, and education about the impact of public policy on the father's role in families: *www.cfpp.org*.

Dads and Daughters is the leading group promoting understanding and connection between fathers and daughters. It provides many resources, including ways to get involved to make the world a better place for girls to grow: *www.dadsanddaughters.org*.

Daughters: For Parents of Girls presents a newsletter to help parents raise emotionally healthy, strong, confident daughters: *www.daughters.com*.

The Fatherhood Project at the Families and Work Institute promotes research and education to support fathers' role in their families, as well as providing information and links to other organizations: *www.fatherhoodproject.org*.

Girl Power: Fathers Are Powerful, sponsored by the U.S. Department of Health and Human Services, provides research, resources, and activities to enhance fathers' and daughters' connections to each other: *www.girlpower.gov*.

The National Center on Fathers and Families engages in research and policy formation to strengthen fathers' role in families: *www.ncoff.gse.upenn.edu.*

The National Organization of Men Against Sexism is dedicated to promoting gender equity and an end to sexism: *www.nomas.org.*

Websites About Eating Disorders

www.about-face-org promotes positive self-esteem in women of all ages through media education, outreach, and activism.

www.ANAD.org provides information, referrals, education, and support groups on eating disorders.

www.andreasvoiceorg is a moving website dedicated to a young woman who died from bulimia. It offers critical and helpful information for sufferers and their families.

www.annawestinfoundation.org advocates for insurance coverage and provides support to families.

www.bulimia.com, sponsored by Gürze Books, is both a resource for information and an extensive bookstore. The company specializes in books and newsletters on eating disorders. Subscribe to a free monthly e-newsletter on eating disorders.

Federal advocacy for the recognition of eating disorders as a major public health problem: *www.eatingdisorderscoalition.org.*

www.freedfoundation.org This foundation raises money for treatment and provides public information about eating disorders.

Sponsored by Harvard University, this site provides training and educational programs: *www.hedc.org.*

www.mentalhealthscreening.org sponsors screening, education, and outreach programs for eating disorders.

This website of author Margo Maine, Ph.D., provides helpful information and links to other sites: *www.mwsg.org.*

National Eating Disorders Association (NEDA), the largest national organization, provides educational materials and referral information, sponsors an annual Eating Disorders Awareness Week, and offers educational programs. It's a great resource for both the general public and professionals: *www.nationaleatingdisorders.org*.

www.redwinggogirls.com shows the power of young women advocating against negative media images that promote eating disorders and pressuring the media to foster more realistic images.

www.somethingfishy.org is a wonderful website full of information and resources for anyone concerned about eating disorders or suffering from them.

www.theelisaproject.com This foundation dedicated to a young woman who succumbed to eating disorders sponsors education and outreach programs in the Dallas, TX area.

www.winsnews.org provides education and media advocacy programs.

Notes

Introduction

1. M. Maine (2000). *Body Wars: Making Peace with Women's Bodies: An Activist's Guide.* Carlsbad, CA: Gürze Books.
2. American Psychiatric Association. (2000). Practice Guidelines for the Treatment of Eating Disorders (Revision). *American Journal of Psychiatry, 157* (1), January Supplement, 1–39.

Chapter 1

1. K. D. Pruett (2001). *Fatherneed: Why Father Care Is As Essential As Mother Care for Your Child.* New York: Broadway Books, p. 2.
2. S. Minuchin, B. L. Rosman, and L. Baker (1978). *Psychosomatic Families: Anorexia Nervosa in Context.* Cambridge, MA: Harvard Press.
3. M.S. Palazzoli (1978). *Self–Starvation: From Individual to Family Therapy in the Treatment of Anorexia Nervosa.* New York: Jason Aronson.
4. C. Dare, I. Eisler (1997). Family Therapy for Anorexia Nervosa. In D. M. Garner and P. E. Garfinkel, *Handbook of Treatment for Eating Disorders,* 2nd ed. New York: Guilford Press, 307–24.
5. H. C. Fishman (1996). Structural Family Therapy. In J. Werne and I. D. Yalom (Eds.), *Treating Eating Disorders.* San Francisco: Jossey-Bass, 187–215.
6. M. S. Palazzoli (1988). The Cybernetics of Anorexia Nervosa. In M. Selvini (Ed.), *The Work of Mara Selvini Palazzoli.* Northvale, N.J.: Jason Aronson, 213–227. Quote on p. 207.
7. R. S.Dixon, J. M. W. Gill, V. A. Adair (2003). Exploring Paternal Influences on the Dieting Behaviors of Adolescent Girls. *Eating Disorders: The Journal of Treatment and Prevention, 11*(1), 39–50.
8. K. Chernin (1985). *The Hungry Self: Women, Eating, and Identity.* New York: Times Books.

Chapter 2

1. J. J. Arnett (2002). The Psychology of Globalization. *American Psychologist, 57* (10), 774–83.
2. M. Maine (2000). *Body Wars: Making Peace with Women's Bodies: An Activist's Guide.* Carlsbad, CA: Gürze Books.
3. S. Elliott (2003). Barbie Makes a Comeback. In *Advertising/NYTimes.com,* 3/11/2003.
4. J. Kilbourne (1999). *Deadly Persuasion: Why Women and Girls Must Fight the Addictive Power of Advertising.* New York: The Free Press.

5. P. McLaughlin (2002). Selling Stuff to Kids: Are We Selling Out Our Children by Turning Their Vulnerable Little Hearts and Minds Over to Madison Avenue? After a Fashion: SCEC Conference. Syndicated Column: Universal Press Syndicate, © Patricia McLaughlin, 9/15/02.
6. S. Linn (2004). *Consuming Kids: The Hostile Takeover of Childhood.* New York: The New Press.
7. M. Dittman (2002). Selling to Children. *American Psychological Association Monitor on Psychology,* Nov 2002, 37.
8. R. Segall (2003). The New Product Placement. *The Nation,* 2/24/2003, 30–33.
9. A. Quart (2003). *Branded: The Buying and Selling of Teenagers.* Cambridge, MA: Perseus Publishing.
10. CASA: The National Center on Addiction and Substance Abuse at Columbia University (2003). *Food for Thought: Substance Abuse and Eating Disorders.* New York: CASA.
11. M. Maine, op. cit.
12. N. Underwood (2000). Body Envy: Thin Is In and People Are Messing with Their Bodies As Never Before. *Maclean's,* 8/14/2000, 36.
13. M. Healy (2001). Britney Leaves Impact on Bellies. *USA Today,* 12/14/2001, 9D.
14. E. Goffman (1978). *Gender Advertisements.* Cambridge, MA: Harvard University Press.
15. S. Plous, D. Neptune (1997). Racial and Gender Biases in Magazine Advertisements: A Content Analytic Study. *Psychology of Women Quarterly, 21,* 627–44.
16. CASA, op cit.
17. D. Then (1992). Women's Magazines: Messages They Convey About Looks, Men, and Careers. Paper presented at American Psychological Association, Washington, DC.
18. J. J. Brumberg (1997). *The Body Project: An Intimate History of American Girls.* New York: Random House, p. 25.
19. C. Schoen, K. Davis, K. S. Collins, L. Greenberg, C. Des Roches, M. Abrams (1997). *The Commonwealth Fund Survey of Adolescent Girls.* New York: The Commonwealth Fund.
20. M.P. Levine, L. Smolak, H. Hayden (1994). The Relation of Sociocultural Factors to Eating Attitudes and Behaviors Among Middle School Girls. *Journal of Early Adolescence, 14*(4), 471–88.
21. S. S. Friedman (2002). *Body Thieves: Help Girls Reclaim Their Natural Bodies and Become Physically Active.* Vancouver, Canada: Salal Books.
22. M. Pipher (1994). Reviving Ophelia: Saving the Selves of Adolescent Girls. New York: Ballantine, p. 44.
23. R. Gordon (2001). Eating Disorders East and West: A Culture-Bound Syndrome Unbound. In M. Nasser, M. A. Katzman, R. A. Gordon, (Eds.). *Eating Disorders and Cultures in Transition.* New York: Taylor and Francis.
24. Anorexia Affects 1 in 20 Schoolgirls (2002). *Boston Globe,* 4/14/2002, A12.

25. A. E. Becker, R. A. Burwell (1999). Acculturation and Disordered Eating in Fiji. Presented at the 152nd Annual Meeting of the American Psychiatric Association.

26. J. Kelly (2002). *Dads and Daughters: How to Inspire, Understand, and Support Your Daughter When She's Growing Up So Fast.* New York: Broadway Books.

27. C. Schoen, et al., op.cit.

28. The National Center for Victims of Crime (2002). Teenagers at Greatest Risk for Crime Victimization: Teen Victims Project. Press Release, 7/16/2002, www.ncvc.org.

29. Media and Women News (2003). The Most Popular Video Game Ever: What *Grand Theft Auto: Vice City* Shows (and Doesn't Show) Millions About Women, Sex, and Violence. Girls, Women, and Media Project, Feb 2003, www.mediaandwomen.org.

30. C.Gandee (1994). Nobody's Perfect. *Vogue,* September 1994, 560–67.

31. A. Wallace (2002). True Thighs. *More,* Sep 2002, 90–95.

32. A. Brashich (2003). Stop Right There. Think About This *(2),* 2/27/2003, www.cultureofmodeling.com.

33. Girls, Women, and Media Project: What Are You Looking At? (2002). What's the Problem? Facts About Girls, Women, and Media, 9/02/2002, www.mediaandwomen.org.

34. R. Segall, op. cit.

35. A. Balsamo (1996). *Technologies of the Gendered Body.* Durham, NC: Duke University Press.

36. J. Croll, D. Neumark-Sztainer, M. Story, M. Ireland (2002). Prevalence and Risk and Protective Factors Related to Disordered Eating. *Journal of Adolescent Health, 31*(2), 166–75.

37. A. E. Swarr, M. H. Richards (1996). Longitudinal Effects of Adolescent Girls' Pubertal Development, Perceptions of Pubertal Timing, and Parental Relations on Eating Problems. *Developmental Psychology, 32,* 636–46.

38. Centers for Disease Control and Prevention (2002). Youth Risk Behavior Surveillance: U.S., 2001. *Morbidity and Mortality Report (MMWR), 51*(SS-4).

39. P. F. Sullivan (1995). Mortality in Anorexia Nervosa. *American Journal of Psychiatry, 152,* 1073–4.

40. Centers for Disease Control and Prevention, op. cit.

41. M. L. Fitzgibbon, et al. (1998). Correlates of Binge-Eating in Hispanic, Black, and White Women. *International Journal of Eating Disorders, 24*(1), 43–52.

42. R. H. Striegel-Moore, et al. (2000). Eating Disorder Symptoms in a Cohort of 11- to 16-Year-Old Black and White Girls: The NHLBI Growth and Health Study. *International Journal of Eating Disorders, 27*(1), 49–66.

43. G. A. Gaesser (2002). *Big Fat Lies: The Truth About Your Weight and Your Health.* Carlsbad, CA: Gürze Books.

44. American Association of University Women, Public Policy and Government Relations Department (2002). Gender Equity in Education: Myth vs. Reality, AAUW Position Paper. Jan 2002, www.aauw.org.

45.K. A. Martin (1998). Becoming a Gendered Body: Practices of Preschools. *American Sociological Review, 63*(4), 494–511.

46.American Association of University Women Education Foundation, Sexual Harassment Task Force (2001). *Hostile Hallways.* Washington , DC: AAUW Education Foundation.

47.N. Wyatt (2000). Background on Sexual Harassment. Updated Jun 2003, www.de.psu.edu/harassment.

48.American Association of University Women, Public Policy and Government Relations Department (2002). Equity in School Athletics, Position Paper. American Association of University Women, Jan 2002, www.aauw.org.

49.L. Smolak, S. K. Murnen, A. E. Ruble (2000). Female Athletes and Eating Problems: A Meta-Analysis. *International Journal of Eating Disorders, 27*(4), 371–80.

50.American Association of University Women, Gender Equity in Education, op. cit.

51.Ibid.

Chapter 3

1. D. L. Braun, S. R. Sunday, A. Huang, K. A. Halmi (1999). More Males Seek Treatment for Eating Disorders. *International Journal of Eating Disorders, 25*(4), 415–24.

2. E. H. Wertheim, G. Martin, M. Prior, A. Sanson, D. Smart (2002). Parent Influences in the Transmission of Eating and Weight-Related Values and Behaviors. *Eating Disorders: Journal of Treatment and Prevention, 10,* 321–24.

3. R. S .Dixon, V. A. Adair, S. O'Connor, (1996). Parental Influences on the Dieting Beliefs and Behaviors of Adolescent Females. *Journal of Adolescent Health, 17,* 303–7.

4. K. D. Pruett (2001). *Fatherneed: Why Father Care Is As Essential As Mother Care for Your Child.* New York: Broadway Books.

5. J. H. Pleck (1997). Paternal Involvement: Levels, Sources, and Consequences. In M. E. Lamb (Ed.), The Role of the Father in Child Development, 3rd ed. New York: John Wiley & Sons, 66–103.

6. H. B. Biller, J. L. Kimpton (1997). The Father and the School-Aged Child. In M. E. Lamb (Ed.), *The Role of the Father in Child Development,* 3rd ed. New York: John Wiley & Sons, 143–61.

7. K. D. Pruett, op. cit.

8. M. E. Lamb (1997). Fathers and Child Development: An Introductory Overview and Guide. In M. E. Lamb (Ed.), *The Role of the Father in Child Development,* 3rd ed. New York: John Wiley & Sons, 1–18.

9. L. B. Silverstein (1996). Fathering Is a Feminist Issue. *Psychology of Women Quarterly, 20*(1), 3–37.

10.K. D. Pruett, op cit.

11.National Vital Statistics Report (2002). Vol. 50(6), Mar 21, 2002.

12. F. Pittman (1989). The Secret Passions of Men. Lecture presented at the 47th Annual Conference of the American Association for Marriage and Family Therapy in San Francisco, CA: Oct 28, 1989.
13. M. Pipher (1994). *Reviving Ophelia: Saving the Selves of Adolescent Girls.* New York: Ballantine Books.
14. H. B. Biller, J. L. Kimpton, op cit.
15. F. F. Furstenberg, K. M. Harris (1993). When and Why Fathers Matter. In R. I. Lerman and T. J. Ooms (Eds.) *Young Unwed Fathers: Changing Roles and Emerging Policies.* Philadelphia: Temple University Press.
16. K. D. Pruett, op. cit.
17. J. Elium, D. Elium (2003). *Raising a Daughter: Parents and the Awakening of a Healthy Woman,* rev. ed. Berkeley, CA: Celestial Arts.

Chapter 4

1. K. D. Pruett (2001). *Fatherneed: Why Father Care Is As Essential As Mother Care for Your Child.* New York: Broadway Books, p. 217.
2. F. Pittman (1989). The Secret Passions of Men. Lecture presented at the 47th Annual Conference of the American Association for Marriage and Family Therapy in San Francisco, CA: Oct 28, 1989, p. 250.
3. J. Bloom-Feshback (1981). Historical Perspectives on the Father's Role. In M. E. Lamb, *The Role of the Father in Child Development,* rev. ed. New York: John Wiley. This article is an excellent overview of the social and historical factors that play an influence in men's parenting. (See quote on p. 81.)
4. J. Kelly (2002). *Dads and Daughters: How to Inspire, Understand, and Support Your Daughter When She's Growing Up So Fast.* New York: Broadway Books.
5. J. H. Pleck (1997). Paternal Involvement: Levels, Sources, and Consequences. In M. E. Lamb (Ed.), *The Role of the Father in Child Development,* 3rd ed. New York: John Wiley and Sons, 66–103.
6. K. D. Pruett, op. cit.
7. S. H. Cath, A. R. Gurwitt, J. M. Ross (1982). *Father and Child: Developmental and Clinical Perspectives.* Boston, MA: Little, Brown, & Co., p. xxi.
8. J. Bowlby (1966). *Maternal Care and Child Health.* New York: Schoken Books, p. 13.
9. M. E. Lamb (1997). The Development of Father-Infant Relationships. In M. E. Lamb (Ed.), *The Role of the Father in Child Development,* 3rd ed. New York: John Wiley and Sons, 104–12.
10. E. M. Hetherington, M. M. Stanley-Hagan (1997). The Effects of Divorce on Fathers and Their Children. In M. E. Lamb (Ed.), *The Role of the Father in Child Development,* 3rd ed. New York: John Wiley and Sons, 191–211.
11. K. D. Pruett, op. cit.
12. C. McEnroe (1991). To Joey with Love from a Guy Who Grew to See Fireballs. *Hartford Courant,* Jun 16, 1991, p. 1.
13. K. Pruett (1980). The Nurturing Male: A Longitudinal Study of Primary

Nurturing Fathers. In S. H. Cath, A. Gurwit, and L. Gunsberg (Eds.). *Fathers and Their Families*. Hillsdale, NJ: The Analytic Press, 389–409.

14. V. Phares (1996). Conducting Nonsexist Research, Prevention, and Treatment with Fathers and Mothers: A Call for Change. *Psychology of Women Quarterly, 20*(1), 55–77.

15. W. K. Redican (1976). Adult Male-Infant Interactions in Non–Human Primates. In M. E. Lamb (Ed.). *The Role of the Father in Child Development*. New York: John Wiley.

16. M. W. West, M. S. Konner (1976). The Role of the Father: An Anthropological Perspective. In M. E. Lamb, Ibid.

17. L. B. Silverstein, V. Phares (1996). Expanding the Mother-Child Paradigm: An Examination of Dissertation Research, 1986–94. *Psychology of Women Quarterly, 20*(1), 39–54.

18. K. D. Pruett, op. cit.

19. M. E. Lamb (1997). Fathers and Child Development. In M. E. Lamb (Ed.), *The Role of the Father in Child Development,* 3rd ed. New York: John Wiley and Sons, 118.

20. H. B. Biller, J. L. Kimpton (1997). The Father and the School-Aged Child. In M. E. Lamb (Ed.), Ibid., 143–61.

21. E. M. Hetherington, M. M. Stanley-Hagan, op. cit.

22. M. E. Lamb, op. cit.

23. K. D. Pruett, op. cit.

24. U.S. Department of Health and Human Services, Office of the Assistant Secretary for Planning and Evaluation (1999). *Trends in the Well-Being of America's Children and Youth*. Hyattsville, MD: U.S. Dept HHS.

25. C. W. Nord, N. Zill (1996). *Non-Custodial Parents' Participation in Their Children's Lives: Evidence from the Survey of Income and Program Participation*. Washington, DC: U.S. Dept HHS.

26. E. M. Hetherington, S. H. Henderson (1997). Fathers in Step Families. In M. E. Lamb (Ed.), *The Role of the Father in Child Development,* 3rd ed. New York: John Wiley and Sons, 212–26.

27. M. E. Lamb, op. cit., p. 9.

28. C. Hanford (2001). NOW Acts. *National NOW Times*, Summer, 2001.

Chapter 5

1. Many have written about this issue, including S. S. Friedman (2002). *Body Thieves: Helping Girls Reclaim Their Natural Bodies and Become Physically Active*. Vancouver, BC: Salal Books; C. Gilligan and L. M. Brown (1992). *Meeting at the Crossroads: Women's Psychology and Girls' Development*. Cambridge, MA: Harvard University Press; M. Pipher (1994). *Reviving Ophelia: Saving the Lives of Adolescent Girls*. New York: Ballantine Books; C. Steiner-Adair (1989). Developing the Voice of the Wise Woman: College Students and Bulimia. In L. C. Whitaker and W. N. Davis (Eds.). *The Bulimic College Student: Evaluation, Treatment, and Prevention*. New York: Haworth Press, p. 152.

2. Abramovitch, H. (1997). Images of "Father" in Psychology and Religion. In M. E. Lamb (Ed.), *The Role of the Father in Child Development,* 3rd ed. New York: John Wiley and Sons, 19-32.
3. D. Kindlon, M. Thompson (1999). *Raising Cain: Protecting the Emotional Life of Boys.* New York: Ballantine.
4 . F. S. Pittman (1993). *Man Enough: Fathers, Sons, and the Search for Masculinity.* New York: G P Putnam's Sons, p. 44.
5. C. Gilligan (1982). *In a Different Voice: Psychological Theory and Women's Development.* Cambridge, MA: Harvard University Press, p. 100.
6. H. G. Pope, R. Olivardia, A. Gruber, J. Boroweiecki (1999). Evolving Ideals of Male Body Image As Seen Through Action Toys. *International Journal of Eating Disorders, 26,* 65–72.
7. Greeting card by Cathy, from Recycled Paper Products. Chicago, IL: Universal Press Syndicate.

Chapter 6

1. J. B. Miller (1976). *Toward a New Psychology of Women.* Boston: Beacon Press, p. 83.
2. J. Bradshaw (1988). *The Family.* Deerfield Beach, FL: Health Communications, Inc.
3. R. Striegel-Moore, L. R. Silberstein, J. Rodin (1986). Toward an Understanding of Risk Factors for Bulimia. *American Psychologist, 41*(3), 246–263.
4 F. Prose (1990). "Confident at 11, Confused at 16." *New York Times Magazine*, Jan 7, 1990; see quote on p. 23. Review of Carol Gilligan (1990). *Making Connections: The Relational Worlds of Adolescent Girls at Emma Willard School.* Harvard University Press, 1990.
5. S. Orbach (1986). *Hunger Strike: The Anorectic's Struggle As a Metaphor for Our Age.* New York: W. W. Norton & Co., p. 36.
6. S. MacLeod (1982). *The Art of Starvation: A Story of Anorexia and Survival.* New York: Schocken Books, p. 69.
7. P. Farb, G. Armelagos (1980). *Consuming Passions: The Anthropology of Eating.* New York: Washington Square Press.
8. G. A. Gaesser (2002). *Big Fat Lies: The Truth About Your Weight and Your Health.* Carlsbad, CA: Gürze Books.
9. J. Kilbourne (1994). Still Killing Us Softly: Advertising and the Obsession with Thinness. In P. Fallon, M. A. Katzman, S. C. Wooley (Eds.). *Feminist Perspectives on Eating Disorders.* New York: Guilford Press, 395418.
10. Testimony at Subcommittee on Regulation, Business Opportunities, and Energy. U.S. House of Representatives Committee on Small Business, March 26, 1990.
11. G. A. Gaesser, op. cit.
12. Historical Tables: Budget of the United States Government, Fiscal Year 1992 (1991). Washington, DC: Executive Office of the President, Office of Management and Budget, p. 46.

Chapter 7

This chapter contains no footnotes.

Chapter 8

1. K. D. Pruett (2001). *Fatherneed: Why Father Care Is As Essential As Mother Care for Your Child.* New York: Broadway Books.

Chapter 9

1. J. R. Kaplan (1980). *A Woman's Conflict: The Special Relationship Between Women and Food.* Englewood Cliffs, NJ: Prentice Hall, p. 10.

Chapter 10

1. P. Caplan, I. Hall-McCorquodale (1985). Mother-Blaming in Major Clinical Journals. *American Journal of Orthopsychiatry, 55*(3), 345–53.
2. Phares, V. (1996). Conducting Nonsexist Research, Prevention, and Treatment with Fathers and Mothers. *Psychology of Women Quarterly, 20,* 55–77.
3 Quote by Robert Bly, a poet and leader of mythopoetic men's movement. Cited by M. Miller in Tough Guys, Wounded Hearts. *Changes,* Jul-Aug 1988, p. 54.

Chapter 11

1. J. Campbell (1972). *Myths to Live By.* New York: Bantam Books, p. 209.
2. S. Keen (1991). *Fire in the Belly: On Being a Man.* New York: Bantam Books. This great resource for men in search of new definitions of masculinity tells how to form a "questing community" to help men address the pain and potential of the male experience.
3. S. Osherson, (1986). *Finding Our Fathers.* New York: Fawcett Columbine, p. 18.
4. A. Napier (1988). *The Fragile Bond.* New York: Harper and Row, p. 84.
5. M. E. Lamb (1997). Fathers and Child Development: An Introductory Overview and Guide. In M. E. Lamb (Ed.), *The Role of the Father in Child Development,* 3rd ed. New York: John Wiley and Sons, 1–18.
6. Parents Educating Parents, Inc. (2002). Top Ten Father Facts from Father Facts, 4th ed., NFI. www.pepinc.org.
7. G. Gaesser (2002). *Big Fat Lies: The Truth About Your Weight and Health.* Carlsbad, CA: Gürze Books.
8. M. Maine (2000). *Body Wars: Making Peace with Women's Bodies: An Activist's Guide.* Carlsbad, CA: Gürze Books, p. 83.
9. Dads and Daughters, 34 East Superior St., Suite 200, Duluth, MN 55802. 218-722-3942 or 888-824-3237, www.dadsanddaughters.org.
10. National Organization for Men Against Sexism, www.nomas.org.

Chapter 12

1. H. Goldhor-Lerner. (1985). *The Dance of Anger*. New York: Harper & Row, p. 11.
2. Ibid., p. 102.
3. Marjorie Hansen Shaevitz (1984) first introduced the term in her book *The Superwoman Syndrome*. New York: Warner Books.
4. C. Steiner-Adair (1989). Developing the Voice of the Wise Woman: College Students and Bulimia. In C. Whitaker and W. N. Davis (Eds.), *The Bulimic College Student: Evaluation, Treatment, and Prevention*. New York: Haworth Press.

Chapter 13

1. M. Williams (1975). *The Velveteen Rabbit*. New York: Avon Books, p. 16–17.

Chapter 14

1. S. J. Bergman, J. L. Surrey (1997). The Woman-Man Relationship: Impasses and Possibilities. In J. V. Jordan (Ed.), *Women's Growth in Diversity: More Writings from the Stone Center*. New York: Guilford Press, 260–87. See quote on p. 263.
2. J. Kelly (2002). *Dads and Daughters: How to Inspire, Understand, and Support Your Daughter When She's Growing Up So Fast*. New York: Broadway Books.

Epilogue

1. Margaret Mead in D. Jackson (1992). *How to Make the World a Better Place for Women in Five Minutes a Day*. New York: Hyperion, p. iv.
2. Attributed to M. K. Gandhi. In G. Van Ekeren (1994). *Speaker's Source Book II*. Englewood Cliffs, NJ: Prentice Hall, p. 33.
3. Attributed to Eldridge Cleaver. In J. Bartlett (1980). *Familiar Quotations*. Boston: Little, Brown, and Co., p. 913.

Index

A

abandonment 94, 168
abuse, preventing 138
achievement orientation 63, 93
adolescence
  boys' development 91
  feelings about opposite sex 117
  girls' character changes 100
  girls' perception of weight 103
  healthy development 162
  identity formation 124
  modern demands on girls 100–102
  separation from parents 148
  sexuality 132–134
  weight concerns 45–46
Adult Children of Alcoholics 248
advertising 23, 33-36, 52, 303, 309
Alcoholics Anonymous 248
alienation 161, 171–172, 176, 179, 271
American Association of University Women 47
anger 136–143, 151, 159, 229, 241
  anger is OK 261
  dread vs. anger 258
  expressing through therapy 261, 275–276
  externalizing 281
  fathers should respect 267
  learning how to be angry 217
  toward father 139–142, 275–276
  women's expression of 169–170, 217–218
anorexia nervosa xiii, ix, xiv, 57, 105, 118, 121, 131–146 141, 143, 155–160, 271
anthropology 33, 79, 106

B

Barbie dolls 33, 91
beauty xi, xiii, 26, 32, 34, 44, 50, 72, 92, 122, 210, 237, 297
  historic ideals 35
  impact of media images 37
  women's identity 102–106
beauty pageants 36, 103
behavior modification 120
Bergman, Stephen 258
birth control 38
Body Image 91, 131, 131–144, 201, 288, 317
Body Wars: Making Peace with Women's Bodies 210
boundaries 137
Bowlby, John 77
bulimia ix, xiii, 57, 121, 131, 139, 141, 169, 271

C

Campbell, Joseph 180
cardiovascular disease 201
Centers for Disease Control and Prevention 45–46
Chernin, Kim 27
codependency 99, 102
cognitive development 23, 36, 80
communication, constricted 58, 117–118, 148

conflict avoidance 148
cosmetic surgery. See plastic
    surgery.
couvade 79

D

Dads and Daughters viii, 52,
    210, 299-300, 305, 307, 310-
    311, 317
Dance of Anger, The 217
denial 63, 93-94, 99-101, 117-
    118, 131, 141, 184, 204,
    220, 240
diet industry 107-108
dieting
    cross-cultural 45-46
    dangers of 44-45
    women and cooking 106-109
divorce 61, 65, 77-78, 80-81,
    125-126, 187-188, 193-194
    223, 228-229, 288, 307
dysfunctional family 287

E

eating disorders vii, viii
    causes 58-60, 157-158, 164
    function 124
    globalization of 39-41
    how fathers can help 203
    impasses in treatment 257-
        280
    prevention 281-283
educator strategies 287-293
extended family 80, 84, 172,
    227, 252

F

family
    common patterns 146-149
    contemporary trends 73-75
    division of labor 163-165
    dysfunction 67, 145-160
    legacy of patterns 214-216
    meals 153-160
    redefining 250-253
    roles 56, 71, 149-152, 162,
        191-195, 213, 224, 252,
        260, 263, 268
family systems 25, 166, 287
family therapy xv, 27, 159-
    160, 166, 169, 172, 185-186,
    198, 209, 222, 234, 253,
    257, 266-267, 303, 307
    mother's role in 222-22
fashion 33-35, 39, 57, 72, 93,
    103, 104, 105, 107, 121,
    170, 237, 297, 304
    historical 72
father
    beliefs about food, weight,
        and body image 201-202
    connecting with daughter
        195-196
    connecting with his father
        184
    connecting with mother
        187-188
    defining fathering 77-80, 199
    feelings 63-64, 181-182
    learning to listen 197-199
    media influence 108
    myths about 55-67
    parenting and eating disor-
        ders 203-204
    relationship with daughter's
        mother 187-188
    role 59, 61-62, 70-71, 75-
        76, 93
    ways to help daughters 179-
        211
father-daughter relationships
    55-56, 83-84, 138-144,
    246-250
    pleasing Dad 118-119

unrequited love 115
helping a daughter 49–51
working with daughter's
  mother 223–229
fatherhood, foundations for
  83–95
female
  early maturation 134–136
  identity 123–130
femininity 26, 28, 55–59, 64–
  65, 99–100, 103, 107, 109,
  116, 119–124, 151, 163,
  171, 189–190, 226, 240
  lessons from mother 64–65
feminist movement 213
Finding Our Fathers 184
food, control issues 120, 142–
  143
Freud, Sigmund 77

G

Gandhi 282
Gilligan, Carol 100
global girls 31–54, 103, 109,
  116, 121, 281
  coping with inner emptiness
    145-147
  food obsessions 100
  guilt 165–176
  media influences 104
  otheration 103, 105
  puberty 134
  sense of self 123, 230
  social cues 101
global village 80–81, 170
Grand Theft Auto 42
Great Depression 73
grief 161, 168, 168–172, 176
guilt
  caring for own needs 109
  cost of connections 99-102
  dealing with 221–222

eating to diminish guilt
  133–134
eating problems 231–232
felt guilty all the time 150
female psyche 101
hunger 161
legacy of loyalty 165–168
punishing self 152
sexuality 133
sexual trauma 136–138
  resulting from father
son's guilt about needs 88

H

Homer 86

I

I-voice 219–220, 231, 248–250
"if only" reasoning 23–24, 26–28
incest 166
Industrial Revolution 61–73
Internet resources 299–302

J

Johnson, Craig ix

K

Kelly, Joe 52, 210, 276

L

Lerner, Harriet 217
lesbian lifestyle 102, 167
loss 170–171, 176
loyalty 161–176

M

male, attitudes toward women
  189–191
male action toys 91
marijuana 126

masculinity 91–94
Mead, Margaret 282
men's feelings 72, 85–87, 140,
    161, 168–169, 219, 281
men's roles 22, 85–87, 276
men's sexuality 91–94
Miller, Jean Baker 98
mothers
    attitudes about food and
        weight 235
    facing own father hunger
        213–223
    goals 220
    how to help 213–236
    working with daughter's
        father 223–229
muscle dysmorphia 91
myths 55–67. See also roles.
    family roles 180, 222
    fathers and daughters 55–67
    gender roles 161
    men 182–183, 219
    parenting 162

N

Napier, Gus 184
National Eating Disorders
    Association viii, 301–302

O

Osherson, Sam 184
otheration 98–99, 101–102,
    109, 129, 140

P

Palazzoli, Mara Selvini 25
parental power
    and food 153–160
parenting vii, 22, 38, 53, 55,
    food and power 153–160
    importance to men 62–63

new directions 80–82
    perspectives on 172–175
Parks, Rosa 279
peer pressure 32–33, 290
perfectionism 48, 59, 187, 221–
    222
physicians
    suggested strategies for 295–
        297
plastic surgery xii, 27, 36, 43–
    44, 104, 116
Playboy 51
Pruett, Kyle 21
puberty 37–38, 47, 51, 92, 104,
    131–134

R

recovery 28, 199, 204, 206–208,
    210, 259, 260, 261, 266, 269,
    271, 277
    as a process 205–206, 263,
        264, 270
    connections 237–239
    from an eating disorder 28,
        232, 257, 260
    importance of support 232,
        235
    reasons for 199
relapse 208
Renaissance 72
resources on eating disorders
    299–302
reverse anorexia 91
roles. See family roles; men's
    roles; women's roles.

S

self-worth xiv, 26, 34, 93, 180,
    218, 239, 281
Seventeen magazine 44
sex roles xvi, 71–72, 74–75, 100,
    279

sexual
harassment 47, 51, 53, 306
trauma 136–139, 142–143
violence 41–42
sexuality iii, vii, 27, 38, 51, 65, 91–93, 116, 131–144, 247
Shakespeare, William 86
Sports Illustrated 50
standardized tests 49
State Department of Protective Services 291
Stop Commercial Exploitation of Children 34
strategies
educators 287–293
physicians 294–297
subsistence societies 70
Superman role 246, 265–266
Superwoman Syndrome 225–226, 311
Surrey, Janet 258
systems theory viii, 24–26

T

television 34, 36, 40, 42, 51, 104, 107
therapy 303, 307
as a process 136
benefits of 208, 242–246
countertransference 272–278
father's role 180, 185–186
father's support 205–206
impasses 257–280
patient discoveries 169
See also family therapy.
thinness
pursuit of 21–29
Title IX 47–48
triangulation 148–149
treatment of eating disorders, impasses 281–283

U

unrequited love 115–116, 239

V

value systems 89–91
Velveteen Rabbit, The 245
Vice City 42
Vietnam War 74–75

W

websites
for or about fathers 300–301
eating disorders 301–302
women
appearance and identity 102–106
emotional connectedness 113–114
power 119–120
roles 22, 27, 59, 72, 98–99, 161, 222, 225, 227
women's movement 190
World War II 40, 74, 225

About the Author

Dr. Margo Maine, Ph.D., cofounder of the Maine & Weinstein Specialty Group, is a clinical psychologist who has specialized in the treatment of eating disorders for more than 25 years. She is a Senior Clinical Consultant at the Institute of Living in Hartford, Connecticut, and is former director of the institute's Eating Disorders Program. Author of *Body Wars: Making Peace with Women's Bodies* (2000) and *Father Hunger: Fathers, Daughters and Food* (1991), she is a senior editor of *Eating Disorders: The Journal of Treatment and Prevention*.

Dr. Maine serves on the board of the Eating Disorders Coalition for Research, Policy, and Action and the board of Dads and Daughters, and is a Founding Member and Fellow of the Academy for Eating Disorders. She is also a member of the Founder's Council and past president of the National Eating Disorders Association, formerly Eating Disorders Awareness and Prevention. She serves on many advisory boards as well, including the National Eating Disorder Screening Project.

Dr. Maine is an Assistant Clinical Professor in the University of Connecticut Department of Psychiatry and an adjunct faculty member at the University of Hartford, Graduate Institute of Professional Psychology. She is a member of the Psychiatry Department at the Institute of Living/Hartford Hospital's Mental Health Network and at Connecticut Children's Medical Center.

A frequent presenter at numerous state, national, and international conferences, Dr. Maine has spoken on a wide range of issues related to the treatment and prevention of eating disorders and women's health. She is also the coauthor (with Joe Kelly) of *The Shape We're In: Overcoming Women's Obsession with Weight, Food, and Body Image* (2004) published by John Wiley & Sons, Inc.

About the Publisher

Since 1980, Gürze Books has specialized in quality books and newsletters on eating disorders recovery, research, education, advocacy, and prevention. Gürze publishes *Eating Disorders Today*, a newsletter for individuals in recovery and their loved ones, and *Eating Disorders Review,* a clinical newsletter for professionals. The company also widely distributes free copies of *The Eating Disorders Resource Catalogue,* which includes listings of books, tapes, and other information. Their website (*www.gurze.com*) is an excellent Internet gateway to treatment facilities, associations, basic facts, and other eating disorder websites.

Order FATHER HUNGER at www.gurze.com or by phone (760) 434-7533

Father Hunger is available at bookstores and libraries and may be ordered directly from the Gürze Books website, *www.gurze.com*, or by phone (760) 434-7533.

FREE Catalogue

The Eating Disorders Resource Catalogue features books on eating disorders and related topics, including body image, size acceptance, self-esteem, and more. It includes listings of nonprofit associations and treatment facilities, and it is handed out by therapists, educators, and other health care professionals around the world.

www.gurze.com

Go to this website for additional resources, including many free articles, hundreds of eating disorders books, and links to organizations, treatment facilities, and other websites. Gürze Books has specialized in eating disorders publications and education since 1980.

Eating Disorders Today
A newsletter for individuals in recovery and their loved ones

This compassionate and supportive newsletter combines helpful facts and self-help advice from respected experts in the field of eating disorders. Request a sample issue!